67

Women and Children First

Royal Festival Hall
Hayward Gallery
on the South Bank

FROM THE SUBLIME TO THE METICULOUS
- SUMMER EXHIBITIONS AT THE HAYWARD

Chuck Close

22 July - 19 September 1999

+

FULL MOON

APOLLO MISSION PHOTOGRAPHS
OF THE LUNAR LANDSCAPE

www.hayward-gallery.org.uk

The *the Sounding Century* Lectures, on the South Bank

Thur 23 September, RFH 7.30pm
Mary Robinson
with Michael Ignatieff
Human Rights:
Meeting The Challenge
Tickets £10 Concs £6

Tue 28 September, QEH 7.30pm
Peter Matthiessen
Human Nature vs Nature
Tickets £8 Concs £5

Wed 13 October, PR 7.30pm
Christopher Hitchens
A Few Kind Words in Closing
Tickets £6.50 Concs £4

Thur 4 November, QEH 7.30pm
Simon Schama
Cleo and The Zip Drive
Tickets £8 Concs £5

A co-promotion between SBC Literature and BBC Radio 3

Royal Festival Hall
& Hayward Gallery **BOX OFFICE 0171 960 4242**

For your FREE Literature and Hayward Bulletins with full details
of all the above and more please call 0171 921 0971. www.sbc.org.uk
The South Bank Centre is a registered charity.

LEONARDO'S GRAVE
GRAVE
Ian Jack

The *Titanic* leaving Belfast, 2 April 1912

1.

My son was three and my daughter five. It was the summer of 1997. James Cameron's film had not yet appeared, but a great human tragedy was unfolding on our living-room carpet.

'Here it comes!' said my son to his sister, and began to push a small toy ship across the floor from the direction of the television set. 'Here it comes, *brm, brm, brm,*' (the noise of marine steam engines, as a three-year-old thinks of them). My daughter moved a scrunched-up ball of white paper towards the course of the toy ship. They would meet, there would be an accident. My son swung his boat to the left, but the paper ball was too quick for him.

'Bang! Crash!' my son said, tilting his toy up and turning it over. 'Glug, glug, glug.'

'Let's get the passengers into the lifeboats,' his more humanitarian sister said. 'Look at all the people in the sea.'

We needed to imagine them, just as we needed to imagine the carpet as the North Atlantic, the paper ball as the iceberg, the toy boat as the *Titanic*.

'Don't worry,' my son said. 'Here comes the *Carpathia*.' Another toy was being pushed across the carpet to the rescue.

They played the game on many afternoons, but there were dissatisfactions. No detachable lifeboats; a funnelling discrepancy. The model ship had three funnels (it was based on the *Queen Mary*), whereas the *Titanic* had four. I explained to my son that the *Titanic* didn't need four to suck the smoke from its boiler furnaces—one funnel was a dummy—but that there was a fashion for over-funnelling in the Edwardian age—'a long time ago', I said—when numerous funnels implied grandness, size and speed; the more funnels the better the ship. Of course, this was just an impression, the equivalent of go-faster stripes and spoilers on family saloons at the other end of the century, but for about twenty years (like many other fashions, it died with the First World War) it held sway among the public and the premier passenger lines of the North Atlantic. Germany's Norddeutscher Lloyd line started the trend with the *Kaiser Wilhelm der Grosse* in 1897. Britain's Cunard Line followed after the turn of the century with the *Mauretania* and *Lusitania*. When the White Star company came to order their trio of *Titanic*-class ships from Harland and Wolff's yard in Belfast in 1909, four funnels were the only way to go.

'Doesn't matter. We'll just pretend it has four funnels,' said my son of his toy. But I could see that it was niggling him and when, a few months later, I spotted a model *Titanic* in a junk shop window in Lancashire, I went in and bought it for £9.95. It was new—the Hollywood film was out by then and *Titanic* souvenirs were everywhere—and, oddly, made of coal, or at least a sort of coal-based resin. 'British coal' said the label on the back with its Union Jack. The same shop window had coal railway locomotives, coal vintage cars and coal English country cottages—all a dull black, like Victorian memento mori. Coal had fuelled Britain and its industrial revolution; when the *Titanic* was at speed, the ship's 196 stokers had shovelled up to a hundred tons of it through 159 furnace-doors during each of their four-hour shifts. Now, to judge from the display in the window, it had dwindled from the country's leading power source to a raw material for folk art. Further back in the shop, I could see shiny brass coal miner's lamps, equally new, which people could put on their mantelpieces above their 'coal-effect' gas fires.

The shop was in a back street of an old cotton town, Nelson, which is high in the Pennines and close to the border with Yorkshire. Nelson had been a considerable town, growing in the last half of the nineteenth century from a crossroads with a pub (the Lord Nelson, from which first a railway halt and then the town had taken its name) to an industrial settlement of 30,000 people, twenty mills and 26,000 steam-driven looms weaving specialist cottons for the clothing trade: flannelettes, poplins, ginghams, twills. But that Nelson had gone. A few old weaving-sheds and their mill chimneys still stood; terrace houses of the local millstone grit still ran straight up the hillside towards the moors; there were still a few Nonconformist chapels, churches and municipal buildings in the centre (though many more had been demolished and replaced by roads and a sad concrete shopping mall).

The shop, like many other shops in small English towns where trade in essentials has been drawn away by supermarkets, sold ornaments—strange and sometimes florid objects in porcelain, clay, wood, imitation bronze, and (in this case) coal, which could be placed on a domestic flat surface and regularly dusted. Many were old, or imitation-old. 'Vic-toari-ana', said the elderly Lancashire man who ran the shop, deliberating over the word, 'they're very keen on it round here.' He was happy to see a customer and even happier to sell me the *Titanic*. A hunch had been proved right. 'I ordered a few of these,' he said as he placed the ship in its cardboard box, 'I thought it would be topical, like.'

At home in London, the coal *Titanic* steamed across the carpet on many voyages, all of them fatal. So many sinkings took their toll on its most vulnerable parts: the funnels. One by one, they split from the upper works. When there were three, my son sometimes imagined his toy as the *Queen Mary*; when there were two, it became the *Queen Elizabeth*; when there was one, it stood in for the *Carpathia*, the single-funnelled Cunarder which had picked up the *Titanic's* survivors and sailed with them to New York in April 1912. It could be all these ships to my son and still, when required, be imagined as the *Titanic*. Then the last funnel came off. A ship without funnels was...a wreck. This was the coal *Titanic's* final form, as a discard buried deep in our cellar, a tiny replica of the funnel-less, broken hull that Dr Robert Ballard and his expedition eventually discovered 13,000 feet down on the seabed of the North Atlantic in September 1985.

In 1998 in our house—in millions of houses and thousands of cinemas, wherever the sea rushed in, the stern tilted vertically, and Rose called to Jack from the screen or the video recorder—art continued to imitate death.

2.

The film *Titanic*, directed by James Cameron and funded by Twentieth Century Fox, is said to be the most commercially successful film of all time. This is a questionable claim; when American receipts are adjusted for inflation, *Gone With the Wind* comes first and *Titanic* fourth. But at least in the span of the 1990s, no other film comes near it. By the end of June 1999, it had earned more than $1,835 million at box offices worldwide and repaid its costs ten times over. Other large sums came from the video release, compact discs, books and general merchandising which ran the gamut from *Titanic* champagne flutes to *Titanic* yo-yos. It won eleven Oscars—only *Ben-Hur* forty years before won as many and no film has won more. Young adolescent girls formed a large part of its audience; newspaper reports from several countries India, Australia, Japan, the United Kingdom and the US—said that some had watched the film scores of times, mainly to see its young lead actor, Leonardo DiCaprio.

But its phenomenal appeal was more than hormonal. According to the London *Evening Standard* (27 April 1998), the Chinese president, Jiang Zemin, saw in the film a parable of the class war, in which 'the third-class passengers (the proletariat) struggle valiantly against the ship's crew (craven capitalist lapdogs and stooges)'. In a statement published in Beijing, the president applauded the film's 'vivid descriptions of the relationship between money and love, rich and poor' and urged all fellow socialists to see it. The French also considered *Titanic* in political terms. Serge July, the editor of *Libération*, wrote: 'The subject of the film is not—this is obvious—the sinking of a famous ship, but the suicide in the middle of the Atlantic of a society divided in classes.' In Germany, according to the *New York Times* (26 April 1998), 'heady articles...with no discernible tongue in cheek, have spoken of the movie as an emblem of the Zeitgeist, an allegory that provides catharsis for all, a surrogate myth in a trivialized era, an icon at the end of history'. In *Die Zeit*, Andreas Kilb, the paper's cultural critic, wrote that the key to the film's appeal lay in its representation of a 'lost wholeness'. Hans Magnus Enzensberger, again in the *New York Times*, compared the durability of the *Titanic* myth with the transience of modern catastrophes, and wondered if the contrast demonstrated that we were losing a proper sense of history. (My son also became a critic. Owing to a lapse in parental attention, he watched the video. We worried that he might have been affected by the disaster and death which Cameron had so realistically evoked, as well as—though this, I admit, was ridiculous—the sight of Kate Winslet's bared breasts. But he was chuckling on the sofa. 'They had smoke coming from the fourth funnel. What a mistake!')

James Cameron's own gloss on his film was similarly myth-driven. He wrote in the 'production information' (the press-pack for critics and other journalists): 'April 10, 1912. Technology had been delivering a steady stream of miracles for the better part of two decades and people were beginning to take this never-ending spiral of progress for granted. What better demonstration of humanity's mastery over nature than the launch of *Titanic* [the missing definite article was important to the film's marketing; 'the', presumably, carried too nautical and traditional a ring], the largest and most luxurious moving object ever built by the hand of man. But four-and-a-half days later, the world had changed. The maiden voyage of the "ship of dreams" ended in a nightmare beyond comprehension and mankind's faith in his own indomitable power was forever destroyed by uniquely human shortcomings: arrogance, complacency and greed.'

Then, perhaps aware that public chastisement had not made good box office since the time of Savonarola and John Knox, the director added that his film was also 'a story of faith, courage, sacrifice and, above all else, love'.

Most of those latter qualities enter the film through its fictional story, a shipboard romance. Briefly: Rose DeWitt Bukater (Kate Winslet) is a seventeen-year-old, upper-class American girl, 'suffocating under the rigid confines and expectations of Edwardian society' according to the press-pack, who meets a free-spirited young American from the Midwest called Jack Dawson (Leonardo DiCaprio). Rose is travelling first class and Jack steerage. They fall in love, have sex, and then, when the ship begins to sink, help each other to survive a villainous sub-plot. In the sea, Jack urges Rose to hold on to life and the wreckage. Jack drowns, but his love and her freshly discovered will-power enable Rose's survival. The story is framed by the present or the near-present. Rose, rediscovered in her hundredth year, narrates the events of the voyage from a perspective which suggests that both experiences—forbidden love across the class boundaries, the awakening of a tougher, unladylike strength—have turned her into a prototype of modern, independent womanhood. The title song, 'My Heart Will Go On', is sung by Celine Dion, but the same sentiments, to better music, can be heard in Edith Piaf.

I saw the film twice at the cinema. There were many things to admire in it. The ship was wonderfully and faithfully recreated (the fourth funnel, in fact, carried the fumes from the kitchen fires; smoke was therefore a possibility). Some scenes had a painterly touch. The

Ian Jack

Titanic overtaking a tiny yawl as the liner leaves Southampton; an officer in a lifeboat casting a torch-beam on the sea to scan it for survivors—scenes such as these could have come from the easel of a Victorian narrative painter seeking, in contrary moods, to capture technological triumphalism and maritime peril. The cleverest aspect of the film, however, depended neither on computer-created images, nor on expensively researched historical detail, nor even on the ninety per cent scale replica of the ship itself, with the stern that tilted almost to the vertical—people falling screaming from it, bouncing from the propellers—before it slid under the sea. Its cleverest aspect, I thought, was how it had taken a previously masculine story—male blunder, male heroism, male sacrifice in that most male of environments, the sea—and feminized it as a monument not to the dead but to a modern notion of...'girl power' is probably the phrase.

The true opposition was not between classes (*pace* the president of China), just as the film's true subject was not the 'suicide' of the society that produced these classes (*pace* the editor of *Libération*). In Cameron's film, the armies that clashed on that calm north Atlantic night represented youth and age, the new and old. To be young and new (to be, in a sense, *now*) was to smoke and spit and wear a flat cap and no tie like Jack; to be creative, an artist, like Jack; to be free and resourceful like Jack; to have heard, improbably, of Picasso and Freud like Rose; to make love in the back of a car, part of the ship's cargo, like Rose and Jack; to drink and dance Irish jigs in the steerage; to be Irish or Italian or Scandinavian or American (though not clipped, rich, East Coast American—Anglo-American). To be young and new was to have, as your soundtrack, the ghastly Celtic-twilight pastiche of James Horner's music.

And to be old? That was to lose, to be part of dying things, an *ancien régime*; to be repressed and repressive; not to have heard of Freud; to have as your soundtrack the hymn 'Nearer My God, To Thee', like Captain Smith (Bernard Hill) as he stood stoically, purposelessly, in the wheelhouse and saw the sea come crashing through its windows; to be smug and autocratic like the ship's officers and owner before the disaster, and then to be weak, brittle and cowardly after it; or to be weak and servile like the crew, before and after.

In other, shorter words: to be old, to be the enemy, was to be British.

I watched the film and felt a slight sense of ancestral, racial injury, and eventually took the train to Lancashire.

3.

Four days out from Southampton on its maiden voyage to New York, the *Titanic* hit the iceberg at 11.40 p.m. on Sunday 14 April, and sank at 2.20 a.m. on 15 April. Its last known position was 41° 46' N, 50° 14' W; about 350 miles south-east of Newfoundland and 1,000 miles and three days away from New York. According to the British Board of Trade inquiry, 1,503 passengers and crew died and 703 were saved. The *Titanic* had steamed into an ice field at twenty-two-and-a-half knots; it had ignored ice-warnings tapped out in Morse from other ships; its lifeboats had room for only 1,178 people; its watertight bulkheads did not rise high enough in the hull. But these reckless errors of navigation and flaws in ship design were largely ignored in the immediate British coverage of the disaster. Tragedies needed heroes. *Titanic*'s band supplied them. To preserve order and calm, they had started to play soon after the iceberg was hit and had gone on playing until the very end, insouciantly, stoically, and finally religiously and comfortingly. Their last number was said to have been the hymn, 'Nearer My God, To Thee'.

'Why is it,' George Bernard Shaw wrote in the *Daily News and Leader* one month later, 'that the effects of a sensational catastrophe on a modern nation is to cast it into transports, not of weeping, not of prayer, not of sympathy with the bereaved…but of…an explosion of outrageous romantic lying?' Shaw listed what he called the 'romantic demands' of a British shipwreck. The first was the cry 'Women and Children First' and the second that all the men aboard ('except the foreigners') should be heroes and the captain a superhero. Finally, Shaw wrote, British romance demanded that 'everybody should face death without a tremor; and the band, according to the *Birkenhead* precedent, must play "Nearer My God, To Thee".' The *Birkenhead* was a troopship which foundered off the South African coast in 1852. While the women and children were got off in the boats, the troops held ranks at attention on deck. In Victorian Britain, the story had a powerful effect.

The evidence from the *Titanic*, according to Shaw, ran in the opposite direction. 'The captain and officers were so afraid of panic that, though they knew the ship was sinking, they did not dare tell the passengers so—especially the third-class passengers—and the band played Rag Times [*sic*] to reassure the passengers, who, therefore, did not get into the boats, and did not realize their situation until the boats were gone and the ship was standing on her head before plunging to the bottom.'

Sir Arthur Conan Doyle replied to Shaw's attack in the *Daily News* of 20 May.

'Mr Shaw tries to defile the beautiful incident of the band by alleging that it was the result of orders issued to avert panic. But if it were, how does that detract either from the wisdom of the orders or from the heroism of the musicians? It was right to avert panic, and it was wonderful that men could do it in such a way.'

Shaw, as usual, was being controversial; he was England's leading controversialist. But he was also being brave, because in the middle of this still familiar London newspaper phenomenon, the columnar spat, the body of its chief subject, the leader of the *Titanic*'s band, had been unloaded from a ship in Liverpool and taken by hearse inland across Lancashire, up past the noisy weaving-sheds of Preston and Blackburn, Burnley and Nelson, to the town of Colne. If disasters need heroes, heroes need burials, and burials need bodies. The body of Wallace Henry Hartley, violinist and bandmaster, had been retrieved from the sea and brought to Halifax, Nova Scotia, on 30 April. In Halifax it had been coffined and taken by train to Boston, and from there shipped by the White Star's *Arabic* to Liverpool, where it arrived at South Canada Dock on 17 May.

Even before his body had been found, Hartley was a hero. Reports of the band's behaviour, how they had continued to play, first appeared in the *New York Times* on 19 April, the morning after that newspaper's reporters interviewed survivors who disembarked from the *Carpathia*. Newspapers in Britain magnified these reports— Shaw was right about 'outrageous romantic lying'—until Hartley became the man who not only went on playing his violin when the ship began to settle by the bows, but continued playing even when he was waist-deep in water.

On 18 May, Hartley was buried in Colne. About 26,000 people then lived in the town. The local newspaper, the *Colne and Nelson Times,* estimated that a crowd of about 40,000 attended the funeral, drawn from across northern England by trains and trams. They made Hartley's funeral the largest single solemnization of the *Titanic* disaster on either side of the Atlantic. The *Colne and Nelson Times* reported that the town had reached 'the highest eminence of its character and tradition... The whole world has been at the feet of Wallace Hartley; then why wonder at the jealous pride of Colne?'

4.

In Lancashire, I went first to Liverpool to consult the newspaper archive and look at the *Titanic* monuments. The city has two of them; the ship, like all of White Star's fleet, was registered here (when the last of the hull slips under in Cameron's film, the sight of the word LIVERPOOL on the stern jolted me into remembering that this was a city of global importance, once). Many Liverpudlians were in the crew, especially as firemen and coal-trimmers in the stokeholds, and it was a Liverpool musical agency that recruited the band. One monument stands at the Pierhead, originally intended for the ship's engineers (no engineering officer survived) but later modified before its unveiling in 1916 to take account of the First World War and 'honour all heroes of the marine engine room'. In the bas-reliefs, stokers with bare chests stand with rags and shovels in hand while an officer in a naval cap and jacket holds a spanner. They stare out at an empty river—a process of desertion which began when White Star moved their finest transatlantic liners to Southampton, so that they could cross the Channel to Cherbourg and embark the rich passenger trade from continental Europe. The legend beside them reads: THE BRAVE DO NOT DIE/THEIR DEEDS LIVE FOREVER/AND CALL UPON US/TO EMULATE THEIR COURAGE/AND DEVOTION TO DUTY.

Inside the city, away from the waterfront, a bronze plaque to the *Titanic*'s musicians is fixed to the wall in the foyer of the Philharmonic Hall. There were eight of them: Wallace Hartley, violin and bandmaster; Theodore Brailey, piano, of Ladbroke Grove, London; Roger Bricoux, cello, of Lille, France; Fred Clarke, bass, of

Liverpool; John 'Jock' Hume, violin, of Dumfries, Scotland; George Krins, viola, of Brixton, London; Percy Taylor, cello, of Clapham, London; Jack Woodward, piano, of Headington, Oxfordshire. They performed in two groups, as a trio and a quintet, in different saloons of the ship. All of them died. The legend in art-nouveau lettering said they had 'continued playing to soothe the anguish of their fellow passengers', followed by the words: COURAGE AND COMPASSION JOINED/MAKE THE HERO AND THE MAN COMPLETE.

According to the *Liverpool Daily Post and Mercury* (18 May 1912), 'scenes of a very affecting character' had been witnessed in South Canada dock when Hartley's coffin came ashore. His father, Albion Hartley, had come from Colne to Liverpool and paced the floor of the dock shed as he waited for the casket to be swung from the ship's hold to the quay. He was, said the *Daily Post*'s report, 'a pathetic figure...suffering from intense mental agony...as he signed the receipt for the delivery of the body his hands quivered with emotion...his eyes filled with tears, and he walked away broken with grief'. Before he left, however, Mr Hartley 'communicated a few particulars with respect to his son's personal history'. These included: that his son had been engaged to be married (Miss Maria Robinson of Leeds); that his son had regretted moving from one of the Cunard Line's bands because the switch to White Star meant that his home port became Southampton rather than Liverpool, taking him further from his parents' home; and that a gentleman who regularly travelled by Cunard had told him, Albion Hartley, that he had heard his son play 'Nearer My God, To Thee' several times on board the *Lusitania*. (The last seemed to be offered as evidence to doubters. Already there were doubts).

Then the hearse's two horses began the slow fifty-nine-mile pull to Colne, where the coffin with Hartley's bruised body inside arrived at one o'clock the next morning.

5.

It was dark when I got there; two changes of train, then a long ride up a bumpy single line which ended at a bare platform. The terminus: Colne. I walked across to the Crown Hotel—Victorian, built soon after the railway came in 1848—where I'd booked a room for the night. Two women were propped against the hotel wall, pawing each other.

'You're a bitch, you're a bitch,' one woman was saying.

'And you're a right cow,' said the other.

In the hallway, a man in a white shirt and black tie ran past me with blood dribbling from his cheek. In the bar, several men, also in black ties, were talking softly and urgently to their womenfolk.

'Now love, just shut it...have another drink and then we'll get a minicab.'

All the men were small and dark, as though they belonged to the same large family. A life-size model of Laurel and Hardy stood in one corner of the bar, and next to it (or next to Hardy at least) these men looked like angry jockeys.

'He's coming back in,' said one man, who was watching the door.

'Nay, he'd never, he wouldn't dare,' said another.

Eventually the Crown Hotel's manager appeared and took me upstairs to my room. 'It's not usually like this,' he said, by way of apology.

Outside the window I could hear a woman shouting: 'Don't give me that shite. You wanted to shag him, didn't you, you bitch.'

The manager smiled and said: 'It's a funeral. Drinking and that. I think it got a bit out of hand.'

6.

Wallace Hartley's funeral began a few hundred yards from the Crown Hotel at the Bethel Independent Methodist Chapel. May the eighteenth was a Saturday. The next week's *Colne and Nelson Times* spared no detail; the idea that Britain, and especially northern Britain, shied away from emotional display at that time, that crying began with the Princess of Wales in 1997, is confounded by this single report. A thousand people crowded into pews which had been built to hold 700. Before undertakers screwed down the coffin lid—'a coffin of an unfamiliar American make, polished to appear like rosewood'—Hartley's parents and sisters came to take a last look at the body. The body is described; 'somewhat discoloured by a blow he had evidently received and by the embalming process'. Then the congregation stood and began to sing in an atmosphere of 'fervid emotion'. Hartley's mother, who remained seated in the front pew, wept bitterly at one point and almost choked with suppressed grief at another. Hartley's two sisters and his fiancée, Miss Robinson, 'shook visibly'; and when 'Nearer My God, To Thee' was sung (for the second time) almost the entire congregation was in tears: 'girls had not the heart to sing...men and women broke under the strain ...voices shook with emotion'.

Mr T. Worthington, an Independent Methodist preacher who had sailed with Hartley on the *Mauretania*, gave the address. Reading it in Colne library almost ninety years later, I was struck by how vividly it had been phrased. 'She [the *Titanic*] had been only a few days out...when she comes into contact with another force, designed in no engineer's office, constructed in no dockyard, possessed by no compass and guided by no rudder, giving off no steam, nor driven by any machinery; but a force with which man's latest and noblest construction coming into contact bolts, shakes, reels, sinks...' Worthington concluded: 'The traditional British character was magnificently shown... Yes, it is brave to be British. It is both brave and noble to be Christian. In fact, it is easier to be British when we are Christian.'

People stepped up to the catafalque to place wreaths on the coffin. 'To Uncle Wallace,' from his sister's children; 'Teach me from my heart to say, Thy will be done,' from Miss Robinson. Then the cortège set out for the cemetery. The procession was half a mile long. Five brass bands came first, followed by a battalion of the East Lancashire Regiment, buglers from the Boy Scouts, the town's ambulance brigade, the congregation of the Bethel Chapel, the Colne Orchestra, the Bethel Choir, the representatives of Colne Town Council and, at last, the carriages with coffin, wreaths and mourners. The bands took it in turns to play the 'Dead March in Saul' with muffled drums: 'the subdued tones of the bands thrilled one with the immense tragedy of the proceedings'. Great whispering crowds lined the route, men doffed their hats as the coffin passed, flags floated at half mast, blinds were drawn in every house. And, unusually, no large amount of coal smoke blew across the town; the town's mills had shut for the morning shift. According to that day's *Manchester*

Evening News, 'workmen and masters assembled together in awed silence on the tramless streets'.

At the cemetery gates, twelve men, all cousins of Hartley, took the coffin. Worthington read the last rites. The reporter from the *Colne and Nelson Times* noticed a lark singing overhead. The hillsides all around were dotted with groups of men who stood silent and bareheaded.

In 1912, it was the most impressive scene Colne had ever witnessed, and—my guess—most probably ever will. But were there no sceptics, people who wondered about the fuss? A week later a letter appeared in the *Colne and Nelson Times*. There were plans for a civic memorial to Wallace Hartley. The anonymous writer hoped, drily, that it would not be a drinking fountain: 'surely there has been enough water in this sad affair'.

7.

I left the Crown Hotel that night and went to look at Hartley's memorial, not a fountain but a bust on a pedestal, flanked by two carved figures representing Music (with a lyre) and Valour (with a laurel wreath). The people of Colne had subscribed £265 to its cost, but when the mayor unveiled it, in 1915, Hartley's death was no longer so remarkable and the mayor took care to connect him with thousands of other young men 'who were giving their lives freely'. In 1992 the bust had been vandalized and four years later repaired. Now, because of the film, in which Hartley makes a fleeting appearance, people had recently begun to bring flowers.

I walked higher up the main street, inspecting the prices of houses in estate agents' windows. There were few people about. I went to a pub—a large saloon with only three drinkers—and heard a middle-aged woman who was slightly tight sing 'Once I had a secret love' to the karaoke machine. The wallpaper and the lamps, like the Crown Hotel's, were new-Victorian. Original Victoriana lined the streets: there were several handsome buildings, but most of them adapted to purposes other than their original. In the ground floor of the old Colne Co-operative Society headquarters I ate spaghetti at Carlo's Pizzeria in a room that pretended to be a red-tiled Tuscan cottage.

Colne and this part of Lancashire once had a singular culture—
a way of thinking and being, which, though many parts of it were
common to northern Britain, had special twists and peculiarities.
Even Nelson, just down the hill, was different, and Colne people
still—a cultural relic—spoke of it disparagingly. Nelson was an
upstart, a pure nineteenth-century invention. Once Colne people had
called Nelson 'Little Moscow' because of its socialism; on my visit I
heard an old man call it 'Little Calcutta' because so many Southern
Asian families lived there. Colne had very few Asians; also it was a
much older town; also it was higher, 600 feet up and surrounded by
moorland which rose another 1,000 feet still.

Did Hartley's stoicism and nobility—if he had been stoic and
noble—depend on Colne, grow in Colne? That would be absurd,
though in Colne in 1912 the claim was often made. On the other
hand, two Colne specialisms had placed him on the *Titanic*, had given
him the chance to behave like a Christian gentleman, if that is what
he had been. Without cotton and Methodism, he would never have
learned to play the violin and, consequently, never have gone to sea.

8.

Cotton came later to Colne than the rest of Lancashire. From the
fifteenth century it developed a thriving woollen business, then, after
the narrow canal from Liverpool reached Colne in the late eighteenth
century, cotton began to be imported from the United States and
India. By 1824, there were only three manufacturers of wool in Colne
but twenty-two of cotton. By 1843, seven of these mills were driven
by steam. More cotton, coal and supplies of Welsh roofing slate came
with the railway. Over the next sixty years, Colne changed from a
riotous little town with bad sanitation, smallpox and public stocks,
into a model of municipal enterprise and self-improvement, with
electric trams, reservoirs, good drains, and libraries. Express trains
from Colne ran all the way to London, as well as to Leeds and
Manchester and Liverpool.

The Hartley family improved with the town. Their addresses and
occupations were listed in each ten-year census, and with every entry
there was change. Wallace's grandfather, Henry, was a weaver of
woollen worsted in 1841 but a weaver of cotton twenty years later.

Henry's son, Albion, was a cotton 'sizer' in 1871 but a cotton-mill manager ten years later. By 1891 Albion had become an insurance agent, about as far away as could be got then, in Colne, from physical work, smoke and machinery. And so Wallace, born in 1878, grew up in the middle stages of his family's social progress. Unlike his grandfather, his father, his uncles and aunts, he never went to work in a mill. He had an education and got a job in a bank.

The education came courtesy of Methodism, which arrived in Colne when John Wesley preached at the opening of the town's first Methodist chapel in 1777. By the middle of the next century it was rampant, evangelizing and schismatic. Wesleyan Methodism became identified with the new middle class of manufacturers and shopkeepers and was seen as autocratic. More radical preachers, anxious to proselytize and uplift the new working class, broke away into new groups: the Bible Christians, the Kilhamites, the Primitives. The Primitives set to work in the poorest and most squalid parts of the town, but they too split into conservatives and radicals, the radicals favouring volunteer rather than paid preachers and renaming themselves the Provident Independent Methodists.

In 1857, the Providents decided to evangelize the growing working-class quarter of Primet Bridge, close to Albion Hartley's house and Wallace Hartley's birthplace. They built a chapel there: the Bethel Independent Methodist Church. Albion Hartley became its choirmaster and the superintendent of its Sunday school and sent his son to Colne's Methodist day school, which existed to educate the children of the poor but self-improving. In Colne, the Methodists stimulated many improving activities—elocution lessons, temperance groups, evening lectures for adults—but music was their special strength: glee clubs, brass bands, choirs, the Colne Orchestra. Sometimes rival choirs would combine to sing a great oratorio: the *Messiah* or *Elijah*. Sometimes a musically gifted millworker left the town and became a professional singer or player. One or two had careers at Covent Garden. At school, Wallace Hartley learned to play the violin. After a few years in the bank, he left Colne for a middling career as a violinist with tearoom trios in department stores and touring opera companies. He played at Bridlington, Harrogate, Leeds, and for the operas put on by Carl Rosa and Moody Manners.

Then he joined Cunard.

That is really all that is known about him. There are no family memoirs or (so far as I could find) surviving members of the Hartley family. Two of his brothers died in infancy; his sisters died childless. In his last letter home, written on board the *Titanic* and collected from the ship at its final port of call, Queenstown, Ireland, he wrote: 'This is a fine ship and there ought to be plenty of money around... We have a fine band and the boys seem very nice.' At his funeral, he was recalled as 'tall, handsome, and of a pleasant disposition—he was popular with passengers and proved a merry companion.'

There are no more clues to his character. And the particular society of Colne that might have influenced it, one way or another, has gone; or almost.

9.

Jack Greenwood took me to see the tombstone. Greenwood was an old Colne man, a retired bus driver, a local historian who specialized in the history of Colne's most famous figure, Wallace Henry Hartley. Like the shopkeeper who sold me the coal *Titanic*, he spoke in the broad, deliberating accent which, in the valleys of the Colne Water, the Calder and the Ribble, takes on a special peculiarity, as though vowels were warm beer twisting down a plughole. He said 'thee' for 'you', 'nowt' for 'nothing', and 'brew' for 'hill'. It would be useless to try to reproduce it.

We met at the library and walked west through the town. It was a grey winter's day with cloud on the hills and a dampness in the air that would later settle into steady, unremitting rain. Eventually we came to a gate. Through the gate, Colne's cemetery ran down a steep hill. 'It's down theer on the left,' Greenwood said. 'I'll stay at the top. That brew's too steep for me.'

I went down on my own. Hartley's tomb was more monumental than the rest and included the names of his father, mother and infant brothers. It was topped by a broken pillar covered in a shroud while at the base a stone violin reposed on its side next to the first words and musical bars of 'Nearer My God, To Thee'. It was here, at Hartley's funeral, that the Bethel Chapel choir sang the hymn for the third and last time to the accompaniment of the Trawden silver band,

and here, as Hartley's coffin was lowered into the earth, that buglers from Colne's Boy Scouts blew the 'Last Post'. Their notes, said the *Colne and Nelson Times*, 'went rolling through the valley and came back again, loth to be done.'

A few old flowers lay at the foot of the monument. Those apart, there was no sign of pilgrimage or a continuing memory. I went back up the hill and asked Greenwood if he thought the grave had the right hymn to the right tune—one of the most vexing questions in the historiography of the *Titanic*. Greenwood didn't doubt it. He'd done his work in the local archives. It was Albion Hartley who had introduced Colne to 'Nearer My God, To Thee' in the musical arrangement by Sir Arthur Sullivan when he was the Bethel choirmaster; it had been regularly sung during Whitsuntide processions. The tune is called 'Propior Deo' and its first notes were those on the tomb. Furthermore, Greenwood added, a Mr Ellwand Moody of Farnley, Leeds, had made twenty-two trips on the *Mauretania* with Wallace and had once asked him, as one cheerful north-countryman to another: 'What would you do if you were on a sinking ship?' And Wallace, according to Moody, according to Greenwood, had replied: 'I don't think I could do better than play "O God Our Help in Ages Past" or "Nearer My God, To Thee".'

We walked back through the centre of Colne and started down the hill which runs towards Nelson. It was raining hard now; in the fading light, the town was wet and black; at the foot of the streets that went off steeply to each side, there were patches of wasteland where the mills had been. I remember feeling how good it would be to take the small, slow train down to the junction at Preston and then sit in a much faster one to London. Or to sign up as violinist with the White Star line.

Instead, we went to Greenwood's terrace house and his wife made tea and biscuits. I asked her about 'Nearer My God, To Thee'. Not many people these days, I said, believed that this was the last tune Wallace Hartley had played on the *Titanic*. Mrs Greenwood said firmly: 'Well, we believe it in Colne, don't we, Jack? Look at the last verse—"Out of my stony griefs, Bethel I'll raise." Bethel, you see. That would have reminded him of the Bethel chapel, his father, this town, everything he'd grown up with and loved.'

10.

The hymn 'Nearer my God, To Thee' was written by an Englishwoman, Sarah Flower Adams, and first appeared in a hymnal compiled in 1840 and 1841 by the Reverend William Johnston Fox for use by the congregation at his Unitarian chapel in Finsbury, London. The first two verses—there are four in all—go:

> Nearer, my God, to Thee
> Nearer to Thee!
> E'en though it be a cross
> That raiseth me.
> Still all my song would be,
> Nearer, my God, to Thee,
> Nearer to Thee.
>
> Though, like the wanderer,
> The sun gone down,
> Darkness comes over me,
> My rest a stone;
> Yet in my dreams I'd be
> Nearer, my God, to Thee,
> Nearer to Thee.

Mrs Adams died (childless and 'of decline' according to the *Dictionary of National Biography*) in 1848 at the age of forty-three. To try to learn a little of her life is to face one of the great problems of the modern secular imagination: how to imagine a time when God was a powerful idea, when Biblical tags and stories were a part of everyday life, when hymns were as familiar and meaningful to most of the population as advertising slogans are now. Mrs Adams might easily be imagined as a Christian sop, disappointed on earth and pining for heaven. In fact, so far as one can tell, she was a spirited woman, a friend of the poet Robert Browning, with whom she corresponded about her religious doubts and difficulties. But perhaps the most surprising thing to discover about her is that she was not, in the strictest sense, a Christian; as a Unitarian she did not accept the Holy Trinity or the divinity of Christ. Neither is her hymn about Christ. It tells, elliptically, the story of Jacob who, fleeing the wrath of his brother Esau, falls asleep on a pillow of stone in the wilderness and dreams of a ladder lined with angels that descends from heaven with God standing at the top. He erects a monument of stones at the site of his dream and calls it Bethel, which in Hebrew means 'the House of God'. According to the Reverend James Hodson's *Hymn Studies*, 'it is a song of the soul in a lonely and gloomy place.'

For many years after it was published, it remained problematic as a Christian hymn. It lacked any mention of Christ; the 'cross' in the first verse is simply a metaphor for human suffering. Various churches tried to amend it, but none of the new versions caught on, until, in 1855, Henry Ward Beecher included it in a general, non-Unitarian collection of hymns (his sister, Harriet Beecher Stowe, published *Uncle Tom's Cabin* four years before and was sometimes miscredited with the words of the hymn). In 1856 another American, the prolific hymnographer Lowell Mason, replaced the original setting, composed by Mrs Adams's sister, Eliza, with a tune called 'Bethany', in 4/4 time, that was altogether more stirring and affecting.

By the time of the Civil War it seems to have reached most corners of North America. One Bishop Martin, fleeing Union troops in Arkansas, heard its tune as he stumbled through backwoods country; located the source as a log cabin; found in the log cabin a poor old woman singing lustily; felt therefore 'an unreserved trust in God, thus ridding him of his fears'.

The books I looked at—old, unvisited books in church libraries, books of earnest, pre-First World War Christian sincerity, books that it now seemed inconceivable that anyone had ever read—told many similar stories. The late Queen Victoria had expressed her love for the hymn. It was the favourite of the late President McKinley, who had repeated it frequently on his deathbed. It was the absolute favourite of His Majesty, King Edward VII, who considered it as 'dear to the peasant as the prince'; and also of the Australian Antarctic Expedition who had sung it 'amid blizzards, in ice caves and at the end of the day's toil'.

A Reverend Dr Moulton, for thirty years a missionary to the Tonga Islands in the South Seas, recounted how he had visited the hut of an old and now dying convert and there met 'a curious sight'. Two friends had propped the old man so that he could hang from a beam in the roof. 'Judge of my astonishment,' wrote the Rev Dr Moulton, 'when I heard these words uttered over and over again—in Tongan of course—"Nearer, O God to Thee! Nearer to Thee".'

The tune, however, was not always the same. North America sang it to Mason's Bethany, while British Christians were divided by denomination; Anglicans favoured a tune called 'Horbury' by John Bacchus Dykes, while Methodists chose Sir Arthur Sullivan's 'Propior Deo'. However they were sung, the words were a hit throughout the English-speaking world. According to the Reverend Canon Duncan in his *Popular Hymns* (1910), the hymn was ranked at number seven in 'The Sunday at Home List' of the hundred best and most popular hymn tunes. He wrote: 'The testimonies are many and from all quarters as to the comfort and help this hymn has been to the souls of men, women and children, even in some of the most depressing circumstances of life.'

Could there be a more depressing circumstance than to stand in a fearful crowd on a slowly tilting deck with a child in your arms, waiting to die in a near-freezing sea? In the early morning of 15 April 1912, the hymn's greatest hour had arrived. Wallace Hartley tapped his violin (the moment is in James Cameron's film) and his band struck up its last tune: 'Nearer My God, To Thee'. So it was said, so it was reported in the newspapers, so it was widely believed. Within days of the *Titanic*'s loss, the words were on memorial postcards, within weeks they were in instant books and the dialogue titles of silent films. By 12 May, according to Reuters news agency, 55,000 copies of a French translation had been sold in one week at the equivalent of a penny each: 'the hymn is even being sung by groups at street corners after the manner of popular songs'.

But which of the three possible tunes had they heard, Dykes's, Mason's or Sullivan's? On 24 May, at a concert for the *Titanic* Relief Fund in the Albert Hall, conducted by Sir Edward Elgar, Sir Henry Wood and Thomas Beecham, London's massed orchestras played Dykes's tune, 'Horbury'. Hartley's grave uses Sullivan's. Cameron's film uses Mason's.

Then again, had anyone heard any of them? As the *Titanic*'s story moved though its various revivals in the century, a new and secular orthodoxy was slowly established.

11.

Mrs Vera Dick, a first-class passenger from Alberta, was the origin of the story. Fresh off the *Carpathia*, she told the *New York Times* (19 April): 'What I remember best was that as the ship sunk [*sic*] we could hear the band playing "Nearer My God, To Thee". We looked back and could see the men standing on deck absolutely quiet and waiting for the end. Their conduct was splendid, splendid.'

Almost all of the *Titanic*'s many historians over the past fifty years have chosen to disbelieve her. Mrs Dick was among the first to leave in the boats, at one a.m., and she was probably at least a quarter of a mile away when the ship went under. On the other hand, it was an unusually still night (everybody attests to that) and on a quiet day the noise of a cello and a couple of violins will carry half a mile across a London park. There is also the private testimony of Mrs Charlotte Collyer, second-class and also in a lifeboat when the *Titanic* sank, whose husband did not survive. She wrote to her parents-in-law in England from Brooklyn in a letter dated 21 April: 'I feel I shall go mad sometimes but dear as much my heart aches it aches for you, too, for he is your son and the best that ever lived... But mother we shall meet in heaven. When that band played Nearer My God, To Thee I know he thought of you and me for we both loved that hymn...'

Other witnesses had different memories. A. H. Barkworth, first-class, from Yorkshire, wrote: 'I do not wish to detract from the bravery of anybody but I might mention that when I first came on deck the band was playing a waltz. The next time I passed...the members of the band had thrown down their instruments and were not to be seen.' Second Officer Charles Lightoller remembered the band playing 'a cheery sort of music... I think it helped us all'. Archibald Gracie, a retired US Army colonel, recalled that the band stopped playing half an hour before the ship sank. 'I did not recognize any of the tunes, but I know they were cheerful and were not hymns. If, as has been reported, "Nearer My God, To Thee" was one of the selections, I assuredly should have noticed and regarded it as tactless warning of immediate death to us all and one likely to create a panic that our special efforts were directed towards avoiding.'

Lightoller and Gracie, unlike Mrs Collyer and Mrs Dick, were among the last to leave, swept overboard by the wave that came rushing up the deck. Harold Bride, the ship's second wireless operator, went into the sea at the same time. Like Mrs Dick he was interviewed by the *New York Times* on 18 April and was quoted as saying. 'The ship was gradually turning on her nose—just like a duck that goes down for a dive...the band was still playing. I guess all the band went down. They were heroes. They were still playing "Autumn." Then I swam with all my might.'

Bride did not specify 'Autumn' as a hymn, and some versions of his interview include an earlier reference to 'the ragtime tune'. But when Walter Lord came to write his book, *A Night to Remember,* published in 1955, he decided that 'Autumn' and not 'Nearer My God, To Thee' was the hymn that had been played. Lord's book, an early example of quick, episodic, narrative history, became a bestseller, the most influential retelling of the story that has ever been published. Three years later, in the British-made film of the book, 'Autumn' is the tune the band plays.

The British hymnologist, Sir Richard Johnson, decided that the *New York Times* reporter had misheard 'Autumn' for 'Aughton', an American Episcopal hymn and tune written by a pupil of Lowell Mason's. The English composer, Gavin Bryars, accepted the idea and incorporated 'Aughton' in his orchestral piece, *The Sinking of the Titanic,* first performed in 1969. In the meantime, Lord had discovered something he did not disclose until he published his follow-up book on the *Titanic* in 1986. In 1957, a former Cunard Line bandmaster wrote to him remembering that *'Songe d'Automne'*, a waltz composed by Archibald Joyce, had been a big hit in London in 1912. The waltz is on the playlist of the White Star line's bands for that year. Books began to reproduce the playlist.

By 1998, God and his comforts were in full retreat.

12.

The Bethel chapel in Colne was demolished in the early 1980s—dry rot—but Independent Methodist services still take place in a smaller outbuilding that used to be the Sunday school. I had told Jack Greenwood I would like to attend one, and somehow the word got round. On the Sunday morning, as I was walking across the waste ground where the chapel used to be, an elderly man came forward to greet me. They were going to sing The Hymn in my honour.

There were eight or nine people inside, all of them, save the woman organist and a couple in their fifties, at least sixty-five years old. We sat on metal chairs and sang several hymns, including 'Nearer My God, To Thee' to Mason's tune. A woman preacher addressed us on St Paul's letter to the Ephesians. Communion wine and bread—small, torn pieces of sliced brown—went between us. Outside, Colne people were doing whatever they now do on a Sunday in March. Waking up, driving to the superstores, looking out from their kitchen windows at bare gardens and wondering when spring will come.

Eric Lambert, the caretaker, took me to see Wallace Hartley's birthplace. On the way I asked about the communion wine, it seemed sweet. 'Vimto,' Lambert said. 'We don't hold with alcohol.'

We walked across a bridge over the Colne Water, and then over a motorway slip road. We were now on the very edge of Colne, among fields. Hartley's birthplace was down a track in a lonely terrace of millstone grit houses: 92 Greenfield Road. 'Don't look in,' Lambert said as we passed the house, 'they don't like folk looking.'

We walked on. 'You know what did for the churches?' he said. 'It was the First World War.' He remembered an old preacher at Bethel, a Mr Diggins, telling him what people had said in 1917: 'There can't be a God or he wouldn't allow this sort of stuff.'

It had made Mr Diggins despair.

I went back up the hill to look at Hartley's bust and now considered the war memorial next to it. There are eight columns of the dead from the First World War and about ninety names to each column. More than 700 young men from a community of about 25,000 people had died in four years, mainly in Flanders. Twenty-one of them were called Hartley: there were even three W. Hartleys. Who in Colne could now remember where, how, and for what they had died? If, at the age of thirty-three, there is ever a right time to die— a time to be remembered for the act—Wallace Hartley had chosen it.

13.

The little train took me down the valley. Two drunk youngish men got on at Accrington. They had no tickets. The ticket inspector and the driver were women. They said the train wouldn't move until the men paid. 'Away ye go to fuck,' said one of the men; they were travelling to Glasgow. Eventually the women gave up and the train moved on. The rest of us studied our newspapers.

One of the questions Cameron's *Titanic* plants in our imagination is: how would we, the modern audience, behave on the deck of a slowly-sinking liner without enough lifeboats, surrounded by a freezing sea? Worse, better, the same? The question implies that we know how people behaved then, and that Cameron's film portrays it accurately. These things are difficult to know. Perhaps Hartley and his men continued playing because it occupied them in what they slowly realized was a hopeless predicament. Perhaps they threw down their instruments long before the end and tried to paddle off on deckchairs, or anything else that would float. The fact is that all eight of them died and many of the people who survived were thankful to them. As to general good behaviour—good in the sense that men hung back and allowed women and children to fill the boats—there are many testimonies and one interesting statistic, which comes from the percentage of passengers saved, arranged by age, gender and class. These are the British Board of Trade Inquiry figures:

In the first class: thirty-four per cent of the men, ninety-seven per cent of the women, a hundred per cent of the children.

In the second class: eight per cent of men, eighty-four per cent of women, a hundred per cent of the children.

In the third class: twelve per cent of men, fifty-five per cent of women, thirty per cent of the children.

The usual juxtaposition is to compare the percentages of the first- to third-class children, or of first-class men and third-class children. These are shameful—by the principle of equity and the code of women and children first. But the interesting statistic in the context of 'good behaviour' is for the second-class men: eight per cent. Unlike the third class, they had easy and early access to the boat deck, and yet only thirteen survived out of 160. Could it be that this class, which on the *Titanic* was largely drawn from the middling tradesmen and professionals of Britain and North America, behaved more nobly and stoically than the men above and below them?

Hartley came from such a class. It may have been a heroic class or a foolish one. 'The old Lie,' Wilfred Owen wrote six years later, *'Dulce et decorum est pro patria mori.'* But it is hard to dismiss the thought that a way of thinking, of being, in Colne and in Britain, must have affected the way people behaved, and that they behaved differently then.

14.

Still hunting for scraps of Hartley's life, I followed his passage back to Halifax, Nova Scotia. It was from Halifax on 17 April 1912 that a Canadian cable ship, the *Mackay-Bennett,* was dispatched under hire to the White Star line. It sailed towards the *Titanic's* last known position with a cargo that included one hundred coffins, several tons of ice, and embalming tools and fluid for use by the professional embalmers who were also on board. By the time the ship returned to Halifax on 30 April, it had recovered 306 bodies. They were often found in clusters; a member of the crew counted more than a hundred floating together in their white life-jackets 'like a flock of seagulls'. Some had drowned in the immediate turmoil of the sinking; others had floated off and frozen to death. As each body was hauled on board, it was given a number before clothes and personal effects were removed and put into a bag with the same number. Bodies that were too damaged or decomposed—though decomposition was not much of a problem in such near-freezing water—were returned to the sea weighted with iron, which had been brought for that purpose. One hundred and sixteen bodies from the *Mackay-Bennett's* haul went back into the Atlantic, but that still left 190 for the voyage home to Halifax.

On board, the bodies, or the identifiable majority of them, were divided in death as in life. The dead from the *Titanic's* crew were stacked unembalmed on the foredeck or in the ice-filled hold. Second- and third-class passengers were sewn up in canvas bags. First-class passengers were embalmed and encoffined and placed at the stern. All of this last class had been successfully identified, perhaps because they carried so many valuables and inscribed memorabilia. When the bodies reached port, some were claimed by relatives and taken for burial at final destinations across North America and in

Europe. Halifax undertakers buried the rest: 150 in all, sixty of them never identified.

Of the band, only three were found. John 'Jock' Hume, the violinist, was body number 193; and Fred Clarke, the bassist, body number 202. Hartley's body was found soon after, perhaps in the same group; body number 224. His details were in the Nova Scotia Archive. Reading through them I cleared up one small mystery. In several accounts of the *Titanic* disaster, Hartley was said to have been found with his music case strapped to his body—as though he had died to save the muse as represented on his memorials. The original handwritten entry for him reads:

> sex: male. est age 25. hair brown. clothing—uniform (green facing), brown overcoat, black boots, *green box*. [my italics]. effects—gold fountain pen, WHH diamond solitaire ring, silver cigarette case, letter, silver match box marked to WHH from Collingson's staff, Leeds, telegram to Hotley [*sic*] , Bandmaster, Titanic, watch, gold chain, gold cigar holder, stud, scissors, sixteen shillings, 16 cents in coins.

A later typed entry amends the 'green box' to 'green socks', which were part of a White Star bandman's uniform. Box/socks. I thought I could imagine the confusion: the undertaker's clerk with his nib-pen scurrying across the page, a colleague opening each of 190 bags and identifying their contents, shouting his list in a noisy warehouse filled with bodies and ice.

That accounted for the music case. I decided I would pay my respects to the grave of John 'Jock' Hume of Dumfries.

The bodies which were buried in Halifax lie in three groups. The identifiably Catholic (such as the bassist, Clarke) were taken to the Mount Olivet cemetery. The identifiably Jewish to the Baron de Hirsch cemetery, from where some of them were quickly removed after an undignified squabble with the local rabbi, who was accused of being too eager to use debatable evidence (circumcision, probably) to call a body Jewish. But by far the largest number went to Halifax's non-denominational cemetery, the Fairview, which is spread across a slope at the head of one of Halifax's inlets from the Atlantic. It was a fine breezy afternoon, with a sparkle from the blue chop in the sound and the rippling green of the cemetery grass. Halifax now advertised itself as a chief port of call on the *Titanic*'s new tourist trail, and a big new sign had been erected: THE TITANIC GRAVES. A path, newly worn, led through the grass to a large oval of small uniform headstones, like those to the dead in Flanders. I bent among them, looking at this name and that, remembering the stories attached to some of them. Here (body 313) was Luigi Gatti, maître d' of the ship's French restaurant, who was found clutching the teddy bear his small daughter had given him before he left home in Southampton. And here (number 193) was 'Jock' Hume, whose parents in Scotland were later asked to stump up for an unpaid uniform bill—it became a small scandal.

There were 121 of these stones, some engraved only with numbers, and other than the occasional flower, very little sign that any of them had recently been remembered.

Then, further down the slope, I came across a grave which was heaped with tributes. Before the headstone to J. Dawson (number 227) candles had been lit and artificial flowers arranged. There were also several keys, some sweets, a crayon or two, a piece of chewing gum still in its wrapper, cinema tickets, and (the most striking thing) a large plastic model of a transatlantic liner—not the *Titanic*, but a three-funnelled ship which could have been the *Queen Mary*.

Someone had written a note: 'Dear James Dawson, I feel sorry about your life. They should have built the *Titanic* stronger. Paula.'

This was the grave of Leonardo DiCaprio.

Keys, flowers, candles: all had been taken to the grave by the young people—girls mostly—who, I was told in Halifax, had towed their parents here from as far away as France and California. Most of the tributes I could understand, but the keys were a puzzle until I remembered that at one point in the film Dawson-DiCaprio is handcuffed to a pipe deep inside the sinking ship, the water rises to his neck, and, despite a frantic search, no keys can be found. (Can he be rescued? Yes. Enter Kate Winslet with an axe.)

But who was the J. Dawson under the headstone? According to the Novia Scotia Archive, he was a fireman, a stoker of coal. His body had been found unmarked and dressed in dungarees with a grey shirt. His estimated age was thirty. He had light hair and a moustache. The only item found on him was a card showing his membership (no. 35638) of the National Seamen's Union. There was some confusion over his address, originally given as 17 Bolton Street, Southampton, then changed to 17 Briton Street, Dublin. Nothing else, so far as I can tell, is known about him, though we have some idea of how he worked.

Terry Coleman describes it well in his book, *The Liners* (1976). Here was the life of a fireman on a four-funnelled, coal-burning Atlantic liner:

> At sea, they worked two four-hour spells in each twenty-four, lifting five tons of coal each a day....They worked in twenty-one minute spells. There were seven minutes to feed coals into furnaces whose heat scorched them, then seven minutes for cutting and clearing clinkers with long slicers, and then another seven for raking over. A man who was behind in any seven minutes could not escape being seen by his fellows to be weaker, and so the weak drove themselves to keep up with the strong. After three periods of seven minutes there was a short pause, and then a gong announced the beginning of another twenty-minutes. This was the fireman's work for four hours on end, scorched by furnaces and choked by coal dust and by gases from white-hot clinkers and ashes. When they had finished their watches they often took the air with chests open to the cold Atlantic wind. They worked, ate, and then slept exhausted. They could not obtain drink aboard, so when they did get ashore they made up for this by getting and staying drunk. As firemen, only the Hungarians were as good as the Liverpool Irish.

It doesn't seem, from this, that one of them would have had time to teach Kate Winslet to spit.

15.

Flying home from Nova Scotia, the *Titanic*'s wreck somewhere in the sea beneath me, I thought: the *Titanic* story is so embarnacled with metaphor and myth that it hardly matters whether Wallace Hartley played his hymn or not (for the sake of Colne, I hoped he had). There are much bigger lies. The first is that the ship was billed as 'unsinkable'. The great paradox of the *Titanic* is that it became unsinkable only after it sank, when White Star officials were anxious to counter early reports of the disaster. Previously the only reference in the company's publicity to 'unsinkability' was a cautiously worded sentence in a 1910 brochure for the *Olympic* and the *Titanic* which said that 'as far as it is possible to do so, these two wonderful vessels are designed to be unsinkable'.

Nor was the *Titanic* a particularly fast ship—her older Cunard and German rivals were three or four knots faster. Nor, though she was briefly the largest ship afloat, was the *Titanic* staggeringly huge; only one foot longer than her earlier sister, the *Olympic*, and significantly smaller than the German *Imperator* which went into Atlantic service later in the same year the *Titanic* went down.

But perhaps the largest untruth is in the hubris metaphor—in James Cameron's words, that 'mankind's faith in his own indomitable power was forever destroyed by uniquely human shortcomings: arrogance, complacency and greed'. What in fact happened was that the lifeboat regulations were redrafted; ice patrols were introduced; hulls given a double lining of steel. Otherwise, Atlantic liners went on growing more luxurious, larger and swifter.

Hubris, if it had ever existed, was killed with the millions of names on the thousands of war memorials like the one in Colne. If it had ever existed, and—I thought, watching *Titanic*'s director holding his final Oscar aloft and calling out 'King of the World!'— if it has ever died.

16.

On 20 May 1999, a cruise liner, the *Sun Vista*, caught fire in the Strait of Malacca and slowly began to sink. More than 1,100 passengers and crew were taken off in lifeboats and other small craft. Ram Yalamanchi, a businessman from India, said: 'It was a true nightmare. I thought we were all going to die. We were on one of the last lifeboats, we watched her [the ship] slip into the water. People were screaming and praying.'

Many passengers sang to keep their spirits up. According to an Australian, Greg Haywood: 'We were singing the Celine Dion song, "My Heart Will Go On".' □

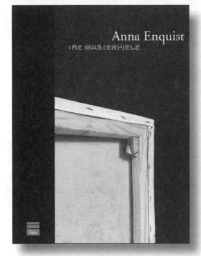

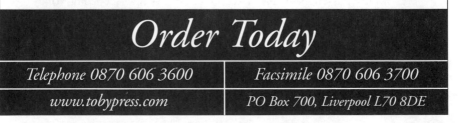

THE DIARY OF
A POLITICAL
IDIOT

Jasmina Tesanovic

BELGRADE
MARCH 1998–JUNE 1999

Jasmina Tesanovic

17 March 1998 I tremble, my feet tremble while I am asleep. Why do my legs tremble as if an electric current is passing through them? Is it because I will need them to run away and fear they will fail me? I fear everything. I fear death and killing. I fear not being able to imagine the future. I watch my children with a sense of guilt. Here in Serbia in the Eighties and Nineties I should have been sensible enough to realize I should never have children.

When I was pregnant, in the Eighties, we didn't have electricity for days. It was winter, and Tito had just died. Tito always told us we had lots of electricity. He said we were a rich country, the best in the world, and I believed him. I liked his face. I'd known it all my life, I thought he was my grandfather. Once, when I was a little girl and lived with my family in Cairo, I was supposed to give him flowers, but then they made me give flowers to President Nasser of Egypt instead, because I was taller and Tito was smaller, and Nasser was taller and the other girl was smaller. Since then I've always associated being small with privilege and beauty.

I grew up abroad, first in Egypt and then in Italy. My father was an engineer who became a businessman and my mother a paediatrician who gave up her career to follow him. I grew up switching between languages and cultures, speaking Serbian at home while the world around me spoke Arabic and then Italian. It was years before I managed to turn this painful Babylon in my head into an advantage, and now I am writing this diary in English, which for me is not the language of intimacy or love but an attempt at distance and sanity, a means of recalling normality.

20 March It has been a terrible month. The killing has started again, this time in Kosovo. Once again we are witnesses who cannot see. We know it is going on, but we are blind. It's not even the killing that makes me die every day little by little, it's the indifference to killing that makes me feel as if nothing matters in my life. I belong to a country, to a language, to a culture which doesn't give a damn for anybody else and for whom nobody gives a damn. And I am completely paralysed. I am not used to fighting, I am not used to killing. I don't believe anybody any more, not even myself. I have stayed here and I have made a mistake: victim or not I have become one of those who did nothing for themselves or for those they love. I have a feeling that I will not survive.

22 March I spent yesterday evening with three young women who seemed so bright and happy—perhaps because their hopes are still intact. Even war and injustice can't completely destroy the hopes of those who haven't lived yet, like my daughter, who is only thirteen. They looked up to me, these girls, they would like to be me in twenty years. They don't see my anxiety, my shattered inner self. They thought I was wise and beautiful and sincere. And so I was—I was fine last night. We laughed about sanctions, about the war, about our destiny as people who will have to flee—because we know we will have to leave for a new life or we'll become like the others. My husband said every country has its terrible political and social upheavals, and some people run away from what they are born into. I know that's true, but here there is nowhere to run to except to places just as oppressive as those you are running away from. I know that despair from my first exile and I fear that choice.

In 1992 I was in Vienna, waiting for Belgrade to be bombed. I was a Serb in Austria, a country whose language I couldn't understand. Then in Italy it was even worse: I understood only too well that I was a bad Serb responsible for the atrocities of war and guilty for not stopping them.

25 March Today they are talking about sanctions again. I don't bother to think what will become of us, I just know I have to survive. They say the mind never dies, well I think the mind dies first, if you are harassed. To preserve the mind one must defend everything that the mind is made up of. I am fighting to save my mind for a better time.

26 March This is another politically correct war rather than a moral one. I have seen it in Bosnia, in Croatia, and now in Serbia: Americans are being Americans and politically correct, which is painful for everybody else who is not American and politically correct in a different way. Americans don't get it. We have a different idea of everyday life, we have different emotions, we have different ideas about help. And we perceive intrusive American help as helping the self-image of the American nation. In many ways we, both victims and aggressors, know that the Americans are right. We would all like to be Americans, but it's impossible. The Americans don't want us to be Americans, they want us to be the Other, they want us to be a territory where new plans can be implemented. I don't like feeling like this. Inside Serbia I have taken the high moral position of a traitor. I defend foreigners, Americans, and foreign intervention against national barbarians. But I don't like to be thought of as the Other by anybody, particularly not the biggest power in the world.

The other night, my neighbours wrecked my car. They did it openly, saying they'd lost their cars, so why should I have mine. I know I should fight back, but how? The law doesn't exist any more, and the police won't protect a woman with a luxury car. They believe only men should have luxury cars in Belgrade today.

One of my neighbours is a poor alcoholic who didn't adapt to the new ways of making money through crime, so he lost his money and his mind and now he drinks beer all day on the pavement. He's neither a good man nor a bad man, just one of thousands of street people who subsist in the moral and physical decay that is modern Serbia. He's not alienated from society. He is in touch emotionally and rationally. He understands the New Order and is following it. We are both part of the New Poor. Before last night, the only thing that divided us was my car parked on the pavement where he drinks his beer. So he tried to do away with the symbol that stood between us. I understand it. There's no point in explaining that cars shouldn't be scratched, or knifed, or spat upon. He has suffered, so why shouldn't my car? And the criminal on the other side of the street with the big red sports car watching us—it goes without saying: we know, he knows, everybody knows—his car is not going to be touched because he carries a gun.

27 March My parents are ashamed of me, ashamed of my choices. They suffer with every word I utter and rejoice at every word I don't. They want me silent and obedient. They say, 'We gave you everything. Don't question it. Just keep this wonderful world we made going.' And the truth is, my generation won't have time to change it. They are such brave parents, ready to sacrifice my life for their country. But

Jasmina Tesanovic

I am a coward child; not ready to die for any country, or fight a war for any just cause. They and people like them fought all those Balkan wars, produced all these leaders who are ready to appeal to people to fight in more wars; for land, for graves, out of pride, out of prejudice. What I resent is that they never told me the truth about their lives. They never told me about their wars, or about how they survived hunger and killings to make their country perfect. Did they kill? Did they see people being killed? Was it all worthwhile?

7 April Do we want to be ruled by foreigners or not? That's the question put to us in the upcoming referendum. Can it really be so simple? Here we have a ruthless dictator convincing us that we are the 'wild Serbs' we are not. He falsifies our thoughts, our roles, our desires, our history. We are drafted into a war we don't understand and don't want by cowards who are afraid to negotiate because they can't be rational.

I think of myself as a political idiot. Idiot, in ancient Greece, denoted a common person without access to knowledge and information—all women, by definition, and most men. I am unable to make judgements. I see no options I can identify with. Is that normal? Is it because I am a woman? All the political options of my fellow men sound aggressive, stupid or far-fetched compared to my simple needs. I need to move, I need to communicate, I need to have children, I need to talk, to play, to have fun. They speak of history, of historical rights and precedents, but it's not my history they speak of, or if it is, I had no part in it. They talk of blood, of pride, of rights, but I am losing my mind because of lack of love and understanding. All our instincts are focused on dying or surviving.

14 April Yesterday I jumped on to a bus, a terrible, stinking, falling-to-pieces bus. It was a dangerous trip for several reasons: the doors wouldn't close and people were hanging out of them, pickpockets were everywhere, and lots of old sick people who can't afford medicine were coughing and spitting on everybody. But once on board I realized I was surrounded by the happy, pretty faces of young schoolgirls. It was a group of ballet dancers coming back from performing a successful show. I thought of their parents somewhere, grey and tired and anxious like me, young-old people gone half mad with fear and worry. But watching the beaming faces of these young girls, their arms and legs long and thin like some African tribe, I thought, my God, you can't stop beauty, you can't stop joy, you can't stop creativity. And I looked through the window at downtown Belgrade, full of young boys and girls on a Saturday night, with the same shoes, the same jackets as kids in New York or Paris, and I thought, I know some of them are criminals, and some of their parents starve in order to make them look like that, but even so, you can't stop joy and beauty. It grows faster than crime and death.

15 April Today I saw a Serbian family on the road in front of the UNHCR office near my flat in the centre of the city. They were terrified, they had bags and suitcases around them blocking the pavement. A middle-aged woman was crying, a young girl was ashamed to look at us, and the men were just sitting and staring in front of them. Men often do that when they become powerless. It made me shiver. They were in my city, in my street, Serbian refugees from Kosovo. And we were part of a common destiny.

Some twenty years ago my aunt had to emigrate from Kosovo with all her family because, as Serbs, they were harassed by the Albanians. They left all their goods, they sold their house at a loss and started life anew here on the outskirts of Belgrade. That is a common experience in my father's family. They came from Herzegovina and are now scattered all over the world.

The family on the road reminded me of other refugee families I have seen in the past few years, though only a few came to Belgrade. This time the Kosovo Serbs will all come here. My city will change once more. But it isn't really mine now. I don't feel safe here, or happy, or free. I'm a refugee in my own city.

18 April The pensioners are being told they have to vote 'yes' in the referendum in order to get their pensions, in order to be able to buy bread and anything else. The result of our referendum is already pretty certain. Nobody dares to alter the ideas of Big Brother and his political murals on which our personal lives are spattered like cheap paint.

20 April This morning I couldn't buy milk. Just as six years ago when the war started, it started with milk, a symbol of maternal need. The message is: death to the children.

24 April The referendum was yesterday. One of my friends said, now they'll come and shoot us because we didn't vote. I told her she was just being paranoid. After the vote the President gave a speech. Everything about him, his face, his voice, his words and emotions, was so familiar—that pathetic, patronizing tone that knows what's best for me, just like my father. This president, whom I know to be a corrupt liar and merciless enemy, worries for my future—that is why he is sending me to war, that is why he is fighting the rest of the world. That is why he makes me weep.

30 April We spent yesterday evening with an American friend. She was asking us how we could still talk to friends who had become nationalists. I was so nervous I could hardly sit down. Then we heard the news: we've got sanctions. Our friend was afraid her plane wouldn't leave. She asked me what the sanctions were about, what our lives would be like. I said, I don't know. I can't control my life any more. I feel utterly depressed, absolutely lonely.

Most Americans we meet are just silent. I remember at the beginning of the Serbo-Croatian war we went to the International PEN Congress party in Vienna. Nobody wanted to sit at a table with me and my husband—with Serbs—but an Austrian writer came with his wife to our table and talked to us without mentioning the war. I thought we were safe in our invisible pain. But at the end of the evening, he simply said: 'If you need money, if you need a flat, any time, we are here.' I started crying and he said: 'I remember when I was eleven, I was a Nazi for five minutes.' His name was Peter Ebner and his father was killed as a German soldier at the Russian front.

6 May Today I went to a meeting of the Women in Black. We were about fifty women—feminists, refugees, activists, women running non-governmental organizations, women driven mad by the past wars—plus a few gay men. Most of the women from NGOs and feminist groups saw a parallel in Kosovo to the wars in Croatia and

Bosnia. I saw it differently: we have had an apartheid state for Albanians in Serbia for the past ten years at least. In Croatia and Bosnia, it wasn't like that. That was about boys' games and loot.

I was so upset I could hardly speak. I started swearing and my voice trembled. 'The police are entering houses to mobilize men all over Serbia...' Some of the women suggested peace caravans, peace protests, pacifist walks and a global protest against mobilization. But we did all that six years ago and nobody listened to us, so why would they listen now?

9 May Today the international community decided on another package of sanctions against Yugoslavia: one more step on the path to total isolation. I was in the market place where people were talking about prices and inflation, but the hole in the middle of their sentences represented their knowledge of what had happened. Today the President's wife opened a maternity hospital in Novi Sad. For two hours everything came to a standstill. Women already in labour were sent away. But no political power in the world can prevent children being born. Only afterwards can power transform a precious little life into a miserable existence without a future. Yes, power can do that.

16 May What are they doing to us? We are entering the long tunnel of fascism: fascism with a domestic face, that of your neighbour who beats his wife when she disobeys, and pisses on the staircase when drunk. The face of a big funny man who is dangerous because he doesn't know his or your boundaries.

26 May Today the nationalists passed a new law against the autonomy of the university. They say students should just study and not care about politics. Those who protested were beaten and some of them arrested. Everybody else was confused and silent. Most people here have been completely broken down by the political shit of the past five—the past fifty years. Maybe there will be strikes, protests, but more likely nothing will happen at all, and we'll be back in the dark ages. Does anybody enjoy this parade of totalitarianism? Are these few in power good for anyone? I don't believe so. Serbs are like women who don't want to be feminists, who are satisfied with the old stereotypes, no equality just invisibility. I can see how that happens. I used to feel that way too: it's a natural state, you're born into it. Once you come out of it, you may lose everything, but there is no going back.

29 May I met some people from the university: there will be no mass protest against the totalitarian laws. My friend who teaches at the university and whose father is a retired professor said he told her triumphantly: 'Now you'll have to obey. Now you'll have no more freedom.' This is a war between us and our parents, between political idiots (like me) and political criminals (like them): no winners, no losers, no right ways, no middle ways, only permanent struggle and bad dreams.

3 June A few days ago a young soldier was killed during his regular training on the Kosovan border with Albania. Yesterday his last letter to his parents was published in the paper. He couldn't have written anything more direct, cruel and true: 'Just stop it, all of you who think you are doing something right, just stop it.' I could imagine what his parents felt. I could have been his mother.

Some years ago, I found myself in the lift in my building with the mother of my next-door neighbour, a soldier who had been killed at nineteen. He was a punk, he wore an earring and played loud music. But when I saw her I started crying, I didn't know what to say. She embraced me and kissed me on both cheeks. She said: 'Now, now, stop it, he was a brave boy and he died for his country.' I wanted to shout at her: 'You're crazy, you know it's not true, he was killed by people who were taking everything from us, our lives, values, goods, children.' But then I saw her face: I knew she knew it. But she knew better, too. She was pleading with me silently: don't say it, don't take his death away from me. Death took him, leave me his death to be my company through life. (Mothers, I thought, traitors to the nation, traitors to their men, bearers of life and death. Mothers are like court jesters: they tell the truth but it has no impact.) She closed the lift door after me. His music will never disturb me again. Very soon I moved out: the silence was too much like my inner solitude. I couldn't bear it.

4 June The cheapest photocopying shop in town is in my street. To reach it, you have to climb a narrow staircase over the cellars where the gypsies live. They are a local institution. In the last few years the son has fathered two babies and now they are seven in one room. They all drink and make scenes, swearing, cursing or making fun of passers-by. Today I went to the store to photocopy my stories for some Swiss friends. Coming out I found the old gypsy woman lying in a pool of blood. She was screaming at her husband, 'Radovan, you are killing me.' He was running round her, and their dog was licking her blood. The babies were a few feet away, but not crying. I stepped over the blood and decided to leave them to it. Other people were doing the same. She lay there screaming for another half-hour until her husband pulled her to her feet and cleaned her up. They were both so drunk they could hardly stand. Then they sat on their usual doorstep and opened another bottle of beer. The babies didn't cry, the dog didn't bark. We're used to their love quarrels. Usually she beats him and he rarely strikes back, he's smaller and less aggressive. She has a big handsome lover who comes over sometimes when the husband is away, then when he comes back they all scream and fight, usually all night. We can't sleep because of the noise, but their quarrels are so interesting we just stand at the window and listen.

8 June All over Belgrade men are huddled together in bars whispering about the future over their beer. They say blood will be flowing on the streets of Belgrade in two weeks. They say we will all die of hunger, disease and street violence. They say our country is finished, our children are doomed, we have no future. I have listened very carefully to these men who both move me and depress me. But I have realized I don't believe their stories. They're like little boys, these men, afraid to be killed but ashamed to cry. They'd rather damn the world than say no to the war. They regard me as a political idiot. And that's what I am. I've chosen the word myself in order to be safe from their language. I still believe more in words than in democracies.

12 June We are expecting NATO troops to bomb selected targets in Kosovo and in Yugoslavia. It might end the war there—I wish it would—or just result in all-out war. Everybody is speculating, but

Jasmina Tesanovic

I'm over the war shivers now. I had them so strongly six years ago when I left for Vienna that the thought of them now seems no more than an echo. Pain, like fear, has a natural limit. After that comes indifference.

17 June Parents from all over the country are protesting against their children being sent to fight in Kosovo. I wish I could see their faces. They must be special people, honest enough to admit that it is still their old war that has been going on for the past sixty years at least.

The woman who is helping me with my housework is a refugee from Knin, Croatia, from the Storm operation in 1995, when they were bombed at five in the morning and fled in nightgowns, on foot or on tractors. She is trembling today, she can't sleep and is afraid it will happen again here. She wanted me to calm her down but I feel exactly like she does. I tremble, too; I don't sleep, either. We both feel guilty for being in the wrong place once again, for having children we can't protect. And our men blame us for the same things. I tried to explain to her that it is not our fault, that our feelings of responsibility and guilt are irrational. But they are as real as they are ridiculous and groundless. Our fear and anxiety is so great that we clean, dust, cook all day long, only pausing to listen to the news. We behave in exactly the same way, me and my cleaning woman. We go on cleaning and feel guilty.

23 June Tension in the air like electricity before a storm. The gypsy woman in the basement is rolling half naked on the pavement covered in spit, rolling on the glass from her broken beer bottle. Not even the conceptual artist Marina Abramovic in her latest performances could be that good. She's drenched in blood. 'Police! Help me!' she shouts. 'They tried to kill me.' Then she gives us a long speech about life, love, war and simplicity. She does this more and more frequently. Every day, I feel as though the social and emotional space between her and me is becoming smaller. When she sees me she says, 'Hello sweetie'.

I dropped by the Women's Centre. A friend asks me if I've heard what the policemen are doing in Kosovo. We continuously receive e-mails: they rape, they kill, the same as in 1992 in Bosnia. On television we hear only about the Serbian people's centuries of suffering. An American woman asks me if I want to go to Kosovo and see for myself. But I don't have to. I can imagine how it is.

5 July Last night, in front of a police station in the centre of Belgrade, I saw a dozen policemen with sleeping bags and machine-guns ready to leave for Kosovo. Their families were with them: mothers, fathers, wives, babies. The policemen were young and completely calm, the families were worried. It was unnerving to have to pick your way through the guns and sleeping bags on the pavement. I didn't dare ask them anything, not even to look after their machine-guns so we could cross the street safely. They behaved as if their guns were in the right place. In my country uniforms always take away the power of speech from citizens because uniforms carry guns, and citizens carry fear, so there is a permanent civil war going on between uniforms and civilians.

The Serbian war criminal who destroyed a city in the war with Croatia and killed many people committed suicide in the Hague. His body was brought back to Serbia for burial. People are talking about him as if he was a hero.

7 July Today is a state holiday, something to do with the Second World War. The shops are closed, old people haven't had their pensions delivered for a month and even then they only received half the miserable sum. The black market is full of people who have dragged themselves through the humid heat to get a carrot, an onion, a tomato for free. The gypsy woman under my window is singing her lungs out in a lullaby for a baby who cannot sleep because of her song. It's like a scene from a cabaret. I feel sick, I can't breathe because of all the dirt and sadness. Everything is falling apart: no pensions, no cash on the streets, and in the shops, no sugar, no oil. Foreigners taking over the decisions, without much knowledge or goodwill, but with energy and anger—Wild Serbs make the world go wild. I wonder if we will have public soup kitchens in a few months' time and coupons for buying clothing, like my parents did after the Second World War. Normality is a myth by now.

12 July Last night I was in a restaurant with a friend. It was dusk and we were sitting on the terrace overlooking the Danube when a swarm of mosquitoes attacked. There was pandemonium: women screaming and rushing inside, men moving chairs and tables out of their way, and I thought if a single bomb landed here by mistake, their nationalism would vanish. Their proud Serbian nationalist small talk would fizzle out like air out of a balloon. My friend and I stayed outside: the mosquitoes drowned in our sauce, and we ate it and them as they ate us. The nationalists left all their food behind on the terrace as if it was free. It reminded me of those stories about the Russian aristocracy during the October Revolution, but a cheaper version.

31 August Today a wonderful light fell on Belgrade from the sky. I nearly said to my husband: 'I love you, let's have another child and stay here for ever.' Otherwise, I'm packing in my head, switching through countries like satellite channels: who would accept me? Hardly anybody, but still, the more countries I exclude the closer I get to the one waiting for me.

30 September My cousin has been hospitalized for AIDS. She is dying. She got better and then at a certain point she got worse. I went to see her the night after we had an earthquake when everybody was out on the streets thinking it was NATO bombs. But she escaped the earthquake, and she would escape the bombs. She looked like a saint, a beautiful medieval picture, small, white and immobile. She smiled at me and I didn't dare to cry, I just wanted to faint. Who cares about bombs or earthquakes when you have a chance to stay alive? She has none. With her will go my childhood, my ideals, my dreams. Who cares about NATO if she is gone? I don't want to be left alone with the ideas of happiness, beauty and bliss we shared as children.

During the night I hold my child tightly, trying to repair the bliss of childhood, but it is no use. There is no bliss in it. I see my dying cousin every day. I feed her like when we were kids. I say, stay alive. She says, I have no place to go. I say, stay alive for me, I will find you a place. Her eyes sparkle, she takes hold of my hand feebly. She still has beautiful hands. I say, promise.

In the hospital ward the water tubs are full of vomit. Most of the expensive medicines are unavailable and food is brought in from outside. The patients share their food. People don't stay long in the AIDS department: relatives just rush in and out, out of duty, out of fear. The nurses don't talk to patients or visitors. They think everybody knows all that they need to know: those who cross this threshold, abandon all hope. But then all hospitals here have had this kind of atmosphere for the past five or six years. Death reigns. My father spent hours waiting for the hospital to open in order to be among the first to get a pacemaker. It wasn't a question of money, but of sanctions: no pacemakers for Serbs. And he got it. When he had a heart attack there was no money for batteries for the machine to regulate his heart. Then the young man in the next bed died. I happened to be there. My father said: 'The poor man, he died; grab his covers, I have none.' And I did, I grabbed the covers from this dead stranger while his body was still warm. And as I did it, I felt a connection to him. Through his warm covers he had suddenly become familiar to me. I thought, this is not death, this is murder. And I got angry. Let's find the murderer.

10 October Yesterday, in the queue to pay new taxes—for the war to come, for the monasteries, for weapons against Kosovan Albanians, for refugees, NATO, the whole world—I saw that people were worse off than I ever realized. They were rude and dirty and untidy, and when I looked at my image in the mirror, my hair was dirty too: I am leaving my hair unwashed as a protest against the war.

These people despise people like me who are afraid, even if I'm their own flesh and blood. They clean their cellars and buy their candles and say they will defend their country until the very end. Is it possible nobody is afraid? Is it possible that pride can win out over fear, and if so, where is my pride? I am not proud of my proud people, they killed and humiliated others. Even if they did it under orders, they still did it. And yet I am not ashamed of my people because I don't consider them any worse than most others, as such, I just see them as people who have no chance to be better.

Yesterday night I went with the Women in Black to demonstrate in the Square of the Republic. The police were protecting us from the crowd who were spitting on us and shouting, 'Whores, whores...'

Kosovan refugees leaving the village of Vucitrin after their houses were burned, November 1998.

We'd all taken small rucksacks with ID, money, spare clothes etc. in case we got arrested and tied to the trees as NATO targets, which is what Seselj, the deputy prime minister of Serbia, promised us traitors. My parents call me a traitor for not supporting them, my husband does the same for not supporting him; my daughter, too.

11 October Can anything be as bad as this feeling that imminent death is a lottery? Last night we had a birthday party. We couldn't get drunk, but we couldn't stop laughing. It was the kind of behaviour I've observed at funerals.

18 October Last night, the night of the new NATO ultimatum, I wanted to die. Just like my gypsy friend I got drunk, drugged and aggressive. I wanted to kill. I wanted to die. I bashed my head and concussed myself, made my nose bleed and ended up with a broken finger. I wanted to excise the conflict inside me—the conflict all around me. There. My war.

13 November My cousin died on 10 November. I had a vision two days before that it would happen, the day, the hour. I went to the hospital. They wouldn't let me in, so I stood in front of her window as she died. It was a beautiful day, sunny and clear. I entered the ward, gave the flowers I had brought to a very thin guy who seemed nice and very sick. The young lady doctor didn't mention the word AIDS when I asked the immediate cause of death. She said: 'You know what this ward is for.' This is exactly how all people involved with AIDS, whether patients or doctors or relatives, deal with it, through evasion. When I left the hospital I went for a long walk. I felt privileged to have been there, for having such a lovely cousin who made even a ghostly sickness like AIDS lovely. She was calm, smiling and at peace. She even confessed her sins to the Head of the Serbian Church when he came to visit the ward, though she wasn't religious and I doubt she thought she had any sins, even if her life, seen from the outside, was a sin. Because my lovely cousin was a junkie, an outcast, and a writer who never published. Telling her story straight would have meant losing her friends, her social security, her job. She preferred faking normality because she was brave, much braver than me.

1999

On 24 March 1999, NATO began air strikes on Yugoslavia.

26 March, five p.m. I hope we all survive this war: the Serbs, the Albanians, the bad guys and the good guys, those who took up the arms, those who deserted, the Kosovo refugees travelling through the woods and the Belgrade refugees travelling the streets with their children in their arms looking for non-existent shelters when the sirens go off. I hope NATO pilots don't leave behind the wives and children I saw crying on CNN as their husbands took off for military targets in Serbia. I hope we all survive, but that the world as it is does not: the world in which a US congressman estimates 20,000 civilian deaths as a low price for peace in Kosovo, or in which President Clinton says he wants a Europe safe for American schoolgirls. When the Serbian president Milutinovic says we will fight to the very last drop of blood, I always feel they are talking about my blood, not theirs.

The green and black markets in my neighbourhood have adapted to the new conditions: no bread from the state but a lot of grain on the market; no information from state TV, but a lot of talk among the frightened population about who is winning. Teenagers are betting on corners—Whose planes have been shot down, ours or theirs? Who lies best? Who wins the best victories?—as if it were a football match.

The city is silent but still working. Rubbish is taken away, we have water, we have electricity, but where are the people? Everybody is huddled together inside waiting for the bombs: people who hardly know each other, people who pretended not to or truly didn't know what was going on in Kosovo, people who didn't believe NATO was serious all along. We all sit together and share what we have. A feminist friend asked me to organize a consciousness-raising workshop. Another wants me to go with her to Pancevo, the bombed district on the other side of Belgrade, to give a reading of my novel. But there is no petrol. We'll have to buy bicycles.

We phone each other all the time, passing information back and forth: I realize the children are best at it, they prefer to be doing something in an emergency. We grown-ups nag at them with our fears but they're too young for speculation, they deal with facts and news. Most of them are well informed through the children's networks, foreign satellite stations and local TV.

I think of our Albanian friends in Kosovo. They must be much worse off than we are, and fear springs up at the thought.

I'm sleeping heavily, without dreams, afraid to wake up, but happy there is no real tragedy yet; we're all still alive, looking at each other every second for proof. And yes, the weather is beautiful, we enjoy it and fear it: the better the weather, the heavier the bombing, but the better the weather, probably the more precise the bombing. I only wish I knew if we needed bad weather or good weather to stay alive.

The sirens are interrupting me, a terrible wailing up and down. I switch on CNN to see why they're going off in Belgrade but they don't know. Local TV will tell us when it's all over.

NATO stepped up air strikes over Yugoslavia.

28 March Belgrade is rocking, shaking, trembling. We are entering the second phase of NATO intervention. The sirens went off today for nearly twenty-four hours. I had to go out to buy some food, though we are not really starving yet, not keeling over. People are taking tranquillizers to stay calm, or just crying. The shelters are crowded. Every evening we go to the shelter in my local underground station. I know people there already. We try to make plans and we watch the news all the time, none of it good, none of it reliable. I watch Jamie Shea at the NATO press conference. He makes what's happening to us here sound irrelevant compared to NATO's aims. But how can it be as simple as he makes it sound?

We've heard from our friends in Kosovo. They are already living through what will probably come to us in a few days: killing, looting of flats and houses, complete anarchy. For the time being most of us are staying underground. Somebody said that there are eight million Serbs underground, though I think it's part of the local propaganda, to keep people from coming out and making trouble. It's the opposite of the demonstrations of 1997 when everybody was out on the streets. Maybe we should set up an underground state with new democratic laws: maybe this time it should be run by women and children, according to their needs, their morality.

People sheltering in the station have been living inside the trains for days. At first they were restless, hanging round the platforms and on the escalators. Now they barely have room to sit down and the air is stale. Some of my friends, a family of refugees from Krajina with two grown-up sons, spent five years in much worse conditions, so to them these are really good ones. To me it looks like a trans-Siberian journey to nowhere, but I visit them regularly, bringing them food and blankets. They can't understand why I go outside. But I tell them, of course I'm afraid, but I'm even more afraid of staying obediently underground for the next twenty years. And anyway, nothing much is happening outside, it's within ourselves that things are happening.

29 March Gloomy, raining, the siren going all the time. I've just heard that martial law has been established, with execution as punishment. I still can't believe we're living through a war. In a few hours my life has changed completely, everybody's has. I think we're all becoming different people.

30 March Today no bombs, no sirens to wake me up. I slept for sixteen hours. Last night the children went to a terrible nationalist rock and folk concert for the people living underground. I heard that afterwards a gang of nationalists destroyed McDonald's.

My father used to dream of bombing long after the Second World War was over. He would wake up during the night and take me out of my bed and carry me down to the basement. I remember him doing it, and last night I did it myself with my daughter several times. I feel sick both emotionally and physically. I feel like sleeping and sleeping for ever, until the peace comes back.

My God, we really are at war, I just heard some of the rules: no contacts with the foreign press, court martial for deserters. Mental patients have been turned out on the streets and the hospitals are being used for the wounded. My women friends are all working in various humanitarian centres—with refugees, gypsies, old, frightened women who live alone. My best friend says it's the only way she can stay sane. I'm different, the only way I can get rid of my emotions is by writing. I have to fight for my computer every hour of the day. It's the only one at home and everybody in the family wants it. I've always hated computers but now I use it whenever I can. Writing in war is not like writing in peace, though for me it's always been a biological necessity, a way of easing the pain of living.

Today Primakov, the Russian prime minister, is in Belgrade. I dare not hope. The café in my neighbourhood isn't called New York any more but Baghdad Café.

The allies rejected Milosevic's offer to pull back from Kosovo if NATO agreed to stop air strikes.

31 March Is it possible that we are all going to be sacrificed for somebody's lack of political judgement, or worse, madness? The conflict is escalating, atrocities are happening daily. I think of buying some pills and sleeping—for ever if it comes to that. I mean it. I am thinking rationally. I hate seeing the fear in the eyes of people around me. I avoid them and spend time with children.

1 April We spent last night in a shelter, three grown-ups, five children and two dogs. Actually it's a private house with a good cellar next to the underground station where I spent the first night of bombing. According to CNN, downtown Belgrade was supposed to be bombed but it wasn't, so once again we have to wait. Instead, three American soldiers were captured by the Yugoslav army. This is a dirty, dirty war—frightened people in basements, bruised soldiers on television, Albanian refugees crying on camera, saying things people should never have to say, especially on TV. Human dignity is at stake here for all of us.

My friend, a half-Albanian half-Serbian Yugoslav who lives in New York, phoned. I am living your European time here, she says, I wish I was there with you. We are living in American time, awake during the night, dozing during the day: you could say we were living both times at once.

One thing I've noticed: every evening at dusk my hands start to tremble uncontrollably. It goes on for a few hours. I heard that some other women have the same symptoms. It is fear of air raids after dark. The men here behave differently, they shout and argue about life and death. We are more afraid of their deaths than our own. Only at certain moments, when images of violence against my children hit me, I feel faint with fear. Then I think I would prefer suicide to that.

My parents, alone in their flat, can hardly hear the siren. They watch state TV and they phone me every now and then saying, 'Don't worry, it will be OK.' And I feel better. Just like when I was a child, my father's voice makes me feel secure. But I don't give that kind of security to my children. It's my deliberate choice not to: the world is not a safe place.

I heard that the French, German and American cultural centres in the middle of Belgrade have been completely destroyed by the mob. I've got no wish to go and examine the ruins, which, like a public corpse, we are invited to witness as a warning.

Some Yugoslav pilots were honoured on television by our President; now we see in the obituary pages of the papers that they are dead.

2 April Today is Catholic Good Friday and people are getting mystical because of the bombs. They see portents everywhere, in the pattern of days, in the clouds that prevent air strikes, as if they were celestial signs of destiny. Another blow to the common sense of ordinary people.

My friend's son phoned from the battlefield last night: he couldn't say where he was, he said he was OK but that some of his friends were not. The age limit for volunteers has been raised to seventy-five for men. On CNN, Arkan, the indicted war criminal, is promising lawful and merciful treatment of the three American soldiers. I watch the sea of refugees being marshalled by both sides on the borders between Yugoslavia, Macedonia and Albania. It reminds me of 1995, when Serbs from Krajina poured into Serbia for days with no real idea of what was happening to them.

NATO targeted its bombing campaign on Belgrade.

3 April It is morning, a beautiful sunny morning, and I am crying. Last night the centre of Belgrade was bombed with appalling precision; sure, they were military targets, but only twenty metres from one of the biggest maternity hospitals in the Balkans, the one where I was born and where I had my baby. The Ministry of the Interior was destroyed: some of my friends remember being interrogated there. I am pleased by NATO's accuracy. But I feel at the mercy of those young pilots, responsible for hitting military targets without harming a single newborn baby.

I heard from a friend who lives in a small village on the Danube near Belgrade that the peasants there are looking for a missing American pilot. They have organized themselves into a guerrilla group like the partisans sixty years ago. My friend said they are probably doing the same thing in villages all over Yugoslavia. 'What would you do to the pilot if you found him?' I asked people at home. Nothing, of course, they all said. Some would give him food and preach about the situation in Serbia—mostly the grown-ups; while the children would feed him and hide him in a cellar.

On the BBC, CNN, Sky News, commentators are already talking about the war as a chess game. What a virtual, playful, cruel war. Personally, my war is made up of terrible pictures in my imagination, of my loved ones being killed, tortured, raped. These are the images that haunt me when the siren goes off, this is what is turning my hair white. The first time I got grey hairs was ten years ago when a drunken customs officer harassed us at the Slovenian border because we were Serbs. I knew then it was only the beginning. I feel solidarity with anybody who has ever lived through a war—we receive e-mails from such people all over the world.

4 April Again a night in the shelter. Two more bridges have been hit and the railway line to Montenegro has been destroyed by SFOR troops in Bosnia. The wire is finally visible around our cage. We wild bad Serbs from the fourteenth century, disguised in jeans, and speaking English, but still aliens... This NATO viewpoint is completely in line with the local nationalists, who said when the maternity hospital shook from nearby bombing, the babies didn't even cry because they were Serb babies. Well, I cried like a baby yesterday when I heard thousands of people on the Square of the Republic singing *Tamo daleko* ('There, far away is Serbia...') during the daily concert. It's a beautiful old song which Serbian soldiers sang in the First World War when they retreated from Thessalonika. Only a few came back and my grandfather was one of them. He used to sing it to me when I was a child, and I always sang it when people abroad asked me for a Serbian song. It always makes people cry. But I couldn't sing yesterday—it's not my song any more, it's not my Serbia. I am in exile in my own country.

I am supposed to get forty litres of petrol per month, but I have nowhere to go, so maybe I will exchange it for forty litres of wine and forty packs of cigarettes, which are impossible to buy. Maybe this is the route to my Serbia now.

5 April In the pharmacy the shelves were fuller than ever, except for aspirin or tranquillizers—which is what everybody's been asking for. People are buying sweets like mad—for emotional distress, lack of love.

6 April Today is the anniversary of the Nazi bombing of Belgrade in 1941, but the major damage to the city was done at the end of the war by Allied bombing and I know everybody will use the parallel to make themselves feel better or worse. This morning I was sitting on the terrace in the sun dreaming of the sea and the sky was clear again as it was last night when we waited for air raids on the terrace. The planes came again, but they didn't bomb Belgrade. I feel more guilty than ever this morning. People from all over the world ask me, 'Do you realize how terrible it is in Kosovo?' I do, I really do, and I feel guilty that we feel bad here without having the horror they do. But our war, whether for the past ten or fifty years, has always been this kind of invisible horror. We still have a long way to go to be free.

7 April Running to the shelter with food, running out of the shelter to buy food. Phoning friends and relatives, exchanging fears: who, where, what was hit? Who will be next? Never a why. I don't watch the news any more, I hate all sides equally. Yugoslavia is crumbling, what a pity for all those bridges, bridges have such good connotations—people building them, crossing them. What a pity for all those wasted innocent lives. Is this the future, running in and out of a shelter like a rat? The schools are closed, the children have the serious eyes of adults.

8 April Last night we sat on the terrace waiting, making bets. After a few big explosions I went deaf in my right ear. A government administration building was hit in downtown Belgrade, only half a mile away. Nobody really knows why that building and not the general headquarters as was expected. Nobody tells us anything: was it a civil or military target? Anyway, good, we're done with that. We've been waiting for it for days. We started laughing with relief when we heard there was no 'collateral damage', as NATO calls the dead, by the 'criminal aggression', as TV Serbia calls NATO. My father phoned, his voice was trembling, he'd heard nothing, he'd seen nothing, he is already deaf and too old to move, but he kept saying: 'What can we do now? Nothing, can we? I thought it was the pans falling in the kitchen but then it was bombs. What can we do now?'

Last night the daily concert moved to the bridge over the Sava that joins new and old Belgrade. Our families are split between the two sides but we don't dare cross over to see them in case the bridges are destroyed while we're away.

I watched a BBC military commentator talking about Serbs as horrible people who cared about nothing except their own lives. I hate this kind of ethnic generalization. I have never thought to generalize about the British, even though I spent twelve years in an English-speaking boarding school. But after his remark I did. I wonder what British people would be like in these conditions?

My old friend Mica, the gypsy woman from the basement, has been rather stable since the bombings started. Her only distress seems to come from the fact that we can't buy cigarettes any more. She asks me for one every time I pass. She speaks calmly, no more foul language. The difference between us, a white girl and a gypsy girl, is marginal now: we both live in basements with too many emotions, too few cigarettes and too much beer.

9 April I remember, shortly before the war, today was considered a good date to conceive if you wanted a child to be born on 1 January 2000. I remember how silly and ridiculous this seemed; I also

SUBSCRIBE

FICTION MEMOIR REPORTAGE PHOTOGRAPHY

There are over 70,000 subscribers to Granta, in every corner of the world.

Why not join them? Or give a subscription as a gift?

You'll save up to £40 on the bookshop price (£8.99 an issue), and get a regular supply of outstanding new writing, delivered to your home.

A one-year subscription (4 issues) is just £24.95. You save £11.
A two-year subscription (8 issues) is just £46.50. You save £25.
A three-year subscription (12 issues) is just £67. You save £40.

'Never take Granta for granted.'
Daily Telegraph

SAVE
as much as
£40

Order form

Subscribe and save:

○ I'd like to subscribe and save:

○ 38% with a 3-year subscription (12 issues) for £67.00

○ 35% with a 2-year subscription (8 issues) for £46.50

○ 30% with a 1-year subscription (4 issues) for £24.95

Please start the subscription with issue no:_____

My name: _____

Address: _____

Country/postcode: _____

Share and save:

○ I'd like to give a gift subscription, for:

○ 3 years (£67) ○ 2 years (£46.50) ○ 1 year (£24.50)

Please start the subscription with issue no:_____

Recipient's name: _____

Address: _____

Country/postcode: _____

Gift message (optional): _____

Postage The prices above include postage in the UK. For the rest of Europe, please add £8 per year. For the rest of the world, please add £15 per year. (Airspeeded delivery).

Payment Total amount: £_____ by: ○ Cheque (to 'Granta') ○ Visa, Mastercard, AmEx:

Card no / _ / _ / _ / _ / _ / _ / _ / _ / _ / _ / _ / _ / _ / _ / _ / _ /

Expires / _ / _ / _ / Signature _____

Return You can either post ('Freepost' if you live in the UK), using the address label below. Or e-mail, fax or phone your details, if paying by credit card.

In the UK: **FreeCall 0500 004 033** (phone & fax).

Elsewhere: tel: 44 171 704 0470, fax 44 171 704 0470. E-mail: subs@grantamag.co.uk

99JBG67

○ Please tick if you'd prefer not to receive information from compatible organizations.

Granta Magazine

**FREEPOST
2/3 Hanover Yard
Noel Road
London
N1 8BR**

remember how suggestive it was. Now the day has arrived nobody here has any such plans. With all the talk about ground troops entering Yugoslavia, women are hoping they are not pregnant, or wondering what to do with their children if they have to take up arms. Already two of my girlfriends, pacifists, feminists, said that if it comes to an all-out ground war they will take up guns instead of staying at home and waiting to be killed, raped, or sent into exile.

Military logic is entering our everyday language. We talk about adapting to war conditions. I thought of starting a school for the children who are suddenly on the loose, without their usual studying routine. Most of us don't go into hiding any more, don't think of leaving the country. We are just here—who cares for how long?—we are held hostage by our lives, we have no decent way out.

10 April The hairdresser next door is working his usual hours despite the alarm that went off in broad daylight. The pilots were probably 'frustrated' last night, unable to drop their bombs because of the weather. The NATO briefing will be tense, no doubt, but we had a peaceful night: no boom-booms, only local aircraft which at least have a more humane sound, like planes used to have.

Tomorrow is Orthodox Easter. My daughter painted eggs—not that we're religious, but she said she was bored and I thought, better let her do something constructive than sulk alone in her room waiting for the sirens to go off. She is a child of the war now. She said yesterday, 'I have a feeling I'm going to be killed when I'm sixteen, so what's the point of going to school any more?' I froze and just said, 'You'll go to school anyway.'

11 April Last night at midnight Belgrade was on the streets, the sirens were going but still people were crowding into the churches for the Easter service. I looked at them: the old, simple and ragged people, the young and middle-aged and better off, and then those in the minority who really believe. They all wore the same tragic expressions, like in a crowd scene at La Scala. At the same time, the rock concert was raging on the Sava bridge, packed with patriots who believe fervently in their own power rather than God's. I don't fit on either side. I don't believe in God but I don't believe in myself, not with the world the way it is.

I'm scared when the siren goes off, and I don't want my children to take any risks, so I went to the video club and took out some films for us. One was a Mickey Rourke film my favourite actor until eighteen days ago—but he seemed so foolish. I just thought, he knows nothing about me any more, he can't share the crucial experiences of my life. So Mickey Rourke and I had to split after all these years.

I went to bed early and slept like a log. The fridge makes a terrible row, worse than air raids, so I decided to switch it off and clean it today, even though my granny used to say it was bad luck to work on Easter Day.

When I was five my grandmother took me to church at Easter, secretly, so that my communist parents wouldn't know. I remember the fear and excitement I felt entering the biggest building I had ever been into in my life, with its strange smells and glimmering candles. After that first moment of joy, I was overcome by a feeling which has never left me: the feeling of powerlessness, of the invisibility of my little person. I started crying hysterically, saying to my granny, 'I will be burned, I will be punished…' So she had to take me out, much distressed at her failed mission. I remember she bought me an ice cream and a toy dog and we never spoke about Easter or church again. It was years before I went into another church, and the feeling was pretty much the same, but I was stronger, my mystical crisis was over—not resolved, but over—and by that time my granny was no longer around to comfort me or try to explain.

12 April I couldn't get to sleep last night so finally I took a tranquillizer—there, I've started too. All these weeks I've put off using drugs to stay normal, but I realize that it's impossible to stay normal without them, impossible to stay here without them. I understand those who leave, I could have been one of them, but I don't want to leave my city, my friends, my language. Other friends from all over the world keep offering me flats, money, help, but the only thing I need from people all over the world is for them to try to stop our war.

Yesterday a newspaper editor was shot in front of his house in the centre of Belgrade in the middle of the day. Who's going to be next?

The kids go to discotheques and hold parties during the day. They say maybe it will be their last bit of fun.

More factories were destroyed last night, more fuel dumps, in Pancevo and Novi Sad, two towns which for the past few years have been full of Serbian refugees from Croatia and Bosnia. I have friends in both. One of them e-mailed me: 'Yes, we will go on with work for our international summer schools, they are more important than ever. But at the moment we have dead people here, though we at the peace movement are still all alive.' He's a better person than I am. I don't want to fake normal life.

Last night the old man next door was taken to hospital during the air raids. He was tied to a chair and carried out of his flat. 'Good night,' he said politely. I guess it was some kind of nervous breakdown: alone all these weeks, he couldn't take it any more. He'll be better off in a crowded hospital.

NATO planes hit a civilian passenger train near Leskovac, south of Belgrade. Ten people were killed.

13 April The old man next door died. 'Good night, ladies, good night, sweet ladies...' Today a woman with facial injuries from the train NATO bombed yesterday was asked on TV: 'What do you think of this NATO aggression?' She said, 'I was just going to visit my relatives for Easter.'

I saw doctors and relatives in the buses leaving Belgrade for Leskovac where the train was hit on the bridge. Nobody was crying or being emotional. I caught sight of my own reflection in a window: I have changed, too. I don't cry any more. I sleep during the raids. I work during the day. I laugh. When you get used to it you forget to ask how and why.

An Albanian refugee convoy on a road outside Pizren in southern Kosovo was hit by NATO planes. At least seventy-two people were killed.

15 April In the middle of the night the windows started to rattle like in a horror movie and the sky was lit up by fire. My daughter woke up screaming and clung to me. She is bigger than I am now but all of a sudden she seemed like a little baby. I was so exhausted I could hardly open my eyes. She was afraid but she didn't want to go down to the shelter. She kept saying, 'What's happening, what's all the noise…?' I said: 'It's our artillery, darling, don't be afraid.' It was the first time since the war started that I made a distinction between 'our' weapons and 'their' weapons. But it was only to calm her, not because I believe in that distinction.

Yesterday more than a thousand people attended the funeral of Slavko Curuvija, the newspaper editor who was found with three bullets in the back of his head, the mark of a contract killing. The more stories I hear the less I am convinced there is any story to it at all, other than that he was a brave, intelligent, powerful, good-looking man. I guess that was enough.

Horrible, horrible pictures of refugees in a convoy in Kosovo hit by NATO bombs. Horrible NATO definition of 'collateral damage to the targeted military convoy'. I saw some soldiers here in Belgrade: they were young and very worried, awkwardly carrying their big guns. I can imagine them in a convoy during the night in the woods in Kosovo: all these city boys could be my sons.

16 April Last night our household exploded in panic. Yugoslav artillery fire covered the sky over Belgrade while 300 NATO planes flew over the city. The children were screaming with a mixture of terror and joy, as though they were at the circus. I rushed them down to the local shelter, gulping down some wine to stop my hands and knees trembling, then after half an hour we went back home where the children say they prefer to be. We slept like logs.

We heard on the radio that children no longer have to pass a state exam to get into high school: they're overjoyed of course, but they're already happy enough in any case—no exams, no school, nothing any more. They say, 'Don't you see now, going to school was useless? Power and money are what matter.' And they don't associate knowledge with power and money, not after this war.

People from abroad ask me how Serbian people are taking the death of the bombed refugees. What a question: the same as all other civilian deaths, of which there have already been too many in this 'humanitarian bombing'. It never occurred to me to think of dead civilians as Albanian or Serb. But obviously people from NATO countries feel differently. Still, I suppose they paid for the bombs out of their taxes, so maybe they can choose their victims. Let's hope these 'humanitarian' bombs really bring us peace, not just the peace of death.

17 April An American journalist on TV quoted an Australian aid worker in Kosovo saying: 'Thanks, NATO, for bombing us, for destroying all our blankets and medicines.' To which a NATO officer at the press conference replied: 'Sorry, but our maps are old.' A woman who sells home-made cheese at the market said to me: 'They're bombing the hell out of us, everything is destroyed. Can't somebody tell them that it's been two years now since the army moved out of our village?' I guess it's the old maps again.

Thousands of Kosovan Albanians attempted to cross the borders with Albania and Macedonia.

18 April It is Sunday, but who cares? We have been living the same day ever since the war started. In Belgrade there are efforts at normality—the traditional marathon was held in heavy rain; there was a big wedding on TV—but personally I'm done with anything that resembles human life. I'd rather be a cockroach, at this point, much safer.

Last night three factories in Pancevo were hit again, including the chemical factory, where there was an acid leak. Some people are being evacuated. We in Belgrade had a good wind, we were lucky once more. In Batajnica, near the airport, a three-year-old girl was killed by falling glass after an explosion. Her father said she'd been difficult in the night. First she wanted to go to the bathroom, then she didn't, then she did. And then he let her go in and she never came out.

19 April Last night my friends were very pessimistic about the future. They are all educated people, impoverished by the last ten years of economic upheaval, in the opposition but with more or less strong patriotic feelings. They definitely don't want to go into exile. There is an increasingly strong feeling here among ordinary people that nobody really wants us anywhere any more, not even here. Writers and commentators from all over the world now refer to the Serbs as being accomplices in the atrocities, and they mean all Serbs. I won't name names, but they were people I admired, some were even my friends. I forgive them, but I don't read them any more. Just as some years ago with our local nationalistic writers: for me they don't exist.

Yugoslavia closed its border with Albania; tens of thousands of refugees were turned back into southern Kosovo.

20 April Oh, and about the atrocities, about the Albanian refugees? Please, all of you reading this, understand that I accept as much blame as you want me to. I know what is going on, even if I have no more proof than what some people say, just as I am telling you all these things about my life, expecting you to believe me. Which cross should I bear—NATO bombs or Serbian deaths? Between compulsive guilt and compulsive patriotism, I guess there is no way out.

23 April I guess you all know, the TV building was hit last night. My windows were blown open by the blast. We live quite near to it, my parents just behind it, and a close friend is in the building next door. We are all OK, but the TV workers sacrificed their lives.

My father said the impact wasn't so bad, the worst part was seeing the decapitated bodies being taken from the building. Some of the foreign journalists who arrived yesterday are afraid for their lives. Serbian TV is broadcasting again, better than yesterday.

24 April Since the NATO celebration in Washington is dazzling all the TV channels, we expected the bridges in Belgrade to be hit, finished off in one big operation to celebrate the new NATO accord. I watched the military waltzes, the flags, the uniforms, the audience, the speeches—it was as surreal as our reality here. In the end, Belgrade wasn't hit. The siren went off anyway, but I had a good sleep. My friend from Rakovica, a badly damaged part of Belgrade, is afraid of radioactivity. She wants to leave, but all she can do is watch videos while the bombs fall around her.

I just heard that the people in the TV building were warned by NATO about the air strikes but apparently decided to follow their orders and stay. My guess is that not all of them had a free choice.

26 April The shops are still full but people are talking about radioactive vegetables. They are also predicting a future without bread, water or electricity. No visible signs of that yet, only fear. The shortages are still cigarettes and petrol—and of course peace.

Today the famous NATO star Jamie Shea announced that we Serbian citizens feel safe with the NATO bombs: we don't stop working when we hear the sirens. Well, maybe not, but that's because the work has to be done, not because we feel safe. I don't feel safe with NATO or any other bombs. I don't feel safe without bridges, I don't feel safe in a boat, on a horse, on a bicycle, against a NATO bomber; I don't feel safe without schools, universities, libraries, against highly technological NATO countries. I am not afraid, not any more, but my legs still tremble when I hear bombers above my head.

27 April Last night we got the same programme on ten channels; the same news the whole day. Then on the BBC I saw my friend Vjosa, an Albanian from Kosovo, a human rights activist, a doctor, describing the horrors she suffered running for her life from Pristina. It made me cry, not so much because of her story, which I already knew, but for her. She had changed so much. Her face had in it something of a person who would never laugh again.

Last night, an enormous blast, as if round the corner. Again it was the former central committee building across the river. I don't even know what's inside it now, but for some reason when it gets hit you can hear it more than much closer targets. We called our friends and relatives, checked they were alive and went to bed.

28 April Last night my friend and I were sitting planning the future of our feminist publishing house, '94'. The last book we published was *The Origins of Totalitarianism* by Hannah Arendt, two days before the bombing. I wonder what Hannah Arendt would say about being published by feminists in the middle of another European war? We were nervous because it was one a.m. and there were no sirens. Like many people in Belgrade we have developed what is called 'siren neurosis' waiting for them to go off. But the explosions started soon enough—and big ones: windows blown open, the building shaking, fireworks in the air. First Yugoslav aircraft responded, then the clouds broke open with thunder, lightning and heavy rain. We all went to bed together in one big bed with the children's toys and lots of cushions.

The cleaning lady came late this morning: no buses, no petrol. She said she spent all night in the shelter and she didn't believe we would win the war any more. One of my children's friends said to me, 'Hurrah! No more music classes, our teacher has become a sniper!' I remembered him, a particularly talented student from the Academy. My friend's son who is serving in the army phones regularly: he is afraid and cold, but alive. My friend has stopped eating and laughs all the time.

Then this morning we heard that NATO has made another mistake. They have hit a village in southern Serbia: more 'collateral damage', this time to children in a 'safe' shelter. I wonder how many people in Belgrade go to the shelters any more. I still see them in front of the entrance every night, smoking and drinking, but I don't know whether they go there to socialize or out of fear.

Petrol has been rationed to twenty litres a month. Petrol prices on the black market have doubled. One bit of good news: on the BBC I see that the Hungarians might be putting up a refugee camp near Budapest, this time for Serbs, though they will be treated officially as tourists. At least it made me feel a bit safer. If we have to leave we'll be in a camp with people like ourselves, where we can share our fears, where our children can play together. It seems the only decent solution for those of us who have suffered somebody else's war.

A friend calls to tell me an ecological catastrophe is on its way: no more vegetables and fruit, only tinned food and bottled water. Many papers have been circulating on e-mail, collecting evidence of the poisoning of air and water. A young friend of mine decided to have an abortion because she believed what they were saying: she's been crying for days.

29 April The washing machine has broken. I wept as if somebody had died. I imagined myself doing all the laundry by hand as well as all the extra housework I've had to do since the war started. Then I remembered hearing how, in NATO phase three, we will have no water, no electricity, no phone lines. I imagined myself with many others, mostly women, washing the laundry in the Danube as they did in ancient Greece: singing, gossiping, laughing, with kids running around us. That will be my summer holidays.

30 April My friend's son, the soldier, sent a message from somewhere in Kosovo: he wants to marry his girlfriend so she can have his flat legally if he is killed.

Step by step, down, down; every day crossing a new border of horror: yesterday's fear, today's habit. Last night a bomb landed only a hundred metres from us. The blast was so strong the building shook for minutes and we hung on to each other laughing with nerves. 'They'll kill us eventually,' somebody said, 'either psychologically or physically.' Then we all went to bed together. After a few hours there were no more explosions but the shaking went on and on: we hung on to each other half asleep.

No news on TV. We are still shaking and feeling sick.

Belgrade was never hit so hard before. Dead bodies are lying round the ruined buildings, car alarms from wrecked cars are wailing, rescue vans are circling with their headlights on. And life goes on—today with no buses or trams; salad, fruit and vegetables from the market forbidden because the earth has been poisoned with uranium. No information because it doesn't help anyway.

After thirty-seven days of air strikes, I finally gave in and let my daughter go out during the alarm: only for half an hour, but I know now there is no way back. We are determined to enjoy life in any way we can. I'm aware of a strange new sensation creeping up my spine. It's the thrill of risk, of death. Fear of death is not the same as fear of dying: the first is pleasurable, the second depressing.

3 May Finally it happened, a blackout, in a city of two and a half million people. It's already lasted sixteen hours, but I think it will last for good. We gathered on the terrace with everything we had

Jasmina Tesanovic

prepared for survival without electricity and water. Before the war we hardly knew our neighbours, but now we're all in the same boat. We collected water in tubs and bottles, offered books for the fire and pooled grain or potatoes. We decided to go to bed with the sun at eight in the evening and hold survival meetings every morning. When will this end? For most people bets are off, the war should have ended already. I guessed 2 June. Everybody felt relieved.

This morning some areas have got their light and water back, but not ours. I am here at my friend's table with my portable computer. The children are baking bread. Tomorrow, we've been told the phone lines and the last bridges will be destroyed. I want to say goodbye to so many people and in the end I say goodbye to nobody.

We've been buying church candles because they last longer and are cheaper; we buy batteries for radios, simple food and plain water; no cigarettes, no alcohol. We've fished out old clothes and rearranged the furniture to suit life in the dark—so we don't trip over it. All of Belgrade is doing the same thing.

4 May Yesterday was a beautiful day, with no electricity, no water. People had despair in their eyes, as if they had no idea what to do with themselves any longer. It's not just the bombs, it's this pointless passing of time which destroys us. There are problems with the children: the small ones cry all the time, the big ones are more angry and spoilt than ever. They can't—don't want to—understand the war. This lack of a bridge between generations is our fault: we didn't want to poison them with old wars and now they are living a new one without any idea of what it means.

The man who came to help me move the furniture asked for a glass of water. I said, of course. After drinking it he said, 'Please, be so kind and give me another one.' It was only then that I realized he must have come from an area of the city that has no water. I said, 'Please, take a bath, whatever, we have water. This is a criminal war.' He looked at me and said, 'But we will win.' I didn't realize that there are people who still think of this existence as a victory.

5 May Last night I went to bed early and lay awake in the dark, alone. I realized I hadn't had a chance to be alone since the bombing began. It's raining, we have no electricity, but no bombs either. It's no use writing because of the blackouts. I heard on the BBC that we were without light for only six or seven hours, but that's not true. I don't know whose propaganda it is, local or foreign, but it doesn't help us here in Serbia to believe news about the Albanians, from either side, when we hear that we have electricity and water because it suits somebody's purpose to say so. All the news suits somebody.

I'm constantly running from one flat to another with my computer, meatballs and the laundry, running after electricity. But I feel as if I'm bringing bad luck: as soon as I arrive the lights go out, the moment I leave to go to another flat that has electricity, the lights come back on. It's like when you queue in one line and the other moves faster. I'm running like the Masai—I heard they never walk, or stop, except to sleep or die.

6 May Everybody I talk to has left, is leaving, has a safe place to go. I don't. I come desperately from this falling city. We change flats for the night fantasizing about which will be safer, what will be hit, as I am sure everybody does. It is a game we play, a game of rats.

7 May Today is my parent's fiftieth wedding anniversary. We planned a surprise party, but yesterday they said they were sick and couldn't have any guests. Who knows what it is like to measure out your marriage with bombs at either end? The second and third largest cities in Yugoslavia have been hit hard: in Nis, where some of my relatives live, the central market has been destroyed. Many civilians are dead. NATO knows nothing about it: a Sky News journalist confirms it. Of course it's true. It reminds me of when the people queuing for bread were killed in the market place in Sarajevo: was it Serbs or was it Muslims who fired the shell? The debate went on for years.

9 May I slept for thirteen hours because there were no bombs; tonight I am sure there'll be many. I feel like a battered woman who expects violence and then feels loved if the punch misses her.

Last night we sat once again on the terrace, drank wine, smoked nasty, expensive cigarettes and fantasized about the future.

Since we have none we're free to dream up anything. I've never had such wild ambitions as during these nights on the terrace. I even offered to lead the country out of war if my refugee friend from Krajina agrees to be the Minister of Finance and my best friend from the Women's Centre, the Minister of Police. Also, I'd like to say something about the bombing of the Chinese Embassy. Of course it was a mistake, a grossly incompetent mistake. But a mistake nonetheless, which happens in all wars. But what a lot of noise about it. What about all the others killed while sleeping in their beds, buying food on the market, drinking wine on the terrace looking at the starry sky above? They are also people who died for no reason.

10 May I thought I should have some kind of escape plan in case I go crazy and start doing strange things so I'm trying to get an Italian visa. After days of long and complicated negotiations, with generous help from my Italian friend, the visa department in the Italian Embassy was hit: my papers are lost, along with all my other shattered hopes.

I went out in my car, which I haven't done for over a month now, and turned on the radio. They were playing some old songs, 'April in Belgrade', 'Green, Green Eyes of Yours', and suddenly I burst into tears. I had to pull over because my sight was blurred, I was sobbing out loud. Calm down, I told myself, you're a reasonable person, control yourself; you never liked that music, you never liked to drive a car. Yes, came back the thought, but what I loved was the life I have lost for ever, and part of it was the luxury of despising sentimental music or a big car. I was overcome by a terrible sense of loss as if I'd been killed by accident and somebody else had stepped into my skin and taken over my life.

Yesterday I heard one of the worst stories I've heard since the beginning of the war. A young man, dealing in gold—but not a criminal—came across a dead person's teeth filled with gold. In order to get the gold out he had to crush the teeth. He did it and then threw up. He didn't want to think about the fate of the people whose teeth were in his hands. He said: 'Lately the price of the gold has gone down a lot in Belgrade because there are so many Albanian jewels around.' I felt a terrible toothache at that moment. Hardly anybody has gold teeth any more, but I do, an Italian dentist did it when I was sixteen.

11 May I passed a young thin girl of about fifteen on the street. She seemed very self-conscious and shy—the tortures of adolescence. I looked at her longer than I should have because I was thinking about my own daughter and myself at that age. Then suddenly a blast shook the ground. In a second she changed from a beautiful girl into a frightened animal, she put her hands to her throat as if somebody was choking her, then to her heart, and then she fainted. I ran over to her. I had an urge to kiss her as I often do to my daughter to wake her up, but people gathered round and carried her to a restaurant where she could lie down and take some water.

Our children got their grades today, officially no more school. One of my daughter's best friends went to Australia with her parents some years ago when the situation here began to get worse. Now they have a house on the sea and she has become a model, while my daughter is here, burdened with our history and fighting for her life. She has grown old very quickly, though part of her is still a child, like the girl on the street. She and her friend in Australia stopped writing to each other because they had nothing in common any more.

12 May I'm running around the city, collecting documents to prove I am myself. I'm also doing this for members of my family so we can get visas. In the meantime I hear that a bridge on the border with Hungary was hit last night; that Hungarian customs officers are armed, and are searching people and asking for bribes, depending on how they feel that day. Of course, if you are a man, you need a special permit to leave the country. The siren goes on night and day.

13 May I just heard an item on Sky News about how Serb men fight differently from British and other soldiers. How stupid that is: racism, militarism, sexism all rolled into one. Serb soldiers are just as good and bad as any other men: they watch the same Bruce Willis films, drive the same cars, dream of Pamela Anderson. I fight with them and their culture but it's an unequal fight: they're the same all over the world, friends or foes.

Jasmina Tesanovic

16 May Last night the planes nearly came right through the windows, followed by the local artillery guns. We have this beautiful old-fashioned Belgrade window, overlooking the courtyard. To avoid the war we have moved from this room with the big windows to rooms looking out over the city. My daughter can't sleep in her room because of the bombs. She says the war will never end.

I learned that the Italian Embassy is no longer willing to give us visas. Well, that's my punishment for being late.

Around 300,000 Serbs are estimated to have left the country, many of them from the educated middle class.

17 May A friend's two-year-old daughter runs around the house all day saying, 'I won't give up Kosovo, I won't give up Kosovo.' Her father can't do anything with her, all she wants to do is watch TV. Everybody is talking about the general mobilization scheduled for 24 May. There is slightly more panic and tension in the air. I wonder what's going on in people's heads: probably the same mess I'm writing about, more or less articulated. One of my friends said that there are an incredible number of decent people in this country but they are incapable of organizing themselves into a party to work together. So we are a country without opposition, a country with no leaders but one, a country of political idiots like me.

20 May We were sitting last night watching a video interview with our Albanian friend who was describing her escape from Pristina. She talked about us, too, and how she had received support from her friends in Belgrade rather than from her Serb neighbours. Then missiles started flying above our heads, followed by lots of explosions, but we went on listening to our friend's horrors, living in Blace camp in no man's land along with another hundred thousand refugees before she finally crossed the border. It was peculiar: we all made a silent decision to put solidarity with our friends before our own survival, as if it could help in some way. Our children said nervously, 'Stop watching that stuff. Turn it off.' And in the end I lost my concentration, there were too many bombs; a hospital was hit among other buildings, and a chemical factory. Yesterday a bunch of nationalists attacked the Democratic Party headquarters just round the corner from here, calling their leader—who is in exile in Montenegro—a traitor. He's a handsome middle-aged man who speaks several languages, with a beautiful wife and two children. Now he's fighting on two fronts, against NATO and in a civil war too.

21 May A complete blackout over most of Serbia. I managed to get a new passport for my daughter, and a new identity card, the first time in her young life. 'Wow,' she said, 'I'm a big girl now. Just watch me. But I won't live that long, I am sure of that.'

Deserters are leaving the battlefield. If I were a mother of a soldier sent against his will to fight by white-haired patriots sitting in Belgrade, I would buy a gun and kill all those responsible, giving my life in exchange for my child's. Watching my Albanian friend's interview, I realized how perverse it was our crying for her, listening to her life story, indifferent to the planes above our heads. We are just a step behind the Albanians—and if we decided to leave, nobody would take us.

My local market used to be a happy place, full of gypsics, peasants, second-hand stalls, smugglers, with police chasing those of us who were buying illegal stuff (though not too fast because they did the same thing privately), but now it's become really ugly. Just when we intellectuals have stopped talking politics the people on the market have started. I heard this morning that there were more than two sides to the war: there was NATO, Milosevic, and now Djindjic, the leader of the Democratic Party who is in exile. So now we have more than one option—at least at the market of ideas. The woman I buy eggs from said: 'Yes, we still have everything except happiness.' Her son is fighting in Kosovo and she hadn't heard from him for weeks. She didn't even cry, she just had a hard sadness in her face.

23 May We are shooting a film of my diary in the streets, and it seems everybody wants to be in it, even the policemen we were hiding the cameras from. Some people are angry with NATO, some with the local leaders, some with the whole world. But they all see the pointless situation they are in and they just want to survive and tell us about it. We're all the same, we fear isolation more than bombs.

We have been without electricity for more than twenty-four hours now. Some people don't even have water. There is absolutely nothing we can do. I phone my parents. They tell me, don't worry, the Russians will give us electricity. They always manage to placate me with fairy stories, just like when I was a child.

25 May We were trying to film at the Tito Museum on Tito's official birthday—it used to be called the Holiday of Youth—and I was feeling young and carefree like I used to twenty years ago when I was a film-maker, when I suddenly realized it was noon, the alarm was on, and I had no idea where my daughter was. My husband was on his way back from a PEN conference in Slovenia. During the night central Belgrade had been hit again, only a hundred metres from where we were standing. It was a terrible feeling. I had wanted to make this film with my friends to remember those things we will immediately forget as soon as we get the chance. We are building a memorial of fear with our film.

26 May Today we went to film in a very dangerous zone near a part of Belgrade which is hit on a regular basis. The siren was going and a military car pulled up next to us. Before we could show our permits the men inside pointed their guns at us: I thought I would faint. But then they were very polite and explained that they were just doing their duty. Finally they advised us to go away. I thought I must be crazy to do this, why am I doing it? But then how can we stay rational if everybody has gone crazy? The politics of high risk, as my husband puts it, have deteriorated into the politics of absolute risk.

This afternoon we went to a restaurant on a boat on the Danube: it's a beautiful place where we used to spend a fortune on a few hours of bliss. The food is still good but there is no seafood—yes, we lost the sea. There was hardly anybody there and it closed at seven p.m., so there wasn't time to regain any sense of being an ordinary person.

Doctors are advising women in the early months of pregnancy to have an abortion. I don't know whether this is medical advice, because of radiation, or political-economic advice. One doctor said it's what she would say to her daughter. I also heard on the BBC that a thousand babies have been born in refugee camps in Macedonia. So life goes on, thank God.

27 May Very heavy raids last night. The place we filmed at yesterday was hit by twenty-five missiles last night, only a few hours after we left it.

29 May We filmed a sequence for our movie in the Zoo: jailed hungry, nervous animals. They sense the danger before we do, especially the peacocks. The director told us that the night downtown Belgrade was heavily bombed some mothers ate their young: wolves, tigers, and some of the birds.

My friend says that our film stocks are being destroyed because of the heat and the lack of electricity. And I thought of all our unwritten, unpublished books or those scattered in our damaged flats and garages all over the city. We are losing our intellectual and historical background in this war, as well as everything else.

2 June I remember more than a month ago when we were betting on the date of the end of the war, I said 2 June without any particular reason. Today is the day. Last night, after midnight, we got electricity after twenty-four hours in the dark. We were listening eagerly to Radio Free Europe by candlelight. When the power came on, we didn't turn to CNN, because foreign broadcasts don't talk about us any more. I had a feeling that maybe this would be the day.

My Italian friend said, 'So you don't have bread, light, water, but you sound in good shape?' I am, I said. I can't remember myself some weeks ago when I was so unhappy. Most people turn their backs on people in trouble, but some don't: if this horror is worth anything it is meeting those few people and seeing what humanity is made of.

We are getting so bored that we can hardly put up with each other any longer: nothing to do. Our children are fighting us for not letting them go out during the bombing and for having nothing to do when darkness comes. I say let's talk, we've forgotten how to tell each other stories, to amuse each other as people used to. But for them, sitting in the dark with their parents sounds like utter defeat. So they cry or sulk, depending on how old they are.

Jasmina Tesanovic

My father went to the bank to pay his electricity and water bills, which nobody pays any more. He said, 'We must help the state in this catastrophe.' But the bank clerk was furious. 'You foolish old man,' she said, 'keeping me here while the siren is on so you can spend your last penny. Can't you change, see what your stupid obedience brought to us all?' My father was deeply offended, as he often is nowadays when people don't pay him the respect he feels he's due as a retired general manager who once had power. But he said to me: 'I understand her, even though it is not right, a state is a state—my father served under the Austro-Hungarian Empire and he did what he had to do.'

Milosevic accepts NATO terms for peace.

3 June Was all this really necessary? Today: bedridden, frightened, impoverished, faithless if not dead.

5 June A storm last night instead of bombs: thunder, heavy oily drops of rain. No euphoria on the streets: people are exhausted, bewildered, disappointed. While the storm was on I walked through Belgrade: the windows were lit up and loud music was playing as if the dark times and silence were over. But people are still afraid to voice their opinions. They still talk quietly and only to their closest friends. It's not clear who the winner is, but it's clear that we are the losers. We knew that beforehand, so let's get it over with.

My daughter got top grades at school, even though she's hardly been there. I wonder what her grades would have been if she had. She seems to be about five years older than when the bombing started. She seems older than me and treats me as if she is. I've lost her.

Serb military leaders refused to withdraw from Kosovo. NATO continued air strikes against Yugoslavia.

6 June A lot of tension in the air. You can see it on people's faces, there have been accidents and quarrels. During the bombings it was the opposite. So now we have to endure a collective nervous breakdown, fits of rage and tears, punishment and self-punishment.

It has already started in some families. Nothing to hold on to.

A friend of mine phoned me last night from somewhere in Kosovo. He is a soldier. He knew nothing of the deal in Macedonia, nor did anybody in his regiment. He said to me, we all want NATO to win quickly so we can go back home. But it's all over, I said. He made me repeat what had happened several times.

We are waiting for news. I wake up very early in the morning to watch the news, as I did when the deal over the Dayton Treaty was being made and when Vukovar was happening. There are so many dates, so many treaties, it's been going on nearly all my adult life, certainly all of my daughter's life. My stepson said it wasn't so bad after all, he just hoped we never went back to what it was like before, and I doubt that will happen, so maybe it's been worthwhile. Young people are stronger and smarter than I am. I would give them all the power in the world so long as they were under thirty and had never ruled before. But I must admit, today I felt life and hope running through my veins, I felt alive and confident, the way you feel at the beginning of a new love affair.

7 June I spent the night listening to the news, most of it bad. The local TV station says the peace talks were adjourned at eleven p.m. In the middle of the night, the alarm went on, then the planes came. The truth was: bombing intensified. People were unsurprised and depressed. They know their leaders and the world too well to hope for an easy, painless solution. But then this morning, my old war adrenalin came back and I know I must cope with whatever is going to happen to us hostages here. I just don't want to be pathetic and ridiculous, that's all. I predicted 2 June, but it turned out I'm a false Cassandra.

8 June Last night, raids again, low planes, bombs, fear, anger. But it's different from before, now we have peace problems, too: the fear that the so-called peace will never be peaceful. We sat on the terrace and dealt with the consequences of peace. We probably won't have money, jobs, schools or democracy: no free space whatsoever. My father said: Don't worry, we will build everything anew, democracy will come slowly...so don't go, but help me in my old age. I don't believe him any more. I know what he needs me for, what he has always needed me for—to keep me down, to serve his wars and ideas. It is my victory, and his defeat, to have the courage to say no, to drink, to smoke in front of him, and not to die for him.

NATO and Serb military leaders signed the peace agreement.

9 June In a way this has been the worst year of my life. Looking in the mirror I don't seem much older, a year or more doesn't make much difference in a middle-aged person. But looking around me I notice a big difference: this is not my life any more, my country, my friends, my relatives. It is not as bad as it sounds, it is just painful and hard to grow centuries in one year under such internal and external pressure. I made it, like most of the people around me. We all made it, holding hands or weapons...except for some who didn't, whose names we don't yet know. I am no longer a political idiot. I know I can't hide behind that mask any more.

Serbian troops began to move out of Kosovo. The first NATO troops entered Kosovo at dawn.

12 June War is slowly dropping out of our daily lives. Last night the bars and restaurants in my neighbourhood reopened and the streets were full of people. The tension has gone, more lights are on, and shops once more sell Coca-Cola, twenty-four hours a day. Today, troops are entering Yugoslavia—people don't feel occupied, but they feel uneasy, just as they did in the first days of bombing. Nobody really knows what it means for the future. The only way to stay calm is to take it as it comes, and to use what we know from our history. But with Russians coming from the north, British from the south, soldiers of every colour, like a Hollywood film, personally I feel fine. I feel less isolated. Let them all come, let our histories mix, anything as long as they don't build a wall. □

HAWK
Joy Williams

Hawk

Glenn Gould bathed his hands in wax and then they felt new. He didn't like to eat in public. He was personally gracious. He was knowledgeable about drugs. He loved animals. In his will, he directed that half his money be given to the Toronto Humane Society. He hated daylight and bright colours. His piano chair was fourteen inches high. His music was used to score *Slaughterhouse-Five*, a book he did not like. After he suffered his fatal stroke, his father waited a day to turn off the respirator because he didn't want him to die on his stepmother's birthday. When Glenn Gould wrote cheques he signed them Glen Gould because he was afraid that by writing the second *n* he would make too many squiggles. He took prodigious amounts of valium and used make-up. He was once arrested in Sarasota, Florida, for sitting on a park bench in an overcoat, gloves and muffler. He was a prodigy, a genius. He had dirty hair. He had boring dreams. He probably believed in God.

My mind said *You read about Glenn Gould and listen to Glenn Gould constantly but you don't know anything about music. If he were alive you wouldn't have anything you could say to him...*

A composer acquaintance of mine dismissed Glenn as a *performer*.

Glenn Gould loved the idea of the Arctic but he had a great fear of the cold. He was a virtuoso. To be a virtuoso you must have an absolutely fearless attitude toward everything but Glenn was, in fact, worried, frightened and phobic. The dogs of his youth were named Nick and Banquo. As a baby, he never cried but hummed. He thought that the key of F minor expressed his personality.

You have no idea what that means my mind said. *You don't really know what it is he's doing. You don't know why he's brilliant.*

He could instantly play any piece of music from memory. On the whole he did not like works that progressed to a climax, and then to a reconciliation. The Goldberg Variations, which Glenn is most widely known for, were written by Bach for harpsichord. Bach was visiting one of his students, Johann Goldberg, who was employed by a Count von Keyserling, the Russian ambassador to the court of Saxony. The Count had insomnia and wanted some music that would help him through the dark hours. The first notes of the Goldberg Variations are inscribed on Glenn's tombstone.

My dog rose from his bed and walked beneath the table, which he barely cleared. He put his chin on my knee. He stood there for a few moments, not moving. I could see nothing but his nose. I loved kissing his nose. It was my hobby. He was a big black German Shepherd with accents of silver and brown. He had a beautiful face. He looked soulful and dear and alert. He was born on 17 October 1988 and had been with us since Christmas Day of that year. He was now almost nine years old. He weighed one hundred pounds. His name was Hawk. He seemed to fear nothing. He was always looking at me, waiting for me. He just wanted to go where I was going. He could be amusing, he had a sense of humour, but mostly he seemed stoic and watchful and patient. If I was in a room, he was in that room, no other. Of course we took long walks together and many cross-country trips. He was adept at ferry crossings and checking into motels. When he could not accompany me, I would put him in a kennel, once for as long as two weeks. I felt that it was good for him to endure the kennel occasionally. Life was not all good, I told him. Though mostly life was good. He had had a series of collars over the years. His most recent one was lavender in colour. He had tags with his various addresses and phone numbers on them and a St Francis medal with the words PROTECT US. He had a collection of toys. A softball, and squeaky toys in the shapes of a burglar, a cat, a shark, a snowman, and a hedgehog that once made a snuffling noise like a hedgehog but not for long. They were collected in a picnic basket on the floor and when he was happy he would root through the basket and select one. He preferred the snowman. His least favourite was a large green and red toy—its shape was similar to a large bone but it was an abstraction, it lacked charm. Hawk was in a hundred photographs. He was my sweetie pie, my honey, my handsome boy, my love. On the following day he would attack me as though he wanted to kill me.

As regards to life it is much the best to think that the experiences we have are necessary for us. It is by means of experience that we develop and not through our imagination. Imagination is nothing. Explanation is nothing. One can only experience and somehow describe—with, in Camus's phrase, *lucid indifference*. At the same time, experience is fundamentally illusory. When one is experiencing emotional pain or grief, one feels that everything that happens in life is unreal. And this is a right understanding of life.

I loved Hawk and Hawk loved me. It was the usual arrangement. Just a few days before, I had said to him, This is the life, isn't it honey. We were picnicking on Nantucket. We were on the beach with a little fire. There was a beautiful sunset. Friends had given us their house on the island, an old farmhouse off the Polpis Road. Somehow, on the first night at the house, Hawk had been left outside. When he was on the wrong side of a door he would never whine or claw at it, he would stare at it fixedly. I had fallen into a heavy sleep.

I was exhausted. I was always exhausted but I didn't go to a doctor. I had no doctor, no insurance. If I was going to be very sick, I would just die, I thought. Hawk would mourn me. Dogs are the best mourners in the world, as everyone knows. In my sleep, in the strange bed in the old farmhouse, I saw a figure at the door. It was waiting there clothed in a black garbage bag and bandages. Without hesitation I got up and went to the door and opened it and Hawk came in. Oh I'm so sorry, I said to him. He settled down at the foot of the bed with a great comfortable sigh. His coat was cool from the night. I felt that he had tried to project himself through to me, that he had been separated from me through some error, some misunderstanding, and this, clearly, was something neither of us wanted. It had been a bad transmission, but it had done the job and done it without frightening me. What a resourceful boy! I said to him. Oh there are ghosts in that house, our friends said later. Someone else said, You know, ghosts frequently appear in bandages.

Before Hawk, I had had a number of dogs that died before their time, from grim accident or misfortune, taken from me unprepared in the twinkling of an eye. *Shadrach, Nichodemus, Angel...* Nichodemus wasn't even old enough to have learned to lift his leg. They were all good dogs, faithful. They were innocents. Hawk was the only one I didn't name from the Bible. I named him from Nature, wild Nature. My parents always had dogs too, German shepherds, and my mother would always say, You have to talk to a dog, Joy, you've got to talk to them. It ended badly for my mother and father's dogs over the years and then for my mother and father. My father was a Congregational minister. I am a Christian. Kierkegaard said that for the Christian, the closer you keep to God and the more involved you get with him, the worse for you. It's as though God was saying...you might as well go to the fair and have a good time with the rest. Don't get involved with me—it will only bring you misery. After all, I abandoned my own child, I allowed him to be killed. Christianity, Kierkegaard said, is related only to the consciousness of sin.

We were in Nantucket during the *dies caniculares*, the dog days of summer, but it was a splendid time. Still, there was something wrong with me. My body had turned against me and was full of browsing, shifting pain. The pain went anywhere it wanted to. My head ached, my arms and legs and eyes, my ribs hurt when I took a deep breath. Still, I walked with Hawk, we kept to our habits. I didn't want to think about it but my mind said *you have to, you have to do something, you can't just do nothing you know...* Some days were worse than others. On those days, I felt crippled. I was so tired. I couldn't think, couldn't concentrate. Even so, I spent long hours reading and listening to music. Bach, Mahler, Strauss. Glenn thought that the 'Metamorphosen' of Strauss was the ultimate. I listened to Thomas de Hartmann play the music of Gurdjieff. I listened to Kathleen Ferrier sing Mahler and Bach and Handel and Gluck. She sang the famous aria from Gluck's opera, *Orfeo ed Euridice*—'What is Life'. We listened to the music over and over again.

Hawk had engaging habits. He had presence. He was devoted to me. To everyone, this was apparent. But I really knew nothing of his psychology. He was no Tulip or Keeper or Bashan who had been analysed by their writers. He knew sit, stay, down, go to your place. He was intelligent, he had a good memory. And surely, I believed, he had a soul.

The friends who had given us the house on Nantucket insisted that I see a doctor about my malady. They made an appointment for me with their doctor in New York. We would leave the Island, return to our own home for a few days, then put Hawk into the kennel and drive into the city, a little over two hours away.

I can't remember our last evening together.

On the morning my husband and I were to drive into the city,

I got up early and took Hawk for a long walk along accustomed trails. I was wearing a white sleeveless linen blouse and poplin pants. My head pounded, I could barely put one foot ahead of the other. *How about Lupus?* my mind said. *How about Rheumatoid Arthritis? Well, we'll know more soon...* We drove then to the kennel. It was called Red Rock and Hawk had been there before, they liked him there, he'd always been a gentleman there. When we drove in, Hawk looked disconsolate yet resigned. I left him in the car while I went into the office. I was looking for Fred, big, loud, gruffly pleasant Fred, but he didn't appear. One of his assistants did, a girl named Lynn. Lynn knew Hawk. He's only going to be here for one night, right? Lynn said. I went out to get him. I put the leash on him, his blue, rather grimy leash, and he jumped out of the car and we walked into the office. Lynn had opened another door that led to a row of cement runs. We stood in that doorway, Hawk and I. All right then, I said. I was bent forward slightly. He turned and looked at me and rose and fell upon me, seizing my breast. Immediately, as they say, there was blood everywhere. He tore at my breast, snarling, I think, I can't remember if he was snarling. I turned, calling his name, and he turned with me, my breast still in his jaws. He then shifted and seized my left hand, and after an instant or two, my right, which he ground down upon, shifting, getting a better grip, always getting a better grip with his jaws. I was trying to twist his collar with my bleeding left hand but I was trying not to move either. Hawk! I kept calling my darling's name, Hawk! Then he stopped chewing on my hand and he looked at me coldly. Fred had been summoned by then and had a pole and a noose, the rig that's used for dangerous dogs, and I heard him say, He's stopped now. I fled to the car. My blouse was soaked with blood, it was dripping blood. I drove home sobbing. I've lost my dog, I've lost my Hawk. My mind didn't say anything. It was all it could do to stay with me as I sobbed and drove, my hands bleeding on the wheel.

I thought he had bitten off my nipple. I thought that when I took off my blouse and bra, the nipple would fall out like a diseased hibiscus bud, like the eraser on a pencil. But he hadn't bitten it off. My breast was bruised black and there were two deep punctures in it and a long raking scratch across it and that was all. My left hand was bleeding hard from three wounds. My right hand was mauled.

At home I stood in the shower, howling, making deep ugly sounds. I had lost my dog. The Band-Aids we put over my cuts had cartoon characters all over them. We didn't take our medicine cabinet very seriously. For some reason I had papered it with newspaper pictures of Bob Dole's hand clutching its pen. I put clean clothes on but the blood seeped around the Band-Aids and stained them too. I put more Goofy and Minnie Band-Aids on and changed my clothes again. I wrapped my hand in a dishtowel. Hawk's water dish was still in the kitchen, his toys were scattered around. I wanted to drive into the city and keep my appointment with the doctor, he could look at my hand. It seemed only logical. I just wanted to get in the car and drive away from home. I wouldn't let my husband drive. We talked about what happened as being *unbelievable*. We hadn't yet started talking about it as being a *tragedy*. I'll never see him again, I've lost my dog, I said. Let's not talk about that now, my husband said. As we approached the city I tried to compose myself for the doctor. Then I was standing on the street outside his office which was on East Eighty-fifth Street trying to compose myself. I looked dishevelled, my clothes were stained, I was wearing high-top sneakers. Some people turned as they were walking by and made a point of staring at me.

He was a cheerful doctor. He put my hand in a pan of inky red sterilizing solution. He wanted to talk about my malady, the symptoms of my malady, but he was in fact thinking about the hand. He went out of the office for a while and when he came back he said, I've made an appointment for you to see an orthopaedic surgeon. This doctor was on East Seventy-third Street. You really have to do something about this hand, the first doctor said.

The surgeon was of the type Thomas Mann was always writing about, a doctor out of *The Magic Mountain*, someone whom science had cooled and hardened. Still, he seemed to take a bit of pleasure in imagining the referring doctor's discomfort at my messy wounds. People are usually pretty well cleaned up by the time Gary sees them, he said. He took X-rays and looked at them and said, I will be back in a moment to talk with you about your hand. I sat on the examining table and swung my feet back and forth. One of my sneakers was blue and the other one green. It was a little carefree gesture I had adopted for myself some time ago. I felt foolish and dirty. I felt that I must not appear to be very bright. The doctor returned and asked when the dog had bitten me and frowned when I told him it had been six hours ago. He said, This is very serious, you must have surgery on this hand today. I can't do it here, it must be done under absolutely sterile conditions at the hospital. The bone could become infected and bone infections are very difficult to clear up. I've reserved a bed in the hospital for you and arranged for another surgeon to perform the operation. I said, Oh, but... He said, The surgery must be done today. He repeated this, with beats between the words. He was stern and forbidding and, I thought, pessimistic. Good luck, he said.

The surgeon at Lennox Hill Hospital was a young good-looking Chinese man. He spoke elegantly and had a wonderful smile. He said, The bone is fractured badly in several places and the tendon is torn. Because it was caused by a dog's bite, the situation is actually life threatening. Oh, surely... I began. No, he said, it's very serious, indeed, life threatening, I assure you. He smiled.

I lay in a bed in the hospital for a few hours and at one in the morning the hand was operated on and apparently it went well enough. Long pins held everything together. You will have some loss of function in your hand but it won't be too bad, the doctor said, presenting his wonderful smile. I used to kiss Hawk's nose and put my hands in his jaws in play. People in the hospital wanted to talk about my dog biting me. That's unusual, isn't it, they said, or, that's strange isn't it, or, I thought that breed was exceptionally loyal. One nurse asked me if I had been cruel to him.

My hand would not be the same. It would never be strong and it would never again stroke Hawk's black coat.

When I was home again, I washed Hawk's dishes and put them in the cupboard. I gathered up all his toys and put them away too. I busied myself thinking I would bury all his things. Meanwhile he waited at the kennel for me to come and get him, like I always had. I was taking Vicadon for the pain and an antibiotic. In a week I would begin taking another antibiotic and an anti-inflammatory drug for my malady. I lay about, feeling the pain saunter and ping through me. My arms felt like flimsy sacks holding loose sticks. If the sticks touched one another, there would be pain. I went back to listening to Glenn Gould and reading about Glenn Gould which is what I had been doing when Hawk and I were last together. I played Glenn Gould over and over. Glenn never wanted to think about what his hands and fingers were doing but as he grew older he became obsessed with analysing their movements. He felt that if he performed with a blank face, he would lose his control of the piano. Frowning and grimacing gave him better control of his hands. My mind said *You would not be able to defend or explain Glenn Gould to anyone who didn't care for him.*

Hawk had to remain in the kennel for fifteen days for observation, it was the law. It was the same number of days we had spent so happily on Nantucket. My husband spoke to Fred. You should talk to Fred, he said. When I called, I got Lynn. She spoke to me in a sort of light-hearted way.

She seemed grateful that I had held on to Hawk during the attack. I was too confused by this comment to reply to it. She said, After you left he attacked the noose but then he calmed down in the cage after we washed the blood off of him. He ate some food. Some dogs get a taste for biting, she said, after they start to bite. Everything she said was wrong.

Finally, she said, He seems to be in conflict. The word seemed to reassure her, it gave her confidence. I couldn't understand a thing she was saying. I wanted someone to tell me why my beloved dog had attacked me so savagely and how I could save both of us. He's just in a lot of conflict now, the girl said. Maybe he had some separation anxiety. He seemed all right for a while after we washed the blood off him, I don't know what to tell you.

Finally, Fred got on the line. He's just not the same dog, Fred said. I know that dog, this isn't him. When I had the noose on him he was attacking the pole and looking right at me. There was no fear in his eyes, there was nothing in his eyes. I'm no doctor, Fred said, but I think it's a brain tumour. I think something just kicked on or clicked off in him and you'll never know when it will happen again.

I said, He was a perfectly healthy, happy, loving dog.

This isn't your dog here now, Fred said.

I couldn't bear to call Fred every day. I called him every other day.

He has good days and bad days, Fred said. Sometimes you can walk right up to the cage and he just looks at you or he doesn't even bother to look at you. Other times he flings himself at the chain link, attacking it, trying to get at you. Some days he's a monster.

I thought of Hawk's patience, of his happiness, of his dear, grave face. Sometimes, when he slept, he would whimper and his legs would move as though he were walking quickly in a dream. What do you think he's dreaming about, I would ask my husband. Then I would call his name, Hawk, Hawk, it's all right, and he would open one startled eye and look at me and sigh, and then he would be calm again. I couldn't bear the thought of him waiting in the kennel for me to pick him up. I was not going to pick him up. I would have him put down, put to sleep, euthanized, destroyed. My love would be murdered. I would murder my love.

The days dragged on. Fred said, He's unreliable. I have no doubt that if you told him to do something he didn't want to do, he could attack you. Anything could set him off, he could turn on anybody. If you slipped and fell, if you were in a helpless position, he could kill you, I have no doubt of it. That's a tough dog. Fred fancied German shepherds and had several of his own whom he exhibited in shows. He's not the same dog any more, Fred said.

I did not really believe this, that he was not the same dog. I did not think that he had a brain tumour. I thought that something unspeakable and impossible and calamitous had happened to Hawk and me. My husband said, You have to remember him the way he was, if you just dwell on this, if this is all you remember from all the wonderful times you had with him, then shame on you. My husband said, I love him too, I miss him, but I'm not going to mention him every time I think of him. You can talk about him all you want and I'll talk with you, but I'm not going to bring him up again, it makes you too upset.

Upset? I said.

On the fifteenth day, Fred would put a soporific in Hawk's food and then the vet would arrive and give him a lethal injection.

His brain would die and his heart would follow. It would take ten seconds. So often I had sat with Hawk while he ate. He would eat for a while and then pick up a toy and walk around the room with it and then eat some more. Oh, that's so good, I said to him while he ate. Isn't that good? Oh, it's delicious...

Fred said, I know this is difficult. If he had been run over by a truck, it would be a different matter, you would grieve for him. This is a harder grief.

If I talked about something else at home or if I ate something or if I had a Martini again, if I took the time to make a Martini rather than just slosh some gin in a glass, my husband said—you seem a little better.

I tried to imagine that Hawk was attempting to reach me teleneurally during these days. I went to all his places, for they were my places too, and tried to listen but nothing was coming through. I didn't expect his apologies of course. For my part I forgave him, but I was going to have him murdered too. We had loved one another and we would never meet again. He never came to me in dreams. I was granted nothing, not the smallest sign.

We had to go to the vet to sign the paper authorizing euthanization. The vet's name was Dr Turco. There had been Dr Franks and Dr Crane and Dr Yang and Dr Iorbar in my life in the last days and now there was Dr Turco. In the parking lot there was a young man with a white pit bull in the back of his pick-up truck. He was fumbling with the dog's leash somewhat and it was taking me a while to get out of our car with my hand in the cast and my aching, crippling malady, my mysterious malady, whatever the hell it was. I passed the dog, sturdy and panting, cute in his ugliness, white and pink with dashes of black about him, a dog with his own charms. Hi there, I said to the dog. The young man seemed unfriendly, he did not seem as nice as his dog. They followed my husband and myself into the vet's waiting room, the dog sliding and scrambling across the waxed floor, his nails clicking.

My mind said *The vet may have an explanation for what happened, an answer. Perhaps some anecdotes at the very least will bring you peace.* Dr Turco said, Fred tells me that Hawk has become quite dangerous.

I said, It was an aberration, a moment's madness seized him. Could it be a brain tumour?

The vet paused. It's possible… he said, indicating that it wasn't very likely. He said, So sad. My sympathy and respect for your decision.

It's unusual, isn't it? I asked, for a dog to attack his owner?

It's quite unusual, the vet said. I've never known a dog to attack its owner. Excuse me for just one moment.

He left the room. My God, I said to my husband, did you hear that! He didn't say that, my husband said in anguish. He did! He just did! I said. I'll ask him when he comes back, my husband said.

I've never known personally of it happening, the vet said, in the course of my practice. I'm sure it's probably happened. I'm so sorry.

I signed the paper with my left hand. My signature looked totally unfamiliar to me. Above it, printed by some other hand, was Hawk's name and breed and age and weight. As we returned to the parking lot the young man we had seen with the pit bull was coming back to his truck from the rear of the vet's office. He was cradling a black garbage bag in his arms, his lips pressed to it. He placed it in the back of the pick-up, got into the cab and sat there for a moment. Then he rubbed his eyes and drove away.

On the sixteenth day, my husband went to the kennel to pay for Hawk's residency there and to pick up his leash. Then he went to the vet and paid for the euthanization, for the cremation that hadn't happened yet. He brought home Hawk's lavender collar from the vet with his tags on it and the St Francis PROTECT US medal. I said, That's not Hawk's leash. I wanted to bury Hawk's leash with his ashes and his toys but I wanted to keep his collar with all the photographs I had of him. That's his leash, my husband said. They bleached it to get the blood out.

Silver Trails is a pet motel but it also has a crematorium and a cemetery where the pictures of beloved pets, made weatherproof in a silvering process, are mounted on a curved tile wall. The wall was supposed to be capable of withstanding freezing temperatures but it has not and some of the tiles are cracked. All the dogs shown have been 'good' and 'faithful'. The wall is in a fragrant pine grove and on the pathway to it there is a plaque which the owners of Silver

Trails are very pleased with. It says IF CHRIST HAD HAD A LITTLE DOG IT WOULD HAVE FOLLOWED HIM TO THE CROSS. There is no devotion, it is known, like a dog's devotion. Dogs excel in love.

Hawk had been taken from Red Rock to the vet's but it would be several more days before he was brought to Silver Trails. Actually, only living dogs come to the place so named. Dead dogs come to Trail's End.

I was waiting for someone to call me and say, Your animal will be ready after four, which, when the day arrived, is what they would say. Hawk still did not come to me in dreams. I dreamed instead about worrying that I had not told my mother. She would feel so badly about Hawk. Surely I must have told her, but I had forgotten if indeed I had. I wasn't sure. Awake, everywhere I looked, I thought Hawk should be there. He should be here with me. How strange it all is, how wrong, that he is not here. My mind said *He wants to come back, he wants to come back to his home and be with you but he can't because you killed him, you had him killed...* My body was my malady, my tedious non-life-threatening banal malady, but my mind was like Job's wife whose only advice to him was to curse God and die. I felt that I wanted to die.

I was utterly unhappy and when, according to Kierkegaard, one becomes utterly unhappy and realizes the absolute woefulness of life, when one can say and mean it, life for me has no value, that is when one can make a bid for Christianity, that is when one can begin. One must become crucified to a paradox. One must give up reason.

I listened to Kathleen Ferrier sing from *Orfeo ed Euridice* in her unearthly contralto.

> What is life to me without thee?
> What is left if thou art dead?
> What is life, life without thee?
> What is life without my Love?

In the myth of the great musician, Orpheus played music that was so exquisite that not only his fellow mortals but even the wild beasts were soothed and comforted by it. When his Eurydice died, he sang his grief for her to all who breathed the upper air but he was not able to call her back so he decided to seek her among the dead. It ended badly, of course, though not typically so.

The lovely Kathleen died when she was forty-one years old. Glenn died when he was fifty-one. My mind said *You haven't done much with your life, think of what those two could have done if they had lived on, you couldn't even keep your own pet from tearing you apart, or what do they call them now, pet, companion animal...*

There was no consolation. Hawk had been my consolation.

When the phone rang, a woman's voice said, Your animal will be ready after four. I arrived at Silver Trails and I was directed to a building with a not unsubtle smokestack. I was told to speak with Michael. But Michael was not there. Michael? I called. I could hear a lawnmower in the distance and over the sounds of the lawnmower were the sounds of the live dogs barking.

I walked into the building which had two rooms, then a larger room, open like a garage. There was a stubby tunnel-like object there, the crematorium oven. There were twenty filled black garbage bags secured with twine on a table and a large sleek golden dog lying free. He was a big dog, lying with his face away from me. He looked fit and not old. One of his ears was folded back on itself in a soft, sad way. I walked outside and just stood there. I didn't know what to do with myself any more. Eventually the lawnmower grew closer with the boy named Michael on it. I've come for my dog's remains, I said. His name is Hawk. The boy led me into the building but he closed the door to the big room. He drew back a curtain that ran along a wall and there were dozens of small black shopping bags on the shelves, the size bag that might contain something lovely, special from a boutique. There was a label on each bag that said TRAIL'S END and it had the name of a dog and then the owner's name. Inside the bag was a blue-and-white tin with a vaguely Oriental motif of blue swallow-like birds flying. The boy and I searched the shelves for the proper bag. Here he is, I said. The boy pointed to another bag. There's another Hawk, he said. He had a strange, half-smiling grimace. There was grass in his hair and grass stuck to his T-shirt. This is my Hawk, I said, there's my name too. I gestured at the shelves. So many! I said. There's so many!

Oh sometimes all four shelves are full, the boy said.

At home, I sat on the porch and with great difficulty pried open the lid of the tin with its foolish scene. I used a knife around it. There was cotton on the top and beneath it was a clear bag of ground bones. Hawk's ashes weighed more than those of my mother or my father. We all end up alone, don't we, honey, I said.

And then, in time, my little dream.

Hawk and I are walking among a crowd in near darkness. I am a little concerned for him because I want him to be good. He can hardly move among the people in the crowd but he pays them no attention. He is close to me, he is calm, utterly familiar, he is my handsome boy, my good boy, my love. Then, of course, I realize that these are the dead and we are both newly among them. □

SELF-CONSCIOUSNESS
Edward Said

Edward, aged seven, with Rosy in Gezira Preparatory School uniform.

My father's strength, moral and physical, dominated the early part of my life. He had a massive back and a barrel chest, and although he was quite short he communicated indomitability and, at least to me, a sense of overpowering confidence. His most striking physical feature was his ramrod-stiff, nearly caricature-like upright carriage. And with that, in contrast to my shrinking, nervous timidity and shyness, went a kind of swagger that furnished another browbeating contrast with me: he never seemed to be afraid to go anywhere or do anything. I was, always. Not only did I not rush forward as I should have done in school games, but I felt seriously unwilling to let myself be looked at, so conscious was I of innumerable physical defects, all of which I was convinced reflected my inner deformations. To be looked at directly, and to return the gaze, was most difficult for me. When I was about ten I mentioned this to my father. 'Don't look at their eyes; look at their nose,' he said, thereby communicating to me a secret technique I have used for decades. When I began to teach as a graduate student in the late Fifties I found it imperative to take off my glasses in order to turn the class into a blur that I couldn't see. And to this day I find it unbearably difficult to look at myself on television, or even read about myself.

It was my mother's often melting warmth which offered me a rare opportunity to be the person I felt I truly was, in contrast to the 'Edward' who failed at school and sports, and could never match the manliness my father represented. And yet my relationship with her grew more ambivalent, and her disapproval of me became far more emotionally devastating than my father's virile bullying and reproaches. One summer afternoon in Lebanon when I was sixteen and in more than usual need of her sympathy, she delivered a judgement on all her children that I have never forgotten. I had just spent the first of two unhappy years at Mount Hermon, a repressive New England boarding school, and this particular summer of 1952 was critically important, mainly because I could spend time with her. We had developed the habit of sitting together in the afternoons, talking quite intimately, exchanging news and opinions. Suddenly she said, 'My children have all been a disappointment to me. All of them.' Somehow I couldn't bring myself to say, 'But surely not me,' even though it had been well established that I was her favourite, so much so (my sisters told me) that during my first year away from home she would lay a place for me at table on important occasions like Christmas Eve, and would not allow Beethoven's Ninth (my preferred piece of music) to be played in the house.

'Why,' I asked, 'why do you feel that way about us?' She pursed her lips and withdrew further into herself, physically and spiritually. 'Please tell me why,' I continued. 'What have I done?'

'Some day perhaps you will know, maybe after I die, but it's very clear to me that you are all a great disappointment.' For some years I would re-ask my questions, to no avail: the reasons for her disappointment in us, and obviously me, remained her best-kept secret, as well as a weapon in her arsenal for manipulating us, keeping us off-balance, and me at odds with my sisters and the world. Had it always been like this? What did it mean that I had once believed our intimacy was so secure as to admit few doubts and no undermining at all of my position? Now as I looked back on my frank and, despite the disparity in age, deep liaison with my mother, I realized how her critical ambivalence had always been there.

Hilda, my mother, was born in Nazareth in 1914, the middle child of five, and she was Palestinian, even though her mother was Lebanese. Her father was the Baptist minister in Nazareth. She was sent to boarding school in Beirut, the American School for Girls, a missionary institution that tied her to Beirut first and last, with Cairo a long interlude between. Undoubtedly a star there and at junior college (now the Lebanese American University), she was popular and brilliant—first in her class—in most things. Then, in 1932, she was plucked from what was—or was retrospectively embellished as—a wonderful life and returned from Beirut to dour, old Nazareth, where she was deposited into an arranged marriage with my father, who was at least nineteen years her senior.

My father, Wadie, never told me more than ten or eleven things about his past, all of which never changed and remained hardly more than a series of set phrases. He was born in Jerusalem in 1895 (my mother said it was more likely 1893), which made him at least forty at the time of my birth. He hated Jerusalem, and although I was born and we spent long periods of time there, the only thing he ever said about it was that it reminded him of death. At some point in his life his father was a dragoman who because he knew German had, it was said, shown Palestine to Kaiser Wilhelm. And my grandfather—never referred to by name except when my mother, who never knew him, called him Abu-Asaad—bore the surname Ibrahim. In school, therefore, my father was known as Wadie Ibrahim. I still do not know where 'Said' came from, and no one seems able to explain it. The only relevant detail about his father that my father thought fit to convey to me was that Abu-Asaad's whippings were much severer than his of me. 'How did you endure it?' I asked, to which he replied with a chuckle, 'Most of the time I ran away.' I was never able to do this, and never even considered it.

Today none of us can fully grasp what my parents' marriage was or how it came about, but I was trained by my mother—my father being generally silent on that point—to see it as something difficult at first, to which she gradually adjusted over the course of nearly forty years, and which she transformed into the main event of her life. She never worked or really studied again, and she never spoke about sex without shuddering dislike and discomfort, although my father's frequent remarks about the man being a skilled horseman, the woman a subdued mare, suggested to me a basically reluctant, if also exceptionally fruitful, sexual partnership that produced six children.

But I never doubted that at the time of her marriage to this silent and peculiarly strong middle-aged man she suffered a terrible blow. She was wrenched from a happy life in Beirut. She was given to a much older spouse—perhaps in return for some sort of payment to her mother—who promptly took her off to strange parts and then set her down in Cairo, a gigantic and confusing city in an unfamiliar Arab country. My parents often returned to my father's family home in Jerusalem—once for my birth, in 1935—but Cairo was where my father had his business (office equipment and stationery), and it was where, mostly, I grew up.

In 1937, when I was two, my parents moved to Zamalek, an island in the Nile between the city of Cairo in the east and Giza in the west, inhabited by foreigners and wealthy locals. Zamalek was not a real community but a sort of colonial outpost whose tone was set by Europeans with whom we had little or no contact: we built our own world within it. Our house was a spacious fifth-floor apartment at 1 Sharia Aziz Osman that overlooked the so-called Fish Garden, a small, fence-encircled park with an artificial rock hill (*gabalaya*), a tiny pond and a grotto; its little green lawns were interspersed with winding paths, great trees and, in the *gabalaya* area, artificially made rock formations and sloping hillsides where you could run up and down without interruption. Except for Sundays and public holidays the Garden, as we called it, was where I spent all of my playtime, always unsupervised and always within range of my mother's voice, which was lyrically audible to me and my sisters.

I played Robinson Crusoe and Tarzan there, and when my mother came with me, I played at eluding and then rejoining her. She went nearly everywhere with us, throughout our little world, one little island enclosed by another one. In the early years we went to school a few blocks away from the house—GPS, Gezira Preparatory School, which I attended from the autumn of 1941 till we left Cairo in May 1942, then again from early 1943 till 1946, with one or two longer Palestinian interruptions in between. For sports there was the Gezira Sporting Club and, on weekends, the Maadi Sporting Club, where I learned to swim. For years, Sundays meant Sunday school; this senseless ordeal occurred between nine and ten in the morning at the GPS, followed by matins at All Saints' Cathedral. Sunday evenings took us to the American Mission Church in Ezbekieh, and two Sundays out of three to Evensong at the cathedral. School, church, club, garden, house—a limited, carefully circumscribed segment of the great city—was my world until I was well into my teens.

During the GPS years I began slowly, almost imperceptibly, to develop a contestatory relationship with two of my younger sisters, Rosy and Jean, which played or was made to play into my mother's skills at managing and manipulating us. I had felt protective of Rosy: I helped her along, since she was somewhat younger and less physically adept than I; I cherished her and would frequently embrace her as we played on the balcony; I kept up a constant stream of chatter, to which she responded with smiles and chuckles. We went off to GPS together in the morning, but we separated once we got there since she was in a younger class. She had lots of giggling little girlfriends—Shahira, Nazli, Nadia, Vivette—and I, my 'fighting' classmates such as Dickie Cooper or Guy Mosseri. Quickly she established herself as a 'good' girl, while I lurked about the school with a growing sense of discomfort, rebelliousness, drift and loneliness.

After school the troubles began between us. They were accompanied by our enforced physical separation: no baths together, no wrestling or hugging, separate rooms, separate regimens, mine more physical and disciplined than hers. When Mother came home she would discuss my performance in contrast to my younger sister's. 'Look at Rosy. All the teachers say she's doing very well.' Soon enough, Jean—exceptionally pretty with her thick, auburn pigtails—changed from tag-along younger version of Rosy into another 'good' girl, with her own circle of apparently like-minded girlfriends. And she also was complimented by the GPS authorities, while I continued to sink into protracted 'disgrace', an English word that hovered around me from the time I was seven. Rosy and Jean occupied the same room; I was down the corridor; my parents in between; Joyce and Grace (eight and eleven years younger than I) had their bedrooms moved from the glassed-in balcony to another room as the apartment was modified to accommodate the growing children.

The closed door of Rosy and Jean's room signified the definitive physical as well as emotional gulf that slowly opened between us. There was once even an absolute commandment against my entering the room, forcefully pronounced and occasionally administered by my father, who now openly sided with them, as their defender and patron; I gradually assumed the part of their dubiously intentioned brother. 'Protect them,' I was always being told, to no effect whatever. For Rosy especially I was a sort of prowling predator-target, to be taunted or cajoled into straying into their room, only to be pelted with erasers, hit over the head with pillows, and shrieked at with terror and dangerous enjoyment. They seemed eager to study and learn at school and home, whereas I kept putting off such activities in order to torment them or otherwise fritter away the time until my mother returned home to a cacophony of charges and countercharges buttressed by real bruises to show and real bites to be cried over.

There was never complete estrangement though, since the three of us did at some level enjoy the interaction of competing, but rarely totally hostile, siblings. My sisters could display their quickness or specialized skill in hopscotch, and I could try to emulate them; in memorable games of blind man's buff, ring-around-the-rosy, or clumsy football in a very confined space, I might exploit my height or relative strength. After we attended the Circo Togni, whose lion tamer especially impressed me with his authoritative presence and braggadocio, I replicated his act in the girls' room, shouting commands like '*A posto, Camelia!*' at them while waving an imaginary whip and grandly thrusting a chair in their direction. They seemed quite pleased at the charade, and even managed a dainty roar as they clambered on to bed or dresser with not quite feline grace.

But we never embraced each other, as brothers and sisters might ordinarily have: for it was exactly at this subliminal level that I felt a withdrawal on all sides, of me from them, and them from me. The physical distance is still there between us, I feel, perhaps deepened over the years by my mother. When she returned from her afternoons at the Cairo Women's Club she invariably interjected herself between us. With greater and greater frequency my delinquency exposed me to her angry reprobation: 'Can't I ever leave you with your sisters without your making trouble?' was the refrain, often succeeded by the dreaded codicil, 'Wait till your father gets home.' Precisely because there was an unstated prohibition on physical contact between us, my infractions took the form of attacks that included punching, hair-pulling, pushing, and the occasional vicious pinch. Invariably I was 'reported' and then 'disgraced'—in English—and some stringent punishment (a further prohibition on going to the movies, being sent to bed without dinner, a steep reduction in my allowance and, at the limit, a beating from my father) was administered.

All this heightened our sense of the body's peculiar, and problematic, status. There was an abyss—never discussed nor examined, nor even mentioned during the crucial period of puberty—separating a boy's body from a girl's. Until I was twelve I had no idea at all what sex between men and women entailed, nor did I know very much about the relevant anatomy. Suddenly, however, words like 'pants' and 'panties' became italicized: 'I can see your pants,' said my sisters tauntingly to me, and I responded, heady with danger, 'I can see *your* panties.' I quite clearly recall that bathroom doors had to be bolted shut against marauders of the opposite sex, although my mother was present for both my dressing and undressing, as well as for theirs. I think she must have understood sibling rivalry very well and the temptations of polymorphous perversity all around us. But I also suspect that she played and worked on these impulses and drives: she kept us apart by highlighting our differences, she dramatized our shortcomings to each other, she made us feel that she alone was our reference point, our most trusted friend, our most precious love as, paradoxically, I still believe she was. Everything between me and my sisters had to pass through her, and everything I said to them was steeped in her ideas, her feelings, her sense of what was right or wrong.

None of us of course ever knew what she really thought of us, except fleetingly, enigmatically, alienatingly (as when she told me that we had all been a disappointment to her). It was only much later in my life that I understood how unfulfilled and angry she must have felt about our life in Cairo; its busy conventionality, forced rigours and the peculiar lack of authenticity. She had a fabulous capacity for letting you trust and believe in her, even though you knew that a moment later she could either turn on you with incomparable anger and scorn or draw you in with her radiant charm. 'Come and sit next to me, Edward,' she would say, inviting you into her confidence, and allowing you an amazing sense of assurance; of course, you also felt that by doing this she was keeping out Rosy and Jean, even my father then, as well.

But who was she really? Unlike my father, whose general solidity and lapidary pronouncements were a known and stable quantity, my mother was energy itself, all over the house and our lives, ceaselessly probing, judging, sweeping all of us, plus our clothes, rooms, hidden vices, achievements and problems into her always expanding orbit. But there was no common emotional space. Instead there were bilateral relationships with my mother, as colony to metropole, a constellation only she could see as a whole. What she said to me about herself, for instance, she also said to my sisters, and this characterization formed the basis of her operating persona: she was simple, she was a good person who always did the right things, she loved us all unconditionally, she wanted us to tell her everything. I believed this unquestioningly. There was nothing so satisfying in the outside world, a merry-go-round of changing schools (and hence friends and acquaintances), in which, as a non-Egyptian of uncertain, not to say suspicious, composite identity, I felt habitually out of place. My mother seemed to take in and sympathize with my general predicament. And that was enough for me. It worked as a provisional support, which I cherished tremendously.

It was through my mother that I grew more aware of my body as incredibly fraught and problematic, first because in her intimate knowledge of it she seemed better able to understand its capacity for wrongdoing, and second because she would never speak openly about it, but approached the subject either with indirect hints or, more troublingly, by means of my father and maternal uncles, through whom she spoke like a ventriloquist. When I was about fourteen I said something she thought was tremendously funny; I did not realize at the time how astute I was. I had left the bathroom door unlocked (a telling inadvertence, since I had gained some privacy as an adolescent, but for some reason wanted it occasionally infringed upon), and she suddenly entered. For a second she didn't close the door, but stood there surveying her naked son as he hastily dried himself with a small towel. 'Please leave,' I said testily, 'and stop trying to catch up where you left off.' She burst out laughing, quickly closed the door, and walked briskly away. Had she ever really left off?

I knew much earlier that my body and my sisters' were inexplicably taboo. My mother's ambivalence expressed itself in her extraordinary physical embrace of her children—covering us with kisses, caresses and hugs, cooing, making expostulations of delight about our beauty and physical endowments—and at the same time offering a great deal of devastating negative commentary on our appearance. Fatness was a dangerous and constant subject when I was nine and Rosy was seven. As my sister gained weight it became a point of discussion for us throughout childhood, adolescence and early adulthood. Along with that went an amazingly detailed consciousness of 'fattening' foods, plus endless prohibitions. I was quite skinny, tall, coordinated; Rosy didn't seem to be, and this contrast between us, to which was added the contrast between her cleverness at school and my shabby performance there, my father's special regard for her versus my mother's for me (they always denied any favouritism), her greater savoir faire when it came to organizing her time, and her capacity for pacing herself, talents I did not at all possess—all this deepened the estrangement between us, and intensified my discomfort with our bodies.

It was my father who gradually took the lead in trying to reform, perhaps even to remake, my body, but my mother rarely demurred, and regularly brought my body to a doctor's attention. As I look back on my sense of my body from age eight on, I can see it locked in a demanding set of repeated corrections, all of them ordered by my parents, most of them having the effect of turning me against myself. 'Edward' was enclosed in an ugly, recalcitrant shape with nearly everything wrong with it. Until the end of 1947, when we left Palestine for the last time, our paediatrician was a Dr Grünfelder, a German Jew, and known to be the finest child-doctor in Palestine. His office was in a quiet and leafy area of the parched city that seemed distinctly foreign to me then. He spoke to us in English, although there was a good deal of confidential whispering between him and my mother that I was rarely able to overhear. Three persistent problems were referred to him, for which he provided his own idiosyncratic solutions; the problems themselves indicate the extent to which certain parts of my body came in for an almost microscopic, and needlessly intense, supervision.

One concerned my feet, which were pronounced flat early in my life. Grünfelder prescribed the metal arches that I wore with my first pair of shoes; they were finally discarded in 1948, when an aggressive clerk in a Dr Scholl's store in Manhattan dissuaded my mother from their use. A second was my odd habit of shuddering convulsively for a brief moment every time I urinated. My mother observed me for a couple of weeks, then brought the case to the world-renowned 'child specialist'. Grünfelder shrugged his shoulders. 'It is nothing,' he pronounced, 'probably psychological'—a phrase I didn't understand but could see worried mother just a little more, or was at least to worry *me* until I was well into my teens, after which the issue was dropped.

The third problem was my stomach, the source of numerous ills and pains all my life. It began with Grünfelder's scepticism about my mother's habit of wrapping and tightly pinning a small blanket around my midsection in both summer and winter. She thought this protected me against illness, the night air, perhaps even the evil eye; later, hearing about it from different friends, I realized it was common practice in Palestine and Syria. She once told Grünfelder about this strange prophylactic in my presence, his response to which I distinctly remember was a knitted brow. 'I don't see the need,' he said, whereupon she pressed on with a rehearsal of all sorts of advantages (most of them preventive) that accrued to me. I was nine or ten at the time. The issue was also debated with Wadie Baz Haddad, our family GP in Cairo, and he too tried to dissuade her. It took another year for the silly thing to be removed once and for all; my mother later told me that still another doctor had warned her against sensitizing my midsection so much, since it then became vulnerable to all sorts of other problems.

My eyes had grown weaker because I had spring catarrh and a bout of trachoma; for two years I wore dark glasses at a time when no one else did. At age six or seven, I had to lie in a darkened room every day with compresses on my eyes for an hour. As my short-sightedness developed I saw less and less well, but my parents took the position that glasses were not 'good' for you, and were positively bad if you 'got used' to them. In December of 1949 at the age of fourteen, I went to see *Arms and the Man* at the American University of Cairo's Ewart Hall, and was unable to follow the action on stage, until a friend loaned me his glasses. Six months later, after a teacher's complaint, I did get glasses with express parental instructions not to wear them all the time: my eyes were already bad enough, I was told, and would get worse.

At the age of twelve I was informed that the pubic hair sprouting between my legs was not 'normal', increasing my already overdeveloped embarrassment about myself. The greatest critique, however, was reserved for my face and tongue, back, chest, hands and abdomen. I did not know I was being attacked, nor did I experience the reforms and strictures as the campaigns they were. I assumed they were all elements of the discipline that one went through as part of growing up. The net effect of these reforms, however, was to make me deeply self-conscious and ashamed.

The longest running and most unsuccessful reform—my father's near obsession—concerned my posture, which became a major issue for him just as I reached puberty. In June 1957, when I graduated from Princeton, it culminated in my father's insisting on taking me to a brace and corset maker in New York in order to buy me a harness to wear underneath my shirt. What still distresses me about the experience is that at the age of twenty-one I uncomplainingly let my father feel he was entitled to truss me up like a naughty child whose bad posture symbolized some objectionable character trait that required scientific punishment. The clerk who sold us the truss remained expressionless as my father amiably declared, 'See, it works perfectly. You'll have no problems.'

The white cotton and latex truss with straps across my chest and over the shoulders was the consequence of years of my father trying to get me to 'stand up straight'. 'Shoulders back,' he would say, 'shoulders back,' and my mother—whose own posture, like her mother's, was poor—would add in Arabic, 'Don't slump.' As the offence persisted she resigned herself to the notion that my posture came from the Badrs, her mother's family, and would routinely emit a desultory sigh, fatalistic and disapproving at the same time, followed by the phrase *'Herdabit beit Badr'*, or 'the Badr family humpback', addressed to no one in particular, but clearly intended to fix the blame on my ancestry, if not also on her.

The Badrs' or not, my father persisted in his efforts. These later included 'exercises', one of which was to slip one of his canes through both my armpits and make me keep it there for two hours at a stretch. Another was to make me stand in front of him and for half an hour respond to the order 'One' by thrusting my elbows back as hard and as quickly as possible, supposedly straightening my back in the process. Whenever I wandered across his line of vision he would call out, 'Shoulders back.' This of course embarrassed me when others were around, but it took me weeks to ask him to please not call out to me so loudly on the street, in the club, or even walking into church. He was reasonable about my objection. 'Here's what I'll do,' he said reassuringly. 'I'll just say "Back", and only you and I will know what it means.' And so 'Back' I endured for years and years—until the truss.

A corollary to the struggle over my posture was how it affected my chest, whose disproportionately large size and prominence I inherited from my father. Very early in my teens I was given a metal chest expander with instructions to use it to develop the size and disposition of the front of my body. I was never able to master the gadget's crazy springs, which leapt out at you threateningly if you did not have the strength to keep them taut. The real trouble, as I once explained to my mother who listened sympathetically, was that my chest was already too large; thrusting it forward aggressively, making it even bigger, turned me into a grotesque, barrel-chested caricature of a well-developed man. I seemed to be caught between the hump and the barrel. My mother understood and tried to persuade my father of this, without any observable result. When he was in America before the First World War my father had been influenced by Eugene Sandow, the legendary strongman who even turns up in *Ulysses*, and Sandow featured an overdeveloped chest and erect back. What was good for Sandow, my father once told me, ought to do 'for you too'.

Yet on several occasions my resistance exasperated my father enough for him to pummel me painfully around my shoulders, and once even to deliver a solid fist to my back. He could be physically violent, throwing heavy slaps across my face and neck, while I cringed and dodged in what I felt was a most shameful way. I regretted his strength and my weakness beyond words, but I never responded or called out in protest, not even when, as a Harvard graduate student in my early twenties, I was bashed by him humiliatingly for being rude, he said, to my mother. I learned how to sense that a cuff was on its way by the odd fashion in which he drew his top lip into his mouth and the heavy breath he suddenly took in. I much preferred the studied care he took with my canings—using a riding crop—to the frightening, angry and impulsive violence of his slaps and swinging blows to my face. When she suddenly lost her temper, my mother also flailed at my face and head, but less frequently and with considerably less force.

As I write this now it gives me a chance, very late in life, to record the experiences as a coherent whole that very strangely have left no anger, some sorrow, and a surprisingly strong residual love for my parents. All the reforming things my father did to me coexisted with an amazing willingness to let me go my own way later on; he was strikingly generous to me at Princeton and Harvard, always encouraging me to travel, to continue piano studies, to live well, always willing to foot the bill, even though my journey took me further from him as an only son and the only likely successor in the family business. What I cannot completely forgive, though, is that the contest over my body, and my father's reforms and physical punishment, instilled a deep sense of generalized fear in me, which I have spent most of my life trying to overcome. I still sometimes think of myself as a coward, with some gigantic lurking disaster waiting to overtake me for sins I have committed and will soon be punished for.

My parents' fear of my body as imperfect and morally flawed extended to my appearance. When I was about five, my long curly hair was chopped down into a very short no-nonsense haircut. Because I had a decent soprano voice and was considered 'pretty' by my doting mother, I felt my father's disapproval, even anxiety, that I might be a 'sissy', a word that hovered around me until I was ten. A strange motif of my early teens was an assault on the 'weakness' of my face, particularly my mouth. My mother used to tell two favourite stories; the first was about how Leonardo da Vinci used the same man as a model for Jesus and, after years of the man's dissipation, for Judas. The other had her quoting Lincoln, who, after condemning a man for his awful looks and being challenged by a friend that no one is responsible for being ugly, was reported to have responded, 'Everyone is responsible for his face.' When I was being upbraided for delinquency against my sisters, or for lying about having eaten all the candy, or for having spent all my money, my father would swiftly thrust his hand out, put his thumb and second finger on either side of my mouth, press in, and hold the area with a number of energetic short jerks to the left and right, all the while producing a nasty, buzzing sound like 'mmmmm', quickly followed by 'that weak mouth of yours'. I can recall staring at myself disgustedly in the mirror well past my twentieth birthday, doing exercises (pursing my mouth, clenching my teeth, raising my chin twenty or thirty times) in an effort to bring 'strength' to my weak droop. Glenn Ford's way of flexing his jaw muscles to signify moral fortitude was an early model, which I tried to imitate when responding to my parents' accusation. It was partly because of my weak face and mouth that my parents disapproved of my wearing glasses; my mother, ever ready to condemn and praise at the same time, stipulated that glasses obscured 'that beautiful face of yours'.

As for my torso, there wasn't much said about it until I was thirteen, a year before I went to Victoria College in 1949. My father met a gentleman at the Gezira Club called Mr Mourad who had just opened a gymnasium in an apartment on Fuad al-Awwal Street in Zamalek, about half a mile from where we lived. Soon after I found myself enrolled in three exercise classes a week, along with half a dozen Kuwaitis who had come to Egypt to attend the university. These classes included knee bends, medicine-ball raises and lifts, sit-ups, jogging and jumping (all inside a tiny circular room). I was soon the butt of our wiry instructor, Mr Ragab. 'More effort,' he would call out hectoringly at me in English—'Up, down, up, down,' etc. Then, a few weeks into the course, came the bombshell. 'Come on, Edward,' he said contemptuously of my sit-ups, 'we must get that stomach of yours into shape.' When I said that I thought the purpose of my being at the gym was my back, he said that it was, but my midsection was not firm enough. 'Anyway, it's what your parents want us to do.' I was too embarrassed ever to raise the matter with my parents. Another tear opened in the relationship to my body. And as I accepted the verdict I internalized the criticism, and became even more awkward about and uncertain of my physical identity.

My problematic hands became my mother's special province of critical attention. Although I was only dimly aware that physically I noticeably resembled neither the Saids (short, stocky, very dark) nor her family, the Musas (white-skinned, of medium height and build, with longer than average fingers and limbs), it was clear to me that I had endowments of strength and athletic ability denied anyone else. By the age of twelve I was a good deal taller than everyone else in my family, and, thanks to my father's curious persistence, I had amassed knowledge and practice of numerous sports, including tennis, swimming, football (despite my noted failure at it), riding, track and field, cricket, ping-pong, sailing, boxing. I was never outstanding in any of them, being too timid to dominate an opponent, but I had developed an already considerable natural competence. This allowed me over time to develop my strength, certain muscles, and—something I still possess—a very unusual stamina and wind. My hands in particular were large, exceptionally sinewy, and agile. And to my mother, they represented objects both of adoring admiration (the long, tapered fingers, the perfect proportions, the superb agility) and of often quite hysterical denunciation ('Those hands of yours are deadly instruments'; 'They're going to get you into trouble later'; 'Be very careful'.)

To my mother they were almost everything except a pair of hands: they were hammers, pliers, clubs, steel wires, nails, scissors, and when she wasn't angry or agitated, instruments of the most refined and gentle kind. For my father my hands were noteworthy for the fingernails, which I chewed on and which for decades he tried to get me not to chew, even to the point of having them painted with a vile-tasting medicine and to promising me a fancy manicure at Chez Georges, the plush barbershop he frequented on Kasr el Nil Street. All to no avail, though I often found myself hiding my hands in my pockets, as I tried not to expose myself to my father's gaze so that my 'back' would not obtrusively draw his, and everyone else's, attention.

The moral and the physical shaded into each other most imperceptibly of all when it came to my tongue, which was the object of a dense series of metaphorical associations in Arabic, most of which were negative and, in my particular case, recurred with great frequency. In English one hears mainly of a 'biting' or 'sharp' tongue, in contrast with a 'smooth' one. Whenever I blurted out something that seemed untoward, it was my 'long' tongue that was to blame: aggressive, unpleasant, uncontrolled. The description was a common one in Arabic and signified someone who did not have the required politeness and verbal savoir faire, important qualities in most Arab societies. It was my state of being repressed that caused these occasional outbursts as I compensated too much in the wrong direction. In addition, I violated all sorts of codes for the proper way to address parents, relatives, elders, teachers, brothers and sisters.

Edward Said

This was noted by my mother, who would escalate my offence into a portent of truly dire things to come. Added to that, I was also singularly unable to keep secrets or to do what everyone else did by way of choosing what *not* to say. In the context of Arabic, therefore, I was regarded as outside the range of normal behaviour, a rogue creature of whom other people should be wary.

Perhaps the real issue was sex, or, rather, my parents' defence against its onset in my life and, when it could no longer be staved off, its taming. Even when I left for the United States in 1951 at fifteen, my existence had been completely virginal, my acquaintance with girls non-existent. Movies like *The Outlaw, Duel in the Sun,* even the Michèle Morgan costume drama *Fabiola,* which I desperately wanted to see, were forbidden as being 'not for children'; such bans existed until I was fourteen. There were no visibly available sex magazines or pornographic videos in those days; the schools I went to in Egypt or the States until I was seventeen and a half infantilized and desexualized everything. This was also true of Princeton, which I attended until I was twenty-one. Sex was banned everywhere, including books, although there my inquisitiveness and the large number of volumes in our library made complete prohibition impossible to enforce. It was my own powerful need to know and experience that broke through my parents' restrictions, until an open confrontation took place whose memory, forty-six years later, still makes me shudder.

One chilly Sunday afternoon in late November 1949, at three o'clock, a few weeks after I had turned fourteen, there was a loud knock on my bedroom door, followed immediately by a sternly authoritative wrenching of the handle. This was very far from a friendly parental visit. My father stood near the door for a moment; in his right hand he distastefully clutched my pyjama bottoms, which I despairingly remembered I had left in the bathroom that morning. I held out my hands to catch the offending article, expecting him as he had done once or twice before to scold me for leaving my things around ('Please put them away; don't leave them for someone else to pick up'). The servants, he would add, were not for my personal comfort.

Since he kept the garment in his hand I knew that this must be a more serious matter, and I sank back into the bed, anxiously awaiting the attack. When he was halfway into the room, just as he began to speak, I saw my mother's drawn face framed in the doorway several feet behind him. She said nothing but was there to give emotional weight to his prosecution of the case. 'Your mother and I have noticed'—here he waved the pyjamas—'that you haven't had any wet dreams. That means you're abusing yourself.' He had never said it accusingly before, although the dangers of 'self-abuse' and the virtues of wet dreams had been the subject of several lectures and were first described to me on a walk around the deck of the *Saturnia* en route to New York in July of 1948.

These lectures were the result of my asking my mother about a stout little pair of Italian opera singers, fellow passengers on the *Saturnia*. She wore very high heels, a tight white dress, heavily painted lips; he was in a shiny brown suit, elevated heels, with carefully slicked-back hair; both exuded a bountiful sexuality to which I could attach no specific practices. In an unguarded moment I had asked my mother confusedly and inarticulately how such people as those actually did 'it'. I had no words for 'it', none for penis or vagina, and none for foreplay; all I could do was to enlist urination and defecation in my question, which, I had somehow gleaned, bore some pleasurable meaning as well. My mother's look of alarm and disgust set me up for the 'man-to-man' talk with my father. A great part of his massive authority, and his compelling power over me, was that strange combination of silence and the ritual repetition of clichés picked up from assorted places—*Tom Brown's Schooldays*, the YMCA, courses in salesmanship, the Bible, evangelical sermons, Shakespeare, and so on.

'Just think of a cup slowly filling up with liquid,' he began. 'Then once it is full'—here he cupped one hand and with the other skimmed off the hypothetical excess—'it naturally flows over, and you have a wet dream.' He paused for a bit. Then he continued, again metaphorically. 'Have you ever seen a horse win a race without being able to maintain a steady pace? Of course not. If the horse starts out too quickly, he gets tired and fades away. The same thing with you. If you abuse yourself your cup will not run over; you can't win or even finish the race.' On a similar occasion later he added warnings about going bald and/or mad as a result of 'self-abuse', which only very rarely did he refer to as masturbation, a word pronounced with quite dreadful admonishment: *'maaasturbation'* (the a's almost o's).

My father never spoke of making love, and certainly not of fucking. When I tried to bring up the question of how children were produced the answer was schematic. My mother's frequent pregnancies, and especially her alarmingly protuberant stomach during them, never settled the question. Her line to me was always, 'We wrote a letter to Jesus and he sent us a baby!' What my father told me after his solemn shipboard warning about 'self-abuse' was a few almost dismissive words about how the man puts his 'private parts' in the woman's 'private parts'. Nothing about orgasm or ejaculation or about what 'private parts' were. Pleasure was never mentioned. As for kissing, he referred to it only once in all my years of being with and knowing him. 'You must marry a woman,' he told me when I was in college, 'who has never been kissed before you kissed her. Like your mother.' There was not even a mention of virginity, an abstruse concept that I had heard about in Sunday school and then through catechism and that acquired some concrete meaning for me only when I was about twenty.

After we returned from America in the autumn of 1948 there were two or perhaps three occasions when we had man-to-man talks, each time with a growing sense on my part of encroachment and guilt. I once asked him how one would know that the wet dream had occurred. 'You would know in the morning,' was his first answer. As with most things then, I was hesitant to ask more, but I did when he next brought it up, along with a still more embellished account of the evils of 'self-abuse' (the man becoming 'useless' and a 'failure' as the degeneracy took final hold). 'A wet dream is a nocturnal emission,' he said. The phrase sounded as if he was reading it off a page. 'Is it like going to the bathroom?' I asked, using the euphemism we all used for urinating ('pee-pee' was the definitely riskier alternative, which my mother always admonished me against: I used it when trying to be 'naughty', along with 'I can see your pants!!' to one of my sisters, as a further act of insubordination and intransigence).

'Yes, more or less, but it's thicker and sticks to your pyjamas,' he said then. So this was why the pyjamas were being clinically transported in his left hand as he stood a few feet from my bed. 'There's nothing on these pyjamas at all,' he said to me with a look of scowling disgust, 'nothing. Haven't I told you many times about the dangers of self-abuse? What's the matter with you?' There was a pause, as I looked furtively past my father towards my mother. Although I knew in my heart that she sympathized with me most of the time, she rarely broke ranks with him. Now I couldn't detect any support at all; just a shyly questioning look, as if to say: 'Yes, Edward, what *are* you doing?' plus a little bit of 'Why do you do nasty things to hurt us?'

I was seized with such terror, guilt, shame and vulnerability that I have never forgotten this scene. The most important thing about these feelings is how they coalesced around my father, whose cold denunciation of me in my bed utterly silenced and defeated me. There was nothing to confess to that he didn't already know. I had no excuse: the wet dreams hadn't in fact occurred, even though for a time during the past year I did wake up anxiously, searching bed and nightclothes for evidence that they might have. I was already down the road to perdition, perhaps even baldness. (I was alarmed after a bath once to notice that my wet hair, normally quite thick, showed a couple of patches of what appeared to be baldness. I also suspected that my father's insistence on frequent haircuts was connected to deterring the premature effects of self-abuse. 'Have your hair cut often and short, like your father,' he'd say, 'and it'll remain strong and full.') My secret, such as it was, had been found out. All I could think of was that I had no place to go as the dreadful retribution was about to occur. For a moment I felt as if I was clinging to 'Edward' to save him from final extinction.

'You have nothing to say, do you?' A quick breath, then the climax. He threw the pyjama bottoms at me with vehemence and what I thought was exasperated disgust. 'All right then. Have a wet dream!' I was so taken aback by this peremptory order—could one, in fact, if one wanted, just have a wet dream?—that I shrank back even further into the bed. Then, just as I thought he was going to leave, he turned towards me again.

'Where did you learn how to abuse yourself?' As if by a miracle

I was given an opening to save myself. I recalled in a flash that only a few weeks earlier, near the end of summer and just before school started, I had been loitering in the boys' dressing room at the Maadi Club. Although it was at the time my father's favourite club for golf and bridge, I knew relatively few people and, with my usual shyness, would go into the dressing room to get into my bathing suit but would also take my time, hoping to strike up a friendship perhaps, or meet a stray acquaintance. My feeling of loneliness was unallayed. This time, however, a gaggle of older boys, wet from swimming, burst in. They were led by Ehab, a very tall and thin boy with a deep voice that exuded confidence. Rich, secure, at home and in place. 'Come on Ehab, do it,' he was urged by the others. I had seen him before but had not really met him: our fathers did not know each other and I was still dependent on this kind of parental introduction. Ehab lowered his trunks, stood on the bench, and while peering over the wall at the pool's designated sunbathing area, began to masturbate. I heard myself blurt out, 'Do it on Colette,' Colette being a voluptuous young woman in her twenties who always wore a black bathing suit and had graced my own private fantasies. No one heard me; I felt like an ass and blushed uncontrollably though no one seemed to notice. We were all watching Ehab as he rubbed his penis slowly until, at last, he ejaculated, also slowly, at which point he started to laugh smugly, displaying his sticky fingers as if he had just won a sports trophy.

'It was at the club. Ehab did it,' I blurted out to my father, who had no idea who Ehab was or what it was I was trying to say. I realized that he was not asking me for anything concrete: it was only a rhetorical question. Of course I was guilty. Of course he now knew it. My sins had also been exposed to my mother, who never said a word, but showed signs of scarcely comprehending horror and even bereavement.

My father did not seem particularly interested either in my explanation or in listening to my clumsy expressions of determined self-reform. He had found me out and found me wanting; he knew what harm I was doing myself, and he had judged me both weak and unreliable. That was all. He had told me about the cup and the racehorse, about baldness and madness. He had repeated the homilies perhaps eight times, so all he could do now would be to repeat them yet again or, 'wisely' (a word he liked to use), he could register the crime and move on, his authority and moral judgement remaining forcibly intact. I was neither punished nor even reminded of my secret vice. But I didn't think I had escaped lightly. This particular failure of mine, embodied in that exquisitely theatrical scene, added itself, like a new and extremely undermining fault line, to the already superficially incoherent and disorganized structure of 'Edward'. □

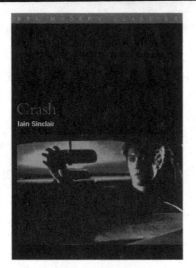

THE WAITER'S WIFE
Zadie Smith

In the spring of 1975, Samad and Alsana Iqbal left Bangladesh and came to live in Whitechapel, London, the other side of town from Archie and Clara Jones. Samad and Archie had a friendship dating back to the Second World War, back to the hot and claustrophobic Churchill tank in which they sat side by side for three months, close enough to smell each other and to recognize those scents thirty years later when Samad emerged from Gate 12, Heathrow, with a young wife and a paisley patterned luggage set in tow. 'Long time no see,' Archie had said, reaching out to grasp his old friend's palm, but Samad converted the handshake into a hug almost immediately, '*Archibald Jones*. Long time no bloody *smell*.'

They fell back into easy conversation, two old boys slipping swiftly into an acquaintance as comfortable as slippers while their wives stood either side of the bags noting they had this thing in common and no more: that they were young, much younger than the men they stood awkwardly beside. They looked an unlikely pair. Alsana was small and rotund, moon-faced and with thick fingers she hid in the folds of her cardigan. Clara was tall, striking, a black girl with a winning smile, wearing red shorts of a shortness that Alsana had never imagined possible, even in this country.

'Hot pants,' said Clara, shyly, in response to Alsana's wide eyes, 'I made dem myself.'

'I sew also,' Alsana replied, and they had a pleasant enough chat about seams and bobbins, materials and prices per yard, in a motorway service station over an indigestible lunch. 'The wives get on like a house on fire,' Archie had said merrily, giving Samad a nudge in the ribs. But this made them nervous, the two young wives, and after the ice-cream sundaes they sat in silence.

So some black people *are* friendly, thought Alsana after that first meeting was over. It was her habit to single one shining exception out of every minority she disliked; certain dentists, certain singers, certain film stars had been granted specialist treatment in the past and now Clara Jones was to be given Alsana's golden reprieve. Their relations were hesitant in the beginning—a few lunch dates here and there, the occasional coffee; neither wished to admit how much time they had on their hands though newly wed, or that Archie and Samad were always together. It wasn't until the Iqbals moved north, two minutes from Archie and his favourite watering hole, that the women truly resigned themselves to their husbands' mutual appreciation society and started something of a rearguard action. Picnics, the movies, museums, swimming pools—just the two of them. But even when they became fairly close, it was impossible to forget what a peculiar couple they made on the bus, in the park.

It took the Iqbals a year to get to Willesden High Road: a year of mercilessly hard graft to make the momentous move from the wrong side of Whitechapel to the wrong side of Willesden. A year's worth of Alsana banging away at the old Singer machine that sat in the kitchen, sewing together pieces of black plastic for a shop called Domination in Soho (many were the nights Alsana would hold up a piece of clothing she had just made—following the plans she was given—and wonder what on earth it was). A year's worth of Samad softly inclining his head at exactly the correct deferential angle, pencil in his right hand, notepad in his left, listening to the appalling pronunciation of the British, Spanish, American, French, Australian:

Go Bye Ello Sag, Please.

Chicken Jail Fret See Wiv Chips, Fanks.

From six in the evening until four in the morning was work and the rest was sleep, sleep without pause, until daylight was as rare as a decent tip. For what is the point, Samad would think, pushing aside two mints and a receipt to find fifteen pence, what is the point of tipping a man the same amount you would throw in a fountain to chase a wish? But before the illegal thought of folding the fifteen pence discreetly in his napkin hand had a chance to give itself form, Mukhul, Ardashir Mukhul, who ran The Palace and whose wiry frame paced the restaurant, one benevolent eye on the customers, one ever-watchful eye on the staff—Ardashir Mukhul was upon him.

'Saaamaad,' he said in his cloying, oleaginous way, 'did you kiss the necessary backside this evening, Cousin?'

Samad and Ardashir were distant cousins, Samad the elder by six years. With what joy (pure bliss!) had Ardashir opened the letter last January, to find his older, cleverer, handsomer cousin could get no work as a food inspector in England and could he possibly...

'Fifteen pence, Cousin,' said Samad lifting his palm.

'Well, every little helps, every little helps,' said Ardashir, his dead-fish lips stretching into a stringy smile. 'Into the Piss-Pot with it.'

The Piss-Pot was a black cooking pot that sat on a plinth outside the staff toilets into which all tips were pooled and then split at the end of the night. For the younger, good-looking waiters like Shiva this was a great injustice. Shiva was the only Hindu on the staff, a tribute to his waitering skills that had triumphed over religious difference. He could make fifteen pounds in tips in an evening if the blubberous white divorcee in the corner was lonely enough, and he batted his long lashes at her effectively. He also made money from the polo-necked directors and producers (The Palace sat in the centre of London's Theatreland) who flattered the boy, watched his ass wiggle provocatively to the bar and back, and swore that the next time someone put *A Passage to India* on the stage, the casting couch would be his. For Shiva then, the Piss-Pot system was simply daylight robbery. But for men like Samad, in his forties, and for the even older, like the white-haired Mohammed (Ardashir's great-uncle), who was eighty if he was a day, who had deep pathways dug into the sides of his mouth where he had smiled when he was young—for men like this the Piss-Pot could not be complained about. It was a boon if anything, and it made more sense to join the collective than pocket fifteen pence and risk being caught (and docked a week's tips).

'You're all on my back!' Shiva would snarl, when he had to relinquish five pounds at the end of the night and drop it into the pot. 'You all live off my back! Somebody get these losers off my back! That was my fiver and now it's going to be split sixty-five-fucking-million ways as a hand out to these losers! What is this, communism?'

And the rest would avoid his glare, and busy themselves quietly with other things until one evening, one fifteen-pence evening, Samad said, 'Shut up, boy,' quietly, almost underneath his breath.

'You!' Shiva swung round to where Samad stood crushing a great tub of lentils for tomorrow's dhal. 'You're the worst of them! You're the worst fucking waiter I've ever seen! You couldn't get a tip if you mugged the bastards! I hear you trying to talk to the customer about biology this, politics that—just serve the food, you idiot—you're a waiter, for fuck's sake, you're not Michael Parkinson. *Did I hear you say Delhi*—' Shiva put his apron over his arm and began posturing around the kitchen (he was a pitiful mimic) '—*I was*

there myself, you know, Delhi University, it was most fascinating,
yes—and I fought in the war, for England, yes—yes, yes, charming,
charming—' round and round the kitchen he went, bending his head
and rubbing his hands over and over like Uriah Heep, bowing and
genuflecting to the head cook, to the old man arranging great hunks
of meat in the walk-in freezer, to the young boy scrubbing the inside
of the oven. 'Samad, *Samad...*' he said with what seemed infinite pity,
then stopped abruptly, pulled the apron off and wrapped it round
his waist, 'you're a sad bastard.'

Mohammed looked up from his pot-scrubbing and shook his
head again and again. To no one in particular he said, 'These young
people—what kind of talk? What happened to respect? What kind
of talk is this?'

'And you, you can fuck off too—' said Shiva, brandishing a ladle
in his direction, '—You old fool! You're not my father.'

'Second cousin of your mother's uncle,' a voice muttered from
the back.

'Bollocks,' said Shiva. 'Bollocks to that.'

He grabbed the mop and was heading off for the toilets, when
he stopped by Samad and placed the broom inches from Samad's
mouth.

'Kiss it,' he sneered: and then impersonating Ardashir's sluggish
drawl, 'Who knows, Cousin, you might get a raise!'

And that's what it was like most nights; abuse from Shiva and
others; condescension from Ardashir; never seeing Alsana; never
seeing the sun; clutching fifteen pence and then releasing it; wanting
desperately to be wearing a sign, a large white placard that said:

I AM NOT A WAITER. THAT IS, I AM A WAITER, BUT NOT JUST A WAITER.
I HAVE BEEN A STUDENT, A SCIENTIST, A SOLDIER. MY WIFE IS CALLED
ALSANA. WE LIVE IN EAST LONDON BUT WE WOULD LIKE TO MOVE
NORTH. I AM A MUSLIM BUT ALLAH HAS FORSAKEN ME OR I HAVE
FORSAKEN ALLAH. I'M NOT SURE. I HAVE AN ENGLISH FRIEND—
ARCHIE—AND OTHERS. I AM FORTY-NINE BUT WOMEN STILL TURN IN
THE STREET. SOMETIMES.

But no such placard existing, he had instead the urge, the need,
to speak to every man, and like the Ancient Mariner to explain,

always to explain, to reassert something, anything. Wasn't that important? But then the heartbreaking disappointment—to find out that the inclining of one's head, poising of one's pen, these were important, so important. It was important to be a good waiter, to listen when someone said:

Lamb Dawn Sock and Rice. Please. With Chips. Thank you.

And fifteen pence clinked on china. Thank you Sir. Thank you so very much.

One evening, shortly after he had put the down payment on the Willesden flat, Samad had waited till everyone left and then climbed the loudly carpeted stairs to Ardashir's office, for he had something to ask him.

'Cousin!' said Ardashir with a friendly grimace at the sight of Samad's body curling cautiously round the door. He knew that Samad had come to enquire about a pay increase, and he wanted his cousin to feel that he had at least considered the case in all his friendly judiciousness before he declined.

'Cousin, come in!'

'Good evening, Ardashir Mukhul,' said Samad, stepping fully into the room.

'Sit down, sit down,' said Ardashir warmly. 'No point standing on ceremony now, is there?'

Samad was glad this was so. He said as much. He took a moment to look with the necessary admiration around the room with its relentless flashes of gold, its thick pile carpet, its furnishings in various shades of yellow and green. One had to admire Ardashir's business sense. He had taken the simple idea of an Indian restaurant (small room, pink tablecloth, loud music, atrocious wallpaper, meals) and just made it bigger. He hadn't improved anything; it was the same old crap but bigger in a bigger building in the biggest tourist trap in London. Leicester Square. You had to admire it and admire the man, who now sat like a benign locust, his slender insectile body swamped in a black leather chair, leaning over the desk, all smiles, a parasite disguised as a philanthropist.

'Cousin, what can I do for you?'

Samad took a deep breath. The matter was…what was the

matter? The house was the matter. Samad was moving out of East London (where one couldn't bring up children, indeed, one couldn't, not if one didn't wish them to come to bodily harm), from East London, with its National Front gangs, to North London, north-west in fact, where things were more...more...liberal. Ardashir's eyes glazed over a little as Samad explained his situation. His skinny legs twitched beneath the desk, and in his fingers he manipulated a paperclip until it looked reasonably like an A. A for Ardashir.

'I need only a small wage increase to help me finance the move. To make things a little easier as we settle in. And Alsana, well, she is pregnant.'

Pregnant. Difficult. Ardashir realized the case called for extreme diplomacy.

'Don't mistake me, Samad, we are both intelligent, frank men and I think I can speak frankly... I know you're not a *fucking* waiter—' he whispered the expletive and smiled indulgently after it, as if it were a naughty, private thing that brought them closer together, 'I see your position...of course I do...but you must understand mine... If I made allowances for every relative I employ I'd be walking around like bloody Mr Gandhi. Without a pot to piss in. Spinning my thread by the light of the moon. An example: at this very moment that wastrel Fat Elvis brother-in-law of mine, Hussein Ishmael—'

'The butcher?'

'The butcher, demands that I should raise the price I pay for his stinking meat! "But Ardashir, we are brothers-in-law!" he is saying to me. And I am saying to him, but Mohammed, this is *retail*...'

It was Samad's turn to glaze over. He thought of his wife, Alsana, who was not as meek as he had assumed when they married, to whom he must deliver the bad news: Alsana, who was prone to moments, even fits—yes, fits was not too strong a word—of rage. Cousins, aunts, brothers thought it a bad sign. They wondered if there wasn't some 'funny mental history' in Alsana's family, they sympathized with him the way you sympathize with a man who has bought a stolen car with more mileage on it than first thought. In his naivety Samad had simply assumed a woman so young would be...easy. But Alsana was not...no, she was not easy. It was, he supposed, the way with young women these days.

Ardashir came to the end of what he felt was his perfectly worded speech, sat back satisfied, and laid the *M* for Mukhul he had moulded next to the *A* for Ardashir that sat on his lap.

'Thank you, Sir,' said Samad. 'Thank you so very much.'

That evening there was an awful row. Alsana slung the sewing machine, with the black studded hot pants she was working on, to the floor.

'Useless! Tell me, Samad Miah, what is the point of moving here—nice house, yes very nice, very nice—but where is the food?'

'It is a nice area, we have friends here...'

'Who are they?' she slammed her little fist on to the kitchen table, sending the salt and pepper flying to collide spectacularly with each other in the air. 'I don't know them! You fight in an old, forgotten war with some Englishman...married to a black! Whose friends are they? These are the people my child will grow up around? Their children—half blacky-white? But tell me,' she shouted, returning to her favoured topic, 'where is our food?'

Theatrically, she threw open every cupboard in the kitchen, 'Where is it? Can we eat china?'

Two plates smashed to the floor. She patted her stomach to indicate her unborn child and pointed to the pieces, 'Hungry?'

Samad, who had an equally melodramatic nature when prompted, yanked open the freezer and pulled out a mountain of meat which he piled in the middle of the room. His mother worked through the night preparing meals for her family, he said. His mother did not, he said, spend the household money, as Alsana did, on prepared meals, yogurts and tinned spaghetti. Alsana punched him full square in the stomach.

'Samad Iqbal the traditionalist! Why don't I just squat in the street over a bucket and wash clothes? Eh? In fact, what about my clothes? Edible?'

As Samad clutched his winded belly, there in the kitchen she ripped to shreds every stitch she had on and added them to the pile of frozen lamb, spare cuts from the restaurant. She stood naked before him for a moment, the as yet small mound of her pregnancy in full view, then put on a long, brown coat and left the house.

But all the same, she reflected, slamming the door behind her, it was a nice area; she couldn't deny it as she stormed towards the high street, avoiding pavement trees where previously, in Whitechapel, she had avoided flung-out mattresses and the homeless. It would be good for the child. Alsana had a deep-seated belief that living near green spaces was morally beneficial to the young and there to her right was Gladstone Park, a sweeping horizon of green named after the Liberal prime minister (Alsana was from a respected old Bengal family and had read her English History), and in the Liberal tradition it was a park without fences, unlike the more affluent Queen's Park (Victoria's) with its pointed metal railings. Willesden was not as pretty as Queen's Park but it was a nice area. No denying it. No NF kids breaking the basement windows with their steel-capped boots like in Whitechapel. Now she was pregnant she needed a little bit of peace and quiet. Though it was the same here in a way; they all looked at her strangely, this tiny Indian woman stalking the high street in a mackintosh, her plentiful hair flying every which way. *Mali's Kebabs, Mr Cheungs, Raj's, Malkovich Bakeries*—she read the new, unfamiliar signs as she passed. She was shrewd. She saw what this was. 'Liberal? Hosh-kosh nonsense!' No one was more liberal than anyone else anywhere anyway. It was only that here, in Willesden, there wasn't enough of any one thing to gang up against any other thing and send it running to the cellars while windows were smashed.

'Survival is what it is about!' she concluded out loud (she spoke to her baby: she liked to give it one sensible thought a day), making the bell above Crazy Shoes tinkle as she opened the door. Her niece Neena worked here. It was an old-fashioned cobbler's. Neena fixed heels back on to stilettos.

'Alsana, you look like dog shit,' Neena called over in Bengali. 'What is that horrible coat?'

'It's none of your business is what it is,' replied Alsana in English. 'I came to collect my husband's shoes not to chit-chat with Niece-Of-Shame.'

Neena was used to this, and now Alsana had moved to Willesden there would only be more of it. It used to come in longer sentences (such as, 'Niece, you have brought nothing but shame...'), but now because Alsana no longer had the time or energy to summon up the necessary shock each time, it had become abridged to Niece-Of-Shame, an all-purpose tag that summed up the general feeling.

'See these soles?' said Neena, taking Samad's shoes off the shelf and handing Alsana the little blue ticket. 'They were so worn through, Aunty Alsi, I had to reconstruct them from the very base. From the base! What does he do in them? Run marathons?'

'He works,' replied Alsana tersely. 'And prays,' she added, for she liked to make a point of her respectability, and besides she was really very traditional, very religious, lacking nothing except the faith.

'And don't call me Aunty, I am only two years older than you.'

Alsana swept the shoes into a plastic carrier bag and turned to leave.

'I thought that praying was done on people's knees,' said Neena, laughing lightly.

'Both, both, asleep, waking, walking,' snapped Alsana, as she passed under the tinkly bell once more. 'We are never out of sight of the Creator.'

'How's the new house, then?' Neena called after her.

But she had gone. Neena shook her head and sighed as she watched her young aunt disappear down the road like a little brown bullet. Alsana. She was young and old at the same time, Neena reflected. She acted so sensible, so straight-down-the-line in her long sensible coat, but you got the feeling—

'Oi! Miss! There's shoes back here that need your attention!' came a voice from the storeroom.

'Keep your tits on,' said Neena.

At the corner of the road, Alsana popped behind the post office and removed her pinchy sandals in favour of Samad's shoes. (It was an oddity about Alsana. She was small but her feet were enormous, as if she had more growing to do.) In seconds she whipped her hair into an efficient bun, and wrapped her coat tighter around her to keep out the wind. Then she set off, past the library and up a long green road she had never walked along before. 'Survival is all, Little Iqbal,' she said to her bump once more. 'Survival.'

Clara was also pregnant. When their bumps became too large and cinema seats no longer accommodated them, the two women began to meet up for lunch in Kilburn Park, often with the Niece-Of-Shame, the three of them squeezed on to a generous bench, Alsana pressing a thermos of PG Tips into Clara's hand, without milk, with lemon. Unwrapping several layers of cling film to reveal today's peculiar delight: savoury dough-like balls, crumbly Indian sweets shot through with the colours of the kaleidoscope, thin pastry with spiced beef inside, salad with onion, she says to Clara: 'Eat up! Stuff yourself silly! They're in there, wallowing around in your belly, waiting for the menu. Woman, don't torture them! You want to starve the bumps?' for, despite appearances, there are six people on that bench (three living, three coming); one girl for Clara, two boys for Alsana.

Alsana says: 'Nobody's complaining, let's get that straight. A boy is good and two boys is bloody good. But I tell you, when I turned my head and saw the ultra-business thingummybob—'

'Ultrasound,' corrects Clara, through a mouthful of rice.

'—Yes, I almost had the heart attack to finish me off! Two! Feeding one is enough!'

Clara laughs and says she can imagine Samad's face when he saw it.

'No dearie,'—Alsana is reproving, tucking her large feet underneath the folds of her sari, 'he didn't see anything. He wasn't there. I am not letting him see things like that. A woman has to have the private things—a husband needn't be involved in body-business, in a lady's...*parts*.'

Niece-Of-Shame, who is sat between them, sucks her teeth.

'Bloody Hell, Alsi, he must have been involved in your parts sometime, or is this the immaculate bloody conception?'

'So rude,' says Alsana to Clara in a snooty, English way. 'Too old to be so rude and too young to know any better.' And then Clara and Alsana, with the accidental mirroring that happens when two people are sharing the same experience, both lay their hands on their bulges.

Neena, to redeem herself: 'Yeah, well how are you doing on names? Any ideas?'

Alsana is decisive. '*Magid* and *Millat*. Ems are good. Ems are strong. Mahatma, Mohammed, that funny Mr Morecambe, from Morecambe and Wise—letter you can trust.'

But Clara is more cautious, because naming seems to her a

fearful responsibility, a godlike task for a mere mortal: 'I tink I like *Irie*. It patois. Means everyting OK, cool, peaceful, you know?'

Alsana is mock-horrified before the sentence is finished, '"OK"? This is a name for a child? You might as well call her "Wouldsulike-anypopadumswiththat?" or "Niceweatherwearehaving"—'

'...and Archie likes *Sarah*. Well, dere not much you can argue wid Sarah, but dere's not much to get happy bout either. I suppose if it was good enough for the wife of Abraham...'

'Ibrahim,' Alsana corrects, out of instinct more than Koranic pedantry. 'Popping out babies when she was a hundred years old, by the grace of Allah.'

And then Neena, groaning at the turn the conversation is taking: 'Well I *like* Irie. It's funky. It's different.'

Alsana loves this: 'For pity's sake, what does Archibald know about *funky* and *different*? If I were you, dearie,' she says patting Clara's knee, 'I'd choose Sarah and let that be an end to it. Sometimes you have to let these men have it their way. Anything for a little— how do you say it in the English? For a little—' she puts her finger over tightly pursed lips, like a guard at the gate, '—*shush*.'

But in response Niece-Of-Shame bats her voluminous eyelashes, wraps her college scarf round her head like purdah, and says, 'Oh yes, Auntie, yes, the little submissive Indian woman. You don't talk to him, he talks at you. You scream and shout at each other, but there's no communication. And in the end he wins anyway because he does whatever he likes when he likes. You don't even know where he is, what he does, what he *feels*, half the time. It's 1975, Alsi. You can't conduct relationships like that any more. It's not like back home. There has to be communication between men and women in the West, they've got to listen to each other, otherwise...' Neena mimes a small mushroom cloud going off in her hand.

'What a load of the codswallop,' says Alsana sonorously, closing her eyes, shaking her head. 'It is you who do not listen. By Allah, I will always give as good as I get. But you presume I *care* what he does. You presume I want to *know*. The truth is, for a marriage to survive you don't need all this talk, talk, talk; all this "I am this" and "I am really like this" like on the television, all this *revelation*— especially when your husband is old, when he is wrinkly and falling apart—you do not *want* to know what is slimy underneath the bed and rattling in the wardrobe.'

Neena frowns. Clara cannot raise serious objection, and the rice is handed around once more.

'Moreover,' says Alsana after a pause, folding her dimpled arms underneath her breasts, pleased to be holding forth on a subject close to this formidable bosom, 'when you are from families such as ours you should have learned that *silence*, what is *not* said, is the very *best* recipe for family life.'

'So let me get this straight,' says Neena, derisively. 'You're saying that a good dose of repression keeps a marriage healthy?'

And as if someone had pressed a button, Alsana is outraged: 'Repression! Nonsense silly-billy word! I'm just talking about common sense. What is my husband? What is yours?' she says pointing to Clara. 'Twenty-five years they live before we are even born. What are they? What are they capable of? What blood do they have on their hands? What is sticky and smelly in their private areas? Who knows?' She throws her hands up, releasing the questions into the unhealthy Kilburn air, sending a troupe of sparrows up with them.

'What you don't understand, my Niece-Of-Shame, what none of your generation understand—'

'But Auntie,' begs Neena, raising her voice, because this is what she really wants to argue about—the largest sticking point between the two of them—Alsana's arranged marriage, 'how could you bear to marry someone you didn't know from Adam?'

In response, an infuriating wink. Alsana always likes to appear jovial at the very moment that her interlocutor becomes hot under the collar. 'Because, *Miss Smarty-pants*, it is by far the easier option. It was exactly because Eve did not know Adam from Adam that they got on so A-OK. Let me explain. Yes, I was married to Samad Iqbal the same evening of the very day I met him. Yes, I didn't know him from Adam. But I liked him well enough. We met in the breakfast room on a steaming Dhaka day and he fanned me with *The Times*. I thought he had a good face, a sweet voice, and his backside was high and well formed for a man of his age. Very good. Now every time I learn something more about him *I like him less*. So you see, we were better off the way we were.'

Neena stamps her foot in exasperation at the skewed logic.

'—Besides, I will never know him well. Getting anything out of my husband is like trying to squeeze water out when you're stoned.'

Neena laughs despite herself, 'Water out of a stone.'

'Yes, yes. You think I'm so stupid. But I am wise about things like men. I tell you,' Alsana prepares to deliver her summation as she has seen it done many years previously by the young Dhaka lawyers with their slick side-partings, 'men are the last mystery. God is easy compared with men. Now, enough of the philosophy. Samosa?'

She peels the lid off the plastic tub and sits fat, pretty and satisfied on her conclusion.

'Shame that you're having them,' says Neena to her aunt, lighting a fag. 'Boys, I mean. Shame that you're going to have boys.'

'What do you mean?'

This is Clara, who has secretly subscribed (a secret from Alsana and Archie) to a lending library of Neena's through which she has read, in a few short months, *The Female Eunuch* by Greer, *Sex, Race and Class* by Selma James and Jong's *Fear of Flying*, all in a clandestine attempt, on Neena's part, to rid Clara of her 'false consciousness'.

'I mean, I just think men have caused enough chaos this century. There's enough bloody men in the world. If I knew I was going to have a boy...' she pauses to prepare her two falsely conscious friends for this new concept, 'I'd have to seriously consider abortion.'

Alsana screams, claps her hands over one of her own ears and one of Clara's, and then almost chokes on a piece of aubergine with the physical exertion. For some reason the remark simultaneously strikes Clara as funny: hysterically, desperately funny, miserably funny; and the Niece-Of-Shame sits between them, nonplussed, while the two egg-shaped women bend over themselves, one in laughter, the other in horror and near asphyxiation.

'Are you all right, ladies?' It is Sol Jozefowicz, the park keeper, standing in front of them, ready as always to be of aid.

'We are all going to burn in hell, Mr Jozefowicz, if you call that being all right...' explains Alsana, pulling herself together.

Niece-Of-Shame rolls her eyes: 'Speak for yourself.'

But Alsana is faster than any sniper when it comes to firing back: 'I do, I do—thankfully Allah has arranged it that way.'

'Good afternoon, Neena, good afternoon, Mrs Jones,' says Sol, offering a neat bow to each. 'Are you sure you are all right? Mrs Jones?'

Clara cannot stop the tears from squeezing out of the corners of her eyes. She cannot work out, at this moment, whether she is crying or laughing; the two states suddenly seem only a stone's throw from each other.

'I'm fine, fine. Sorry to have worried you, Mr Jozefowicz. Really, I'm fine.'

'I do not see what so very funny-funny,' mutters Alsana. 'The murder of innocents—is this funny?'

'Not in my experience, Mrs Iqbal, no,' says Sol Jozefowicz in the collected manner in which he says everything, passing his handkerchief to Clara. It strikes all three women—the way history will: embarrassingly, without warning, like a blush—what the park keeper's experience might have been. They fall silent.

'Well, as long as you ladies are fine, I'll be getting on,' says Sol, motioning that Clara can keep the handkerchief and replacing the hat he had removed in the old fashion. He bows his neat little bow once more, and sets off slowly anticlockwise round the park.

Once Sol is out of earshot Neena says: 'OK, Aunty Alsi. I apologize. I apologize... What more do you want?'

'Oh, every-bloody-thing,' says Alsana, her voice losing the fight, becoming vulnerable. 'The whole bloody universe made clear—in a little nutshell. I cannot understand a thing any more, and I am just beginning. You understand?'

She sighs, not waiting for an answer, not looking at Neena, but across the way at the hunched, disappearing figure of Sol winding in and out of the yew trees. 'You may be right about Samad...about many things...maybe there are no good men, not even the two in this belly...and maybe I do not talk enough with mine, maybe I have married a stranger...you might see the truth better than I...what do I know, a barefoot country girl who never went to the universities...'

'Oh, Alsi,' Neena keeps saying, weaving her regret in and out of Alsana's words like tapestry, feeling bad, 'you know I didn't mean it like that.'

'But I cannot be worrying-worrying all the time about the truth.

I have to worry about the truth that can be lived with. And that is the difference between losing your marbles drinking the salty sea, or swallowing the stuff from the streams. My Niece-Of-Shame believes in the talking cure, eh?' says Alsana, with something of a grin. 'Talk, talk, talk and it will be better. Be honest, slice open your heart and spread the red stuff around. But the past is made of more than words, dearie. We married old men, you see? These bumps,' Alsana pats them both, 'they will always have Daddy-long-legs for fathers. One leg in the present, one in the past. No talking will change this. Their roots will always be tangled.'

Just as he reaches the far gate, Sol Jozefowicz turns round to wave, and the three women wave back. And Clara feels a little theatrical, flying the park keeper's cream handkerchief above her head. As if she is seeing someone off on a train journey which crosses the border of two countries. □

A DIFFERENT CENTURY
Larry Towell

Larry Towell

Mennonites trace their roots to the sixteenth-century Protestant Reformation and to Menno Simons, a renegade Catholic priest from Holland who converted to Anabaptism. He led a church founded on pacifism, the baptism of believing adults, and the separation of church and state. Its early members were persecuted; German and Dutch Mennonites fled to what is present-day Poland and later to the Ukraine to establish rural communities, but the demand that Russian should be taught in their schools, the threat of military conscription and the nationalization of their farms prompted 7,000 Mennonites to leave the Ukraine in the 1870s and settle in western Canada. At the end of the First World War, anti-German sentiment and the Mennonites' refusal to send their children to English-speaking provincial schools led to fines and imprisonment. In the 1920s, 7,000 of the most conservative Mennonites loaded their animals and farm implements on to trains and headed for Mexico.

Today, 50,000 Mennonites make up twenty-three colonies throughout Mexico, where they strive for economic independence and 'separation from the world'. The strictest among their church leaders reject electricity, the automobile, and rubber tyres on their tractors. Those who break with the customs are excommunicated. The old Colony Mennonite education system has not changed in 200 years. Girls finish school at twelve, boys at thirteen. A Bible and a hymn book are their main guide to language. As both are written in High German, a language the Mennonites neither speak nor comprehend well (they speak Low German, an unwritten dialect), many children leave school almost completely illiterate. Their parents and ministers believe education is, in itself, worldly.

But the Mennonites can no longer sustain themselves on the Mexican peso. Their farm produce—principally cheese—has been replaced on supermarket shelves by goods from the United States, and high interest rates make farm investment impossible. Many of them live a transient life between Mexico and Canada and feel they belong in neither place. As migrant workers in Canada, without their own colonies, they face the threat of assimilation into mainstream culture.

These photographs were taken over the past decade in the Mennonite colonies of Mexico and in Canada.

"Every man is, or hopes to be, an idler"
Dr Johnson

The Idler · 1999 · out now
< 0171 691 0317 >

INSIDE IRAQ
James Buchan

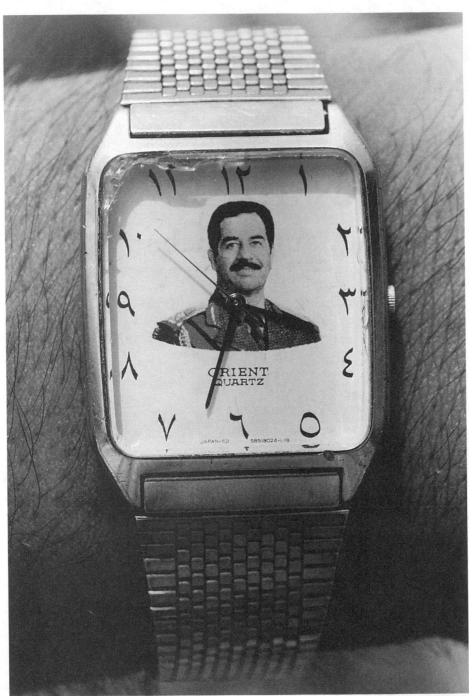

ORIENT
QUARTZ

JAPAN-5D   58518024-L19

The Amiriyeh civilian shelter is in a smart residential district about five miles to the west of Baghdad. It was completed in 1984 during the war with Iran. You come to it by Airport Road, a neat motorway lined with palms, gum trees and oleanders, another survivor of those years of prosperous tyranny.

The shelter, grey and four-square, looks from the outside to be intact. When I went there a few months ago, at the hottest time of a blazing afternoon, during the daily power cut, when my escorts from the Ministry of Information had crept off to their scalding apartments in the sticks, I was met by a woman in a dress of deep mourning set off at the chest by a golden amulet in the shape of the Koran.

Her name was Umm Ghaida. We needed a kerosene lamp, because of the power cut, and she took me into her makeshift office, which was papered with curling photographs, including one of her son, Maisan, being presented to the President of the Republic. Maisan, she told me, was the sole survivor of her ten children. The rest were killed when the shelter was hit by two bombs early in the morning of 13 February 1991. Umm Ghaida had gone home the evening before to do the washing, and Maisan was too small to be left behind with his brothers and sisters.

The photograph of Maisan and the President confirmed Umm Ghaida's authority over the Amiriyeh. It meant the shelter had been entrusted to her by the person in Iraq who has the power to give and take away.

Beyond the five-ton steel double doors, designed to close on impact, was the upper storey of the shelter. Ahead was a dirty light that defeated the lamp. It came down through the perforations made by the two bombs. Sparrows squeaked among the torn steel reinforcing bars and vegetation. There were air vents there, she said, so the concrete was only two metres thick. She showed me the remains of the bathrooms, with the toilets still embedded in the floor, and the place where the boys and men slept, separate from the women and infants.

The first bomb—Umm Ghaida called them missiles, though they came from a US Stealth bomber—had struck at 4.30 a.m., the second four minutes later. Of the 1,200 people in the upper storey, she said,

1,186 were incinerated in the 4,000 degree heat. A lower number of dead—394—had been scratched out wherever it occurred on the official photographs nearby. In the two craters in the floor were gritty plastic bouquets left by visitors, and along the carbonized walls photographs of the dead families, including Umm Ghaida's own. She pointed out her thirteen-year-old daughter, 'Pretty, wasn't she?', and ran her fingers over the photographs, muttering: 'George Bush says this was a military position. But was little Feyziye military? And Resha and Mehdiye?'

Umm Ghaida was reluctant to go downstairs. I told her I'd come a long way. The lower storey housed the shelter's services: the Amiriyeh was supposed to be self-supporting for twenty-one days in the event of a nuclear or chemical attack. We passed scorched storerooms and a door marked 'Doctor'. Along the flickering walls, the lamp picked out the scummy marks made by water burst from the pipes and heated to boiling by the fire. In the shadows, I sensed Umm Ghaida lose her self-control. She scampered through the darkness. Here, under the stairs, bring up the lamp, look, feel it with your fingers, a matting of skin, a hank of girl's hair, the imprint of a backbone, the shadow of the heads of a boy and his sister, two hand-prints, an eyeball.

In Umm Ghaida's devastated mind, the world was losing its order. The lower storey had passed to the demons of dead children. It didn't matter that, given time and the lamp, I could find routine explanations for these phenomena: the trash left by the flood, graffiti, the egg sacs of spiders. Down here, more than any place in Iraq, you confronted a society going off its head.

Humiliated in war by the West, terrorized by their own government, reduced to paupers, unwelcome anywhere in the world, the Arabs of Iraq are falling to pieces. It is not simply that with their money and savings destroyed and their goods embargoed, their living standards have fallen to the level of at least thirty years ago. In their own eyes, as Iraqis, and above all as Arabs, they have been reduced to nothing. I have never seen a people so demoralized. Everybody I met, even the most repellent Ba'athi thug and extortionist, felt himself a victim.

Out in the glare, Umm Ghaida withdrew into herself, hooded,

dark, nine-parts crazy, waiting for her bundle of money, which she nonetheless left untouched on the table. Her amulet glittered against the dirty black of her dress. I wrote idiocies in the visitors' book.

I first saw Iraq in 1972, from across the Euphrates in Syria. I was eighteen years old and had £5 in my pocket which, unfortunately, I needed so I could get back to Britain. As I turned for home, I felt a regret that I would not see the marshes between the Tigris and Euphrates and the famous Marsh Arabs and their amphibious way of life. Over the next few years, as a reporter in Saudi Arabia, Lebanon, Iran, Turkey and the Arab Gulf States, I watched Saddam Hussein consolidate his control over his political party, the Ba'ath, and his country, seize the leadership of the Arab world from Egypt in 1978, then risk it all in an eight-year war with Iran and an invasion of Kuwait.

I was in Egypt when the Iraqis were expelled from Kuwait by a campaign of British and American bombing which included the attack on the Amiriyeh and the land assault of 24–28 February 1991, known in the West as Desert Storm and in Iraq as The Mother of Battles. On television I saw the country's industrial fabric, including its power plants and its water and sanitation networks, knocked out of action. In the chaos, there were violent uprisings against Saddam in the mountainous north, where the Kurds had been fighting rule from Baghdad since the very foundation of Iraq in 1920, and in the disaffected Shia cities of the south. (The Shia, the religious majority in Iraq and also in Iran, had felt neglected by Saddam's regime, which draws its chief support from a secularized Sunni Arab minority.)

Saddam had kept his Republican Guard units in reserve. They escaped the military collapse in Kuwait, loyal and intact, and put down the southern rebellion with extreme brutality. The most holy cities of the Shia martyrs—the seminary town of Najaf, where the Caliph Ali is buried, and the shrines of his sons Hussein and Abbas in Kerbela—were shelled into submission. It is said that Saddam's son-in-law, Hussein Kamel, strode into the shrines of the saints with his boots on.

John Major, the British Prime Minister, called for 'safe havens' from Saddam's vengeance for the Kurds in the north, and Allied troops were ordered into Iraqi Kurdistan on 16 April 1991. The Iraqi army and administration were forced to withdraw. The mountain country was transformed into a United Nations quasi-protectorate, patrolled by British and American aircraft, riven by factional fighting among the Kurds and infiltrated by the agents of Iraq and also Iran and Turkey, which have their own unruly Kurdish populations. Without formally demanding independence from Iraq, which they feared would provoke intervention from all three countries, the Kurdish parties were calling for autonomy within some fanciful democratic, federal Iraq: in other words, an Iraq without Saddam Hussein.

On 6 August 1990, soon after the Iraqi army entered Kuwait, the UN Security Council had imposed a full embargo on trade to and from Iraq excepting only food, medical supplies and other items described as of humanitarian need. The UN 'ceasefire resolution', SCR 687, of 3 April 1991, confirmed that the trade embargo against Iraq would remain in place. Its wording was vague, but Paragraph 22 reads as if sanctions would not be lifted for so long as Iraq failed to account for all its unconventional weapons: these included the sorts of chemical weapons deployed against the Iranian army and Kurdish civilians in the 1980s. The resolution also created a Special Commission to carry out 'immediate on-site inspections of Iraq's biological, chemical and missile capabilities'.

Unlike most cases of sanctions in the world, the Iraq embargo was enforced by neighbouring countries. They had reason to fear Saddam Hussein and the party that brought him to power in a succession of *coups d'état* in the 1960s, known as the Arab Renaissance Socialist Party, or *al-Ba'ath* in Arabic. Two of Saddam's bitter enemies, Iran and Kuwait, guarded his only outlet to the open sea at the head of the Persian Gulf. The sanctions after the Gulf War were effective in that, apart from an incursion into Kurdistan in 1996, Saddam took no large military action. Their other result was that the living standards of the Iraqi population fell to the level of the poorest countries. Trade ground to a halt, such industry as had survived the bombing shut down, private employment dwindled, the Iraqi currency collapsed and average incomes fell to the equivalent of a few dollars a month.

From the summer of 1991, the Security Council offered to allow Iraq to export $1.6 billion in oil every six months to buy food and medicine. The oil revenues would be paid into an account controlled by the United Nations and spent on goods ordered by Baghdad but approved by a committee in New York. Saddam rejected the offer. He wanted, and still wants, to sell Iraqi oil for cash to spend as he pleases. In 1995, amid gruesome reports from the UN specialised agencies—including evidence from UNICEF that infant and maternal mortality rates had doubled since 1990—the Security Council improved its offer, allowing Iraq to sell $1 billion of oil every ninety days. At length, Saddam relented and, on 20 May 1996, the United Nations and the Iraqi government signed a Memorandum of Understanding, the so-called 'oil-for-food' deal, which has been refined and renewed, with much grumbling and grandstanding by the Iraqi regime, every six months, most recently on 24 May this year.

Iraq is now exporting over $4 billion worth of oil every half year from its battered oilfields. Yet because the government must pay thirty per cent of its oil earnings in reparations to Kuwait, cover the costs of the UN's monitoring programme and do repairs to its oil industry, the sum available for food, medicine, civilian reconstruction, household and school goods was only $2.6 billion in the last six-month phase, or little more than $120 per Iraqi Arab and Kurd.

In Kurdistan, the aid is administered by the UN. The Kurdish officials I met in Europe complained bitterly about the quality of the food and medicines ordered by Baghdad: a government that once had only the best from Europe and the US can now only afford rancid cooking oil from Egypt and Syrian antibiotics. But none of the Kurdish leaders wanted the sanctions lifted. The Kurds have suffered indescribable cruelties since 1975 and fear that, once he has cash, Saddam will merely rearm. In the centre and south of Iraq, where rations are distributed by the Iraqi government and monitored by the UN, the oil-for-food deal has staved off famine and epidemic while doing nothing to repair the country's fabric damaged in the war or improve the general health of the public.

As for the Special Commission, usually called Unscom, in its early years it was quite successful in tracking down Iraq's nuclear and ballistic missile experiments, but I met nobody among the European and Asian diplomats in Baghdad who believed it had found and destroyed the regime's chemical and biological weapons. By 1998, Unscom had become an arena for US–Iraqi rivalry, the symbol of an unfinished military campaign. After a set of staged crises, the Iraqis withdrew all cooperation last December. Whatever formal link existed between sanctions and so-called 'weapons of mass destruction' in Iraq, it is fading from sight.

In the West, the drama of Iraq can be reduced to a pair of questions. Can sanctions be lifted without demolishing the peace of mind of Iraq's neighbours and the Kurdish population? Or must Saddam and his Ba'ath party first be driven from power?

The effect, in the modern world, of the hostility of the United States is to freeze a country in time. There are no civilian flights to Baghdad, and most visitors must come across the desert from Amman. My first sight of modern Iraq was a colossal fairy-lit head of Saddam Hussein hurtling out of the darkness, as if from another galaxy of despotism and violence. Beside it Iraqi officials stood in the shadows, smiling, their arms crossed, like shearers waiting for the sheep. The Jordanian drivers shed their swagger and began to whine. This was the Iraqi frontier post of Trebil.

Beyond was an empty motorway, the black desert, tanker trucks swerving like terrified deer in the headlights, then the silent, unlit city sleeping among its palms. At the Rasheed Hotel, a nightingale was singing in the dark garden. Crossing the threshold, visitors must step on a mosaic portrait of a snarling George Bush, a gesture of defiance at one with the antique anti-aircraft artillery on the roofs of the quiet ministries.

I had expected a city under siege. I was surprised to find the shreds of both private and public civility: a pianist plinking out the song from *Titanic* to an empty coffee shop, Belorussian businessmen in the lobbies, cinema marquees painted with gigantic negligéed women, liquor stores, money changers, brand-new police motorbikes, Brazilian Passats bumping and bouncing on potholed streets, fish restaurants beside the Tigris, cranes towering over the sites of presidential palaces and mosques. It was a day or two before my eyes became accustomed to the Potemkin character of Baghdad. Brush against the scenery, and you come on a sort of despair.

The loafers on the pavements will still buy a stranger a Coke at midday; and that vestige of Arab hospitality came from men who can't remember when they last ate meat. At the site of a new mosque Saddam is building at the old racetrack, engineers sped past in clouds of dust, but no building was being done because the site manager had no piledrivers. The shops in the hotels and middle-class districts, which at first seemed so elegant, were in reality selling off the personal property of all three generations of the Iraqi middle class: Rolexes and Parker pens at the front, then cocktail shakers and silver cigarette cases engraved with railway bridges, and, at the back, tulip vases and tobacco pipes of painted Bohemian glass. In Mutanabbi Street, where books are sold in the open air and the city's literary intellectuals gather every Friday, I saw stacks of *The American Home* and *The New England Journal of Medicine* from the 1950s and realized some man had sold everything he had to buy his grandson or -daughter a passage to Jordan. Anybody with a halfway paying job will be supporting two dozen family dependants.

When oil revenues dried up in 1990 and the regime's foreign assets were frozen, the Iraqi government continued to print money. As a result, the Iraqi dinar lost ninety-eight per cent of its value. At the money changers' on Saadoun Street, the chief commercial district of Baghdad, men staggered out with plastic bags full of bundles of badly printed 250-dinar notes, known in Arabic as *dinar fotokopi,* 'photocopy money', or as *shabah,* 'phantoms'. This money was sometimes refused by beggars.

Since wages and pensions are paid at the old pre-inflation rate, all but the most favoured sections of the civil service and military have been reduced to penury. I was baffled that men and women went obediently to their offices for a few dollars a month. Some said things were difficult at home, or they liked company or the air-conditioning for the few hours a day it is working. The truth is that Iraqi Arabs treasure any symbol of normality. Like Saddam, they will not make peace with their misfortune. (I visited a young farmer out in the suburbs who had four unmarried sisters. Like many market gardeners, he was doing well out of sanctions. But nobody could afford the pre-war dowries he was asking for his sisters. He wouldn't budge and so the girls will remain spinsters, a despised condition in the Iraqi villages.)

I had been allocated two escorts by the Ministry of Information. Both were time-serving Ba'athis, creatures of an Arab bureaucratic culture that had not changed from my days as a junior reporter in Saudi Arabia in the 1970s: a culture of turning fans, cigarettes and elaborate excuses, of dozing on steel beds behind the filing cabinets and sitting for hours in Mr Director's office watching junk TV and neither giving nor taking responsibility. Of the pair, Hassan spoke English well. He was reading *Independence Day* by Richard Ford. He was intelligent, depressed and a bully. Jaafar spoke French, less well, and was less depressed.

Hassan took me to Baghdad University, a neat campus in Waziriyeh where the well-dressed boys and girls looked like American high-school pupils. I was received by the head of the English department, Mrs Ibtesaam Jasim, a glowing Ba'athi whose brother had been 'martyred' in Kuwait. She read me long passages from the paper on modern American poetry she had just given to a university symposium, 'America: A Long History of Aggressiveness and Violation of Human Rights'. I said Iraq was doing quite well in both those areas.

Her handsome face went through a violent contortion. I saw that I must take care, not for myself, but for my interlocutors. Mrs Jasim could complain about America because it didn't matter, I didn't care, and nor did the Americans, but she couldn't complain about anything in Iraq without some unspeakable penalty. I was surprised the students milling around outside bothered to attend. They had almost no chance of a job after college. Opposite the gate to the Kazimain mosque the evening before, I had met a cheerful Ph.D. selling black georgette for ladies' *abayas* who ran off a list of his fellow students who were cab drivers. It is what Count Hans Sponeck, the UN humanitarian coordinator in Baghdad, called 'the deprofessionalization of Iraq under sanctions'.

Hassan dragged me away and we set off across the hot campus. He stalked ahead with his demons. I looked up and a boy named Raad was trotting by my side. He said, 'After you'd gone, the other students came to me and said, "Run after the English reporter and tell him our problem. It is unfair! We cannot even get Thomas Hardy!" And this writer,' he looked down at *The Great Gatsby* in the old pastel Penguin, 'Scott Fitzgerald. You must tell your government to let us have books. You must tell your government to let us visit. We are human beings, aren't we? For God's sake let us come.'

Hassan sprang between us.

'Sir, I'm just telling him about our academic situation under sanctions...'

'Get out of here!'

I got on badly with both my minders. I tried tipping. I was paying the Ministry $50 a day, but that, I was told, didn't count because it went to the bank, and ultimately, to the President's Office, the *diwan al-riyasah*. I began to see, faintly, and then much more clearly, how the Iraqi revenue system works: provided officials collect foreign currency for the President, they can make their living as they like. A British-style civil service, based on hierarchies and the book, is reverting to an Ottoman system, based on corruption and punishment. Even so, the President's income, mostly from oil and petrol products smuggled to Jordan and Turkey, may be no more than $1 billion a year. But nobody else in Iraq has anything. In that respect, if no other, sanctions have strengthened Saddam.

With Hassan or Jaafar I went to primary schools, where little children sprang up and bawled at me, '*Long live Saddaham Hissayin! Long live the Ba'ath party, nurse of the generations!*' but needed paper and pencils. We saw jerry-rigged water-treatment plants struggling with the worst drought in memory and railway tracks without power to work the signals. In the hospitals, the leukaemia wards were filled with dying children and their resigned parents: I was told that the disease was increasing in the south, as a result of depleted uranium used in the Allied ordnance in the Kuwait war. In the paediatric department of the Hussein Hospital in Kerbela, sanitary conditions were so bad that the children in the emergency rooms were perpetually infected and reinfected with gastric illnesses. The only salbutamol nebulizer was held together by tape, and I was told asthma patients had to be sent the seventy-five miles to the Saddam Children's Hospital in Baghdad.

I remembered being told by a high-ranking Egyptian official in Cairo in 1991 that Saddam should be left in place: weakened, his army and revenue cut down to size, but still an element in the strategic equation, the balance of threat and violence in the Middle East. Here was the reality of a weakened Saddam: asthmatic children bundled into taxis to choke to death on the road to Baghdad.

Yet the paediatric hospitals had their elements of sham. Dr Ghaith, a young houseman in Kerbela, scrabbled at noon through the empty shelves of the hospital pharmacy, counting off syringes into his left hand: '...thirty-four, thirty-five. Thirty-five is all I have for the whole hospital until eight o'clock tomorrow morning!' I told him what the United Nations had told me, but the Ministry had not permitted me to verify for myself: that the central Ministry of Health warehouses in Baghdad had on their shelves undelivered medical supplies worth $275 million. Dr Ghaith looked at me in bafflement. It occurred to me that the Ba'ath has been quite successful in blaming sanctions for evils that are of its own creation: the collapse of the currency, for example, or the hostility of the other Arab countries dumping their low-grade medicines and stale food on the country, or the incompetence, corruption or malice of the local administration. 'I haven't discovered,' said Count Sponeck, picking his words carefully, 'a deliberate attempt to obstruct medical deliveries. Perhaps there is no determined effort to make things move.'

Basra, the second town of Iraq, 350 miles to the south and 105 degrees in the morning, makes Baghdad seem a paradise. The walls of the Sheraton Hotel were still riddled with cannon holes from the Shia uprising of 1991, much of the population had no clean water, and the town was vulnerable, I was told, to infiltration from both Iran and Kuwait. It was the most morose city in Iraq.

We attended a ceremony arranged by the Ba'ath to celebrate the 1,364th anniversary of the founding of the city. In the phantasmagoria that is Ba'athi Iraq, nobody found the choice of anniversary contrived: there had been unrest in the spring, and no doubt the Party needed to show it cared. Along the waterway known as the Shatt al

Arab, there are ninety life-size statues of men in uniform gesturing heroically at the Iranian shore. They are commanders who fell in the Iran war (or were executed by Saddam). Comrade Abdul Baqi Abdul Karim al-Saadoun, deputy leader of the Ba'ath for the Southern Region, laid a plastic wreath at the base of the statue of General Khairallah Adnan, Saddam's brother-in-law (who died in a mysterious helicopter accident). The air-raid warning sounded for the daily American patrol.

A man leaped out of the crowd and began to shriek. The crowd bent like a bow in shock. I thought he must be felled by a bullet. Then I heard what he was saying: 'We adore the Great President Leader Saddam Hussein! We invite our dear Saddam Hussein to visit this town and see how its inhabitants live! With soul and blood we sacrifice ourselves for Saddam! Long live Saddam Hussein! Long live the Great President Leader!' The women wailed in sympathy. Comrade Saadoun got back into his Mercedes. Later, when Jaafar ducked into a restaurant for a moment, I stopped a man coming out of a mosque to ask what the government was really doing for the town. 'Actually, he hates Basra,' the man said, pushing past me.

'Voilà l'Euphrate,' said Jaafar, pointing to the Tigris. We were travelling back northwards, across an immense plain of mud and salinity, brickworks pouring out acrid black smoke and stagnant pools crowded with wading birds. To my left was the expanse of marshes between the Tigris and the Euphrates which I had dreamed of visiting since my schooldays, but the Ministry had forbidden it. At every mile was a tiny police fort with the name of the unit and the day's date picked out in white stones and a machine-gun at each corner under a roof of rusty corrugated tin.

Jaafar followed my gaze. 'Peut-être ils sont des voleurs, je ne sais pas.'

I said: 'I want to see the First World War cemetery at Kut.'

'Mais, c'est défendu. Absolument défendu, monsieur. Mamnu.'

'Nonsense. It won't take a moment.'

It didn't. Behind the Commonwealth War Graves Commission railings, the cemetery had been engulfed by esparto grass, garbage and shit. The sculpted lettering, Kut War Cemetery 1914–1918, was defaced by illegible graffiti. The central cross had been snapped at the trunk. The tombstones of English infantrymen and Indian muleteers, mementoes of a war between the British and Ottoman Empires in which the local Arabs hardly figured, were marked by thick scum, where the Tigris floods the cemetery every winter.

'*Allez, monsieur, allez,*' Jaafar was beside himself with alarm. '*C'est dangereux ici.*'

I looked up to see hundreds of men's faces gaping at me through the railings. I kicked through the trash and said, in Arabic, 'Well, I suppose if the British are bombing you, why should you care for...'

'No, no,' one of them said and pinched at my wrist. The crowd parted to reveal a tea-stall at the gate where, pinned to the wall above the teapot, was a Polaroid photograph of the cemetery in the days of its prosperity, the cross intact, the gravestones in their straight white lines, Indian gardeners laughing and dragging a motor-mower over the grass. It was a picture from another world, of order and routine and self-respect. I realized the chief emotion of the crowd was not hostility, but shame. They hated me only in as much as they hated everybody, including, certainly, themselves.

My escorts tired easily, could not bear the heat, or technical discussion, and since I was fresh from Europe, and enjoy the company of professional people, they became prey to gastric complaints and family tragedies. By the third week, neither Hassan nor Jaafar was coming to work. On Abu Nuwas Street by the Tigris, at the foot of the steps leading up to the Jumhuriyeh Bridge, I was detained by a young man with the moustache, white shirt and black pants that I had come to recognize as a uniform of the internal security service. Fortunately, he was alone and had no vehicle, it was scalding hot and he was too idle to take me away on foot.

I stopped going about on my own.

My chief friend in Baghdad was a man whom I addressed as Mr Abdullah. A retired professional with a wide acquaintance in Europe, he had dismissed all his staff in January 1993 and was running through his savings at the house he had built in the suburbs. Mr Abdullah's wife was dead, his children were abroad, but he stays in Baghdad because he loves the town, and because the dinar is so cheap that with $200 a month sent from abroad to be exchanged in Saadoun Street you can live in Baghdad like an ambassador.

Since neither of us had much to do, Mr Abdullah took me to visit his friends. I met writers and architects and poets and engineers and picture dealers and sculptors—all of a certain age, when they had begun to cease to care about governments any more. Some were Party members, or were active in the Women's Federation or the Union of Iraqi Journalists or some other organ of the Ba'ath's near total social organization. I never heard a word of criticism of the President from these people: indeed, they praised him for his monuments and patronage of writers. I was witnessing the last survivors of a patrician, Anglophile, art-deco civility. Just evident beneath their kindness was an authentic regret: that they, who had absorbed the values of Britain and the United States, should now be abandoned by those countries; and also a well-bred anxiety, that as members of the privileged Sunni minority, in any revolution in Iraq they would share the big fellow's fate when it came.

They professed an intense nostalgia for the 1980s. Sitting in her fine house by the Tigris, Mrs Salma Mishlawi, an Iraqi gentlewoman of the old school, the first woman in her family to go unveiled, the first to attend university in England, said: 'The 1980s were a sort of climax for us. We became spoiled. Everything we needed the government gave to us. The war with Iran didn't really affect us for the first year or two. Until, of course, the boys started to disappear: from here, and here, and here...' She gestured with her fingers towards the river and Saadoun Street and Thawra and the western suburbs. Iraq is said to have lost 200,000 men in the war with Iran.

Another of these people said: 'After the war [with Iran] ended, we had such plans: for reconstruction, economic development, social advance. The attack on Kuwait came as a complete surprise. We could not believe it. I promise you that ninety-five per cent of the Iraqis were opposed to it.' A third, a well-known man now long retired, voiced the nearest that I heard in Iraq to remorse at the regime's belligerence: 'All our misfortunes can be put down to two unnecessary wars: first Iran, then Kuwait.'

We were having lunch out in the suburbs, or rather I was having lunch and they were having whiskies-and-soda. On the way, we had passed the marble villas of the smuggling profiteers, nouveaux riches who must soon displace the old professional class.

A third person said: 'In 1991, from 17 January to 28 February, we had no electric power, no water, no police, no security. There was no radio, no government, no soldiers, except some days we saw them in the streets in their *disdashas* [robes]. We were happy! We were happy because we were looking after ourselves. And those missiles were streaking across the sky each night or raining down pieces on us as we sat in the orchards.

'I was fortunate enough to have some money with me, and those of us with money helped those who hadn't. Even when the banks did finally open, you could only get one or two dinars each day. One day, I had a few litres of petrol, and drove up to my orchard. People were waiting all over for buses, but there weren't any. I picked up three soldiers who had been withdrawn or run away from Kuwait and Basra. Then in March or April, we started listening again to Baghdad Radio.'

The room was silent for a while.

In the street portraits which stand at crossroads or outside government or commercial buildings the President is shown in different characters in a sort of trashy international Iraq: as a weekend sportsman in a shop-new outfit and holding a twelve-bore shotgun, as an Austrian hiker with loden coat and feathered hat, as a pool lizard in a panama, as a short-order cook, as a Bedu prince, as an Arab officer of the Ottoman army circa 1907, as a French judge with sword and scales, as a landowner with robe and chequered head-cloth, as a brilliant scientist with extra-large glasses, as a grandfather with child and cigar, as a big-band musician, as a Kurdish *peshmerga*, or warrior, creeping forward through long grass, as a cult leader with garland and sunburst, as a war hero, as a young and promising constitutional monarch, as Stalin in a fur hat, as a Russian gangster in a leather coat, as a navvy with spade, waistcoat and cloth cap.

Those pictures are often signed not only by the painter but also by the donor or commissioner: Iraqi Airways, for example, or Sheikh Hamed bin Folan, a Shia landowner at Rasheed village east of Baghdad. Their purpose is both to remind the public of its Great

Leader, particularly in the years after Kuwait when he was not much seen in public, and also to act as a superstitious protection, a species of devil-worship. At a somewhat deeper level, they are like old portraits of monarchs in Europe, even certain photographs of the Prince of Wales today, and promote a dynastic notion: that the President embodies Iraqi male society in all its variety and in a sort of super-ideal form. ('You know,' said one of the Kurdish leaders I met in the north, 'that Saddam wants his son Qusay to succeed him. Republican monarchies! Frankly, we'd be better off with the real thing.') Beyond this is the President's passionate love of fine clothes, and that is really all that matters. He is in love with clothes because he believes that they can somehow transform his fortunes and his personality. To dress as a generalissimo is to win battles, rather as to pat a little boy on the head is to be, just for an instant, Stalin.

We visited the Sahat al-Ehtefalat, or Festival Square, Saddam's monument to victory in the war with Iran, a ceremonial parade ground in Soviet or Chinese style closed at both ends by monumental forearms holding aloft the swords of Ali, the son-in-law of the Prophet and patriarch of the Shia. I was told the forearms were modelled on those of the President. To enter it, you drive over Iranian helmets embedded in the concrete, or tumbling from nets at the base of the monumental wrists. It expresses all that the Ba'ath has by way of ideology. It is a monument to pure violence.

Some of the portraits of Saddam move. In the evenings I would sometimes go to Baghdad railway station to walk the platform in the horizontal glare with the stationmaster and his children and watch the Basra Express limp in. Once, when I was there, Saddam arrived. My heart leaped. I saw a clean Mercedes, olive-green military uniform, moustache, paunch, the look of a man who has long despaired of his life, a dead man walking.

'His Excellency the Minister of Transport,' somebody hissed. My heart subsided.

Later, watching a cabinet meeting on television, or attending Party rallies in Basra, I saw Saddam repeated endlessly in flesh. Each had the same utterly absorbed look in his eyes and the same laboured speech. Saddam speaks Arabic with a nightmarish slowness, but that, I was told, is to conceal his Tikrit accent, which is considered bucolic in Baghdad.

The strangest portrait of Saddam was at the shrines of the Prophet's murdered grandchildren, Hussein and Abbas, in Kerbela. The gold domes were visible for miles above the fields, where the millionaire sheikhs who have done well from high food prices are running up mini-antebellum mansions among the palms. In this place, the most sombre in the Islamic world, I was received with extreme courtesy.

The custodian of the shrine of Abbas, Seyyid Ali Fadel Al-Ghorayi, wearing the green turban of a descendant of the Prophet, was telling me, in his beautiful classical Arabic, of all that Saddam Hussein had done for the shrine: how the President had, out of his very own pocket, provided forty kilograms of gold to regild the dome and even more silver.

'Well, he should do,' I replied. 'He shelled the place in '91.'

The custodian sighed: 'That is a lie you have read in European newspapers.'

'On the contrary,' I said, 'I have seen a video of tanks coming up the street from the east shooting at everything and everybody.'

He smiled as if to concede me one point.

'And I was told his son-in-law, the late Hussein Kamel, strode into the shrine of His Highness Imam Hussein without taking off his boots.'

'Hussein Kamel was never in Kerbela!'

I gaped at him.

'And what about the disturbances earlier this year?' I asked.

'I swear by the Tomb of Abbas that there have been no disturbances.'

The oath reverberated round the mirrored room: I suppose I expected a thunderbolt. Instead, a German clock chimed the quarter. The custodian beamed at me. He was delighted by my novelty. Above his head, I saw a framed family tree showing the President's descent, in the thirty-sixth generation, from Ali, Commander of the Faithful. I tried one more time.

'Does that picture mean that the President of the Republic is a *seyyid* like your honourable self?'

He paused. I sensed his mind whirring like the clock. At length, he said: 'Of course.'

I gave up.

The warren of streets between the two shrines, which I knew from photographs, had been turned into a public park: for recreation, of course, and to give a clear field of fire. Round the edges were stalls selling cheap ladies' novelties from Dubai. There were no men about, except the stallholders, which added to the defeated air of the place.

While my escorts were buying things for their families, I talked to a stallholder in a black mourning shirt who called himself Abu Ali. In no time, he was telling me that Saddam is the Imam Hussein of his age, the only man in the world to stand up to oppression, and the British and Americans are the latter-day Omayyads, persecutors of the righteous.

'Saddam Hussein has withstood thirty-three countries!'

It seemed to me that if Saddam ever did die, the Iraqis would drag his bloody body through the streets as they did the ministers of the Hashemite monarchy in the revolution of 1958. But, as a writer said to me in Baghdad, the Iraqis had lost hope that Saddam would ever die; and while he was alive, they wished him success. The upper classes, even among the Shia, preferred him to chaos or Iran. What I found deceitful in Saddam—his victories that weren't victories, the bombastic verses of the Laureate of the Mother of Battles, the Festival Square in Baghdad—seemed to strike a chord with much of the Iraqi public, which had learned over years of humiliation to feed on such cut-price symbols because there was nothing else. I sensed that the Iraqi Arabs yearned for a military success, however tiny.

Since the departure of Unscom in December last year and the US retaliation known as Desert Fox, Saddam has sought to provoke a new crisis by challenging the daily British and American air patrols in the north and south of the country. His air defences illuminate the aircraft with their radar, the aircraft retaliate with missiles, the missiles sometimes kill people or animals. It has become routine. But to shoot down an American aircraft—that would be something!

James Buchan

When in the Kurdish villages you see the plinths of portraits of Saddam destroyed by a tank round, where you meet men who do not look like Saddam and can mention his name without shaking uncontrollably, you feel an intoxicating pleasure, and also a certain anxiety, as if you had been cut adrift in a boat.

At Feish Khabur in Kurdistan, where the Tigris flows out of Turkey and is joined by the Khabur tributary, you can stand at a place where three countries meet: Iraq, Turkey and Syria. There is nothing in this wild place except snowy mountains and thirty-seven Kurdish boys, in Kevlar suits and baby-blue United Nations helmets, on their knees clearing anti-personnel mines.

Here, in the late summer of 1990, fearing an Allied invasion through Turkey, the Iraqi army sowed a strip of anti-personnel and anti-tank mines which stretches some forty-five kilometres. On a small ridge above the river junction, there is a rusty observation tower. The Italian, Chinese, Russian, German and Yugoslav mines now poking through the weeds were laid, I guess, to protect it. While the mines might have held up a modern army for a good thirty seconds, they blow Kurdish villagers and flocks to smithereens. A field which took a morning to lay will take the United Nations nine months to clear.

I watched a black kite quartering the minefield and realized I was happy. For the first time in four weeks, in this cartographical rarity, among these diligent young men and their Australian and South African supervisors, I could breathe in and breathe out. I was delighted with my liberty and that of the men around me: that they were removing Saddam's careless little fortifications and there was nothing he could do about it.

This was not strictly true. Earlier this year, on 24 April, Nicholas Speight, a thirty-two-year-old New Zealander employed by one of the de-mining contractors, was shot dead on a picnic near Irbil airstrip. The Australian supervisor of the UN mine-clearing operation in Kurdistan, Dave Edwards, counted out the possibilities with his left hand: targeted hit, mishit, target of opportunity. Tentatively, he selected the last. Though it is in the interest of the Ba'ath to create insecurity in Kurdistan so that the UN will leave and the army come in and whack the Kurds as it did in 1996, the shot might just as easily have come from one of the squabbling Kurdish parties. When I questioned them about Speight, they became very pious.

We had to radio back our position at every crossroads. A little later, we heard the coded signal that meant that the boys had finished for the day, posted sentries on the road, detonated that day's haul of mines, and moved out.

Khorshid was the driver assigned to me by the Ministry of Information in Baghdad. He was a nineteen-year-old Kurd from the village of Koya Sanjaq, but his family lived and prospered in Baghdad. He was given to me when I lost my temper at the Ministry and said, like the bully I'd become, that I could not be responsible for the safety of Jaafar or any Ba'athi in Kurdistan. Khorshid played both sides of the street. At the checkpoints that cluster thick and fast as you drive out of Iraqi government territory, he soothed and flattered the swaggering secret policemen, which suited me just fine.

'There are people here who want the Government of Iraq back.'

'Nonsense, Khorshid, I've met nobody here in four days who ever wants to see Mr Saddam again.'

'They do, too. The Kurdish parties don't care about the people, only about their own power and money.'

Khorshid was dress-conscious, like the President. He had learned his English from BBC cameramen. As we drove south from the Feish Khabur minefield down wide, green valleys, past immense blockhouses in the wheat that date from British battles with the Kurds in the 1920s, or the rubble of villages destroyed by Saddam during the war with Iran, we were driven off the road by a truck carrying smuggled diesel to Turkey. 'Cor blimey, what a tosser,' Khorshid said.

In Salahuddin, a breezy little resort above Irbil taken over by Massoud Barzani's Kurdish Democratic Party, I was received by a man now known as Sami Abdul Rahman. Over and over I asked him why, in 1996, he allied with Saddam to drive his rivals, the Patriotic Union of Kurdistan, out of Irbil. I said I thought Washington would not tolerate another outbreak of fighting between the parties or have any truck with Saddam. He listened politely.

'We know we are walking a tightrope.'

And what happens if sanctions are lifted or materially alleviated?

'You know precisely what our fate will be.'

I had seen the vestiges of Iraqi rule in Kurdistan: the filthy concrete concentration camps along the main roads, the dynamited villages. Between 1975 and 1990, the Ba'ath is reckoned by the Kurds to have destroyed more than 4,000 villages in order to cut off support to the Kurdish fighters. In the so-called Anfal campaign at the end of the Iran war—the word is a Ba'athi joke: Anfal is a chapter heading in the Koran and means The Spoils of War—Saddam tried to extirpate Kurdish rural existence. In command was Saddam's cousin, Ali Hassan Majid, known in Kurdistan as Ali Kimawiya, 'Ali Chemical'. On the morning of 16 March 1988, aircraft clearly marked as Iraqi dropped napalm and phosphorus on the Kurdish town of Halabjeh, and then followed up with nerve gas. At least 3,800 people were killed that morning. Both the Kurds and the Iranians were so shattered by Halabjeh that they sued for peace.

If sanctions are lifted, it is hard to imagine Saddam spending the resulting $10 billion a year or more in oil revenues solely on medicine and education and repairs to the electricity and sanitation systems. He will spend it to restore his prestige and his security. He will spend it on palaces and motorways and hospitals. He will spend it on weapons of every sort.

I said: 'What if Saddam is restrained by the normal instruments of deterrence, like the old Soviet Union? This country is all but land-locked. He has no friends but Russia, which is weak. Provided the West doesn't sell arms to him, there is not much he can do.'

Mr Sami looked at me as if I'd lost touch with reality. He said: 'Won't you try the apricots? They're sweet.'

Back in Baghdad, Mr Abdullah picked me up in his Buick. It was dark and he had two things to say to me. The first he would say in his car, the second in his library. As we drove through the underpass beneath the Zawra Park, he gathered himself together in that way even the bravest Iraqis have when they are going to talk about Saddam. He said: 'Don't touch the President. Everything we have here, everything you see,' and here he pointed at the new shops by the racetrack where, in December 1996, Saddam's son Uday had been ambushed and wounded, 'everything you see is designed to protect him. Nothing else matters.'

He was right, of course, for modern Iraq is merely the physical embodiment of a single man's fears and misjudgements. What Mr Abdullah meant, in the elusive way of speaking people have in Iraq, is that Saddam is the Last Iraqi. To get to him, the US will have to kill every single other Iraqi, Arab and Kurd. What Mr Abdullah meant was that it isn't worth it: that, as the boy said at Baghdad University, it isn't fair.

In his library, we settled down with some ceremony. We waited for the power to go off on the dot of nine, and the housekeeper to bring a lamp and glasses of orange squash. Mr Abdullah unrolled an old map of the marshlands between the two rivers and spoke technically, of the Marsh Arabs and their ancient history, their Shiism, their amphibious agriculture and their cult of saints. He spoke of the government schemes, going back to the 1950s, to regulate the salinity of the marshes, to control flooding, and bring the people schools and services. His eyes glistened as he spoke.

Then I told him what I'd heard of Shia rebels, slipping down to Kut from Iranian territory, crossing the main road—*Peut-être ils sont des voleurs*—vanishing into the marshes, till they shot up a Ba'ath bureau or a remote police station or an officer and his driver as they sped along the canal roads.

He said: 'The plans I mentioned to you, for the improvement of the condition of the marsh inhabitants, are now being implemented for the purposes of internal security.'

'Indeed!' I had heard the marshes were being deliberately polluted by chemicals, the people driven from their villages; but could not myself investigate.

'But don't you think it right that people should have clean water and schools, even if those are not the prime intention of the government but—as it were—a by-product?'

I couldn't answer. Mr Abdullah was asking me to adjudicate his life and that of the entire Iraqi professional class. Progressive, optimistic, secular, authoritarian and patriotic, they were the puppets of Saddam Hussein. Everything they had sought to do for their country, the Ba'ath had distorted or debauched or ruined. That crime was as great, in its way, as the shelling of Kerbela or the brutalities

James Buchan

against the Kurds. But of course I couldn't say that. I said only that I thought it would have been best to leave the Marsh Arabs alone.

Mr Abdullah had lost interest. He must have known we would disagree, but he is the sort of man who likes to talk through his conclusions: 'Well,' he said finally, 'if this drought continues, there will be no marshes, whatever we or the government do.'

He called his housekeeper to light the lamp and put it in the garden. 'We will have our drinks there.' □

Some of the names in this piece have been changed.

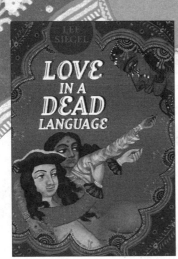

TELLING HIM
Edmund White

Austin invited his friend Joséphine, a children's book illustrator, to lunch. He wanted to know what she, as a woman, thought of Big Julien, though he realized she wasn't very typically female. Was any woman? Would he have felt right about speaking for all men? Gay men?

Joséphine was from Tours, reputed to be the home of the best French accent, and she did speak her own language clearly and elegantly, with not too much slang and no dropped syllables. She had the fully awakened, gently satiric response to the absurdities of her friends which is characteristic of someone from a big family, a family of talkers and observers rather than TV watchers. Her beauty was regal: her long neck lengthened still more by blonde hair swept up and stabbed haphazardly at the top by a comb or gathered into a ponytail by a red rubber band; a pointy chin and hollow cheeks, crowned by prominent cheekbones. She wasn't fussy at all or coy or full of feminine wiles. He'd read somewhere that women imagined men want to feel useful to women and that they delight in performing acts of gallantry; Joséphine was not labouring under any such misapprehension. She knew exactly how ungallant men could be.

At first, Austin could never tell whether Joséphine was stupid or intelligent. Perhaps because he'd grown up in the 1950s he believed in something called 'general intelligence', an uninflected, abstract power akin to reasoning or problem-solving or originality—but how did you measure that through daily chit-chat?

One thing was certain: she was as naive as a Kansan in Paris. Irony sailed right over her head. She never got a joke and the least bit of teasing reduced her to tears rather than sulky, annoyed amusement. No matter how much Austin exaggerated or, in a New York reflex, said the opposite of what he meant in exasperated italics, Joséphine, wide-eyed, would say, '*Vraiment?* Really?'

Now Austin talked across the restaurant table about Big Julien. 'He's very *vieille France*, don't you think?'

'*Vieille...?*'

'God, Joséphine, sometimes I have the feeling *I'm* the Frenchman and *you're* the American. You know, Old France, proper, stuffy, *comme il faut.*'

She blinked, confused, in the lamplight that shed its warmth over their table on this grey, rainy late April day. 'He has nice manners,' she said hopefully, afraid to venture more.

'Do you think he's gay?'

'What? *Isn't* he gay?' she asked, alarmed again. Until she'd moved to Paris, apparently she'd never met a single homosexual or even thought about the whole vexing subject of sexual variety. She'd dealt with impotence, premature ejaculation, violence, baldness, infidelity, logorrhoea, prostate problems and all the other things men might contrive to irritate a woman, but she'd worked from the simple axiom that all these men more or less desired her.

'Well, he *says* he's bisexual,' Austin insinuated with a pretended scepticism and a vocal raised eyebrow, although in truth he had no doubts at all about either side of Julien's sexuality; he simply wanted to provoke a spate of girl talk.

'You *have* been to bed with him, haven't you?' she asked, going with chat-deflecting directness to the sore heart of the matter.

'Not really.'

'Now Austin...' she admonished, raising one translucent forefinger with its small, unpolished nail. She was calling for a truth that was just as unvarnished. She pronounced his name as though it were Ostend, the Belgian port. Her habit of catching him out was something she'd picked up from his friend Gregg, a tic that she'd learned was considered generally amusing.

'Well,' he spluttered, 'I think even he is puzzled, but I don't dare seduce him before I've explained to him about being seropositive. Or what would you say?' He was half hoping for some superior French worldliness that would get him off the moral hook.

Joséphine acknowledged Austin's health status only during those rare times when he mentioned it. Then she'd frown and narrow her eyes as though she were staring into a sunset that had given her a very bad headache. 'Yes, you must,' she said in hushed tones, but he wasn't sure she wasn't speaking out of some mere ethical mimeticism.

'Should we have sex first a few times and *then* should I mention it? Won't he drop me right away if I tell him first?' Austin knew that if a gay American was overhearing him he'd be horrified at Austin's wobbling, even his insouciance.

'Yes,' Joséphine said, as she disappointed Austin by waving off the dessert menu and ordering an espresso for both of them, a mother's disabused glance over imaginary glasses to show she'd brook no whining objections to her spartan good sense from her greedy friend. 'Maybe it would be best if you got him hooked (*accroché*) before you sprang any unpleasant news on him.'

Austin was surprised to hear his possibly imminent death demoted to the status of the 'unpleasant' (*désagréable*). In truth, he had no symptoms and even looked embarrassingly robust.

Austin and Peter, his American ex-lover, had been tested together in Paris in 1986, three years earlier, because their French doctor had insisted. People said that the doctor himself was infected with the virus. Peter, a genuine escapist, had objected to the whole process, arguing they'd be thrown out of France if positive and sent home to the States in leg-irons. 'And you won't be able to travel and practise your profession,' Peter said with such energy and fussy precision that Austin suspected he must be repeating something he'd read in the paranoid gay press. 'In Sweden, they're sending seropositives to a prison island.' Neither Austin nor Peter was certain you said 'seropositives' in English, which Peter in particular found annoying and disorienting in his capacity as a super-patriot who'd never condescended to learn any French beyond the most approximate bar-room gabbling. 'In Munich they test you at the border and to stay in India more than a month you must undergo a blood test.'

'So those places would be eliminated in any event,' Austin pointed out. 'Anyway, who wants to go to Munich, European capital of vulgarity and fascism, all those middle-aged men linking arms and wearing lederhosen? And India is too creepy-crawly for those-who-are-positive,' he said, hoping he'd found a formula for their condition that was both graceful and good English.

Cut off from America, from the massive protests and the underground treatment newsletters, from the hours and hours of frightened midnight conversations with friends by phone and the organized safe sex and massage sessions, far from the hysteria and the solace, Austin did not know what to think of this disease that had taken them by chance, as though he had awakened to find himself in a cave under the heavy paw of a lioness, who was licking him for the moment and breathing all over him with her gamy, carrion smell but who was capable of showing her claws and devouring him today…or tomorrow.

Soon after they were diagnosed, Peter moved back to the States. He bore a lingering resentment against Austin for having insisted they be tested.

And Austin, too, felt that he'd gained nothing by knowing, since the only available treatments didn't seem to work. He'd had a cheerfully defiant conviction that being informed is always liberating, but since moving to Europe he'd come to doubt his democratic frankness, his 'transparence', as the French called it, as though it were no more interesting than a clear pane of glass. He'd learned not to blurt out whatever happened to be passing through his mind and, out of the same curbing of instinct, he'd started to shy away from bald declarations of the facts, even when other people made them. If another American called out anything in a loud, unironic voice, he'd exchange amused but slightly alarmed glances with his French friends—can humankind bear so much candour? he seemed to be asking. Isn't there something inherently alarming about so much explicitness, even when the subject is safe?

The worst thing about knowing he was positive was that now he was under an obligation to tell his partners. Not that he informed the man he picked up in the park or the guy he lured over on the phone chatline. Austin had an American friend in Paris, a well-known gay novelist, who'd come out as positive on TV and in the press and now he was obliged to be honest with everyone, but Austin was a nobody. At least he'd never made any public statements. His friend the writer was apparently having trouble getting laid these days; so much for honesty.

No, truly the worst thing was studying one's body every morning in the shower for auguries. Even in that regard he envied all those hysterical gay guys back in New York or San Francisco who knew to become alarmed about the slightly raised, wine-coloured blemish, not the flat, black mole or whatever, who could tell just when a cough became 'persistent' enough to be worrying or whether a damp pillowcase and a wet head counted as 'night sweats'.

He both feared and embraced the French silence in the face of this disease (or of all other fatal maladies). Something superstitious in him whispered that if you didn't think about it, the virus would go away. From one month to the next he never heard the dreaded three letters (*VIH* in French rather than HIV, as if the French version of the disease itself were the reverse mirror image of the American, just as the French acronym *SIDA* was an anagram of AIDS). Americans sat up telling each other horror stories, but they were later astonished when their worst fantasies came true, as if they'd hoped to ward off evil by talking it into submission or by taking homeopathic doses of it. The French, however, feared summoning an evil genius by pronouncing its name. Neither system worked. When the lioness awakened and felt the first hunger pains, she would show her claws.

He knew in his heart that the French approach was especially unsuited to the epidemic. His friend Hervé last year had been so ashamed of falling ill that he'd slunk back home to his village in the Dordogne without calling a single friend. Only his ex-lover Gilles had stayed in touch, although Hervé's grandmother irrationally blamed Gilles for having given him AIDS. Each time Gilles called she'd say that Hervé was sleeping but would call back later. A month later, the next time Gilles phoned, Hervé had already been dead and buried for eleven days.

It was as if a few young men in the provinces managed to escape to Paris where they lived for a few seasons, where they clipped their heads, lifted some weights, danced on Ecstasy, tattooed one haunch with a butterfly and had sex with hundreds of other underemployed *types*—and then they were driven home to Sarlat by their sombre families, all dressed in black as if out for their Easter duties, and they disappeared in a whispered diminuendo, the score marked *ppppp*...

What didn't work out about this system was that no young bright kid coming up to Paris ever saw his predecessor, skinny and crippled, hobbling back down to the provinces. The best prevention, the most convincing proof of the necessity for safe sex, was ocular evidence, actually *seeing* KS blotches on skinny arms or watching rail-thin old men of twenty staggering into a restaurant on two canes, sharpened cheekbones about to rub through the parchment-thin skin, the eyes as bulbous as an insect's. But in Paris, magical city of elegance and romance, men with AIDS were no more visible than the retarded, the mad or the lame—they'd all been whisked off to some shuttered house in Aquitaine. The French were masters of silence, and as ACT-UP claimed, 'Silence = Death.'

Austin invited Big Julien away for the weekend. In his Michelin guide he'd found a luxury hotel only forty-five minutes by train outside Paris, not far from the royal chateau of Rambouillet. They didn't need to rent a car to get there; theoretically they should be able to find a taxi at the train station. Fatuous as it sounded, Austin was relieved to be going away, for once, with a capable adult male, one who regularly submitted construction plans to the mayor's office and rode a train to other cities.

It was the beginning of May. They took an electrified double-decker commuter train that quickly left the historic city behind and rushed past planned communities in the suburbs, the ugly apartment blocks oriented to one another at rakish angles (to prove how humane the planner had been) rather than laid out in the usual stultifying cemetery grid. When Austin said something dismissive about the buildings and the orange and black graphics on an aubergine-coloured wall in the station shelter, Julien said he knew the architect, an Albanian refugee famous for his sound engineering skills ('No division of labour in Tirana,' Julien said matter-of-factly), and his remark put paid to Austin's facile sneering. Austin was happy to have this handsome man beside him, someone so eccentric in his views, his way of referring everything back to his time in Ethiopia, his indifference to gay life and his ignorance of its tyrannies, his unlikely clothes (the wrinkled pear-green linen blazer he often wore); Austin thought maybe Julien didn't even notice a detail like age: their twenty-year age difference. For Austin was wired very peculiarly. He wasn't like some of his contemporaries who felt they could reduce the gap by doing 300 sit-ups every day until their thickened waists and slack skin looked like melting chocolate bars, the hot flesh oozing over the lines between the tablets. He didn't want to dance all night on drugs, his steps an anthology of four decades of approximated wriggling. He didn't want to pretend not to know any dated slang, not to recognize the words *groovy, mellow* or *get down, girl.*

He liked this intense, brooding married man with the unclassifiable preoccupations, which permitted Austin, by contrast, to appear relaxed and relatively normal, even of a normal age. As they rode side by side in the train they kept stealing glances at each other. They were virtually alone on a Saturday morning in this commuter train heading out of the city. The walls lining the tracks were like ramparts; if Austin looked up he could see the windowless sides of houses rising above. Austin's only other French lover, Little Julien, had never gone anywhere with him in France, perhaps out of fear of being recognized by friends in the company of a much older foreigner. But Big Julien was here with his dark blue eyes, black hair, neat, courtly gestures, his deep, deep voice thrumming and resonating in Austin's ear, his sudden, utterly fake booming laugh, so out of character that Austin assumed it must be a private homage to a friend or relative he'd emulated in the past. No, he wasn't interested in the general impression he was making, even if Austin was his only audience. Julien was a loner, seriously alone now that he was getting divorced, alienated from his father, too, for some reason. Austin would look over at this man whose body he'd never held and imagine they were about to be married, as old-fashioned virgins were once married; he daydreamed his way into the mind of a nineteenth-century bride who looked at these pale male hands beside her, tufted with glossy black hair, and thought she'd know them the rest of her life, that he'd explore her body with them for fifty years.

They had to phone for a taxi from the suburban station and drive out beyond Versailles, but the hotel was worth the trip: a former abbey with its low stone-faced Gothic buildings looming up over an ornamental lake with swans. The chapel was roofless, the empty, glassless rose window nothing but brambles of vacant masonry, the colourful petals long since shed and swept up. Separating the grounds and the fields beyond was a partially destroyed wall, once perhaps the side of a cloister garden; at least it had empty ogival windows and under them stone seats worn smooth and deep by centuries of monastic meditation. The man at the desk, who had registered them with impassive good manners, now added, as a well-judged hint at friendliness, 'The death scene of Depardieu's *Cyrano* was shot out there by the ruined cloisters.'

A moment later they were in their suite with its copper tub and its long antechamber leading to double doors and, beyond, the bedroom with its double bed and its flung-open gauze-covered high windows that floated like panels of bird-riddled silence, empty and twittering, twin paintings by an abstractionist who'd turned wryly metaphysical. They couldn't wait for the bellboy to leave them alone.

They'd gone so long without ever having had sex that Austin felt a certain stage fright, but for the next two days they were all over each other, above, below, behind, like two boys wrestling with hard-ons they don't know how to discharge. Half the hotel had been turned over to a giant wedding party and whenever they descended for another long meal with its succession of courses they were isolated from the other diners with their flowered dresses, big hats and corsages, their decorous toasts and gentle teasing, their restless children in rumpled organdie or clip-on bow ties and their game old grandparents. No, Austin and Julien were blissfully irrelevant to the machinery of a big country wedding and as they wandered the grounds, feeling formal and drained from their furious, tangled bouts of lovemaking, they were always gliding past uniformed waiters stacking rented chairs or testing the microphone in the ballroom by tapping on it and whispering numbers. The weather shifted unpredictably between moments of magnifying-glass heat and cold, cloud-propelling wind.

They sat at opposite ends of the big copper tub in the daylight filtered through smoked glass. The bubble bath lost its suds to reveal their strong, intertwined legs and their body hair undulating like algae.

They'd lie in the hotel's white terry-cloth robes on the bed and Julien would talk about his divorce. 'We were fine in Ethiopia—'

'Except you had that affair with the Englishwoman. How happy could you have been?'

'No, no, *mon pauvre petit*,' Julien said, smiling at Austin's touching gay naivety, 'I loved her, Sarah, the English know the names of all the birds and plants, we French are always astonished by their expertise. We went with her children in her old car to a wonderful lake crowded with pink flamingos. But that doesn't mean I ever hesitated in my feelings for Christine… She's dying to meet you, by the way.'

Austin could feel the blood flooding his face and neck. 'Me? But—'

'She's very interested in old furniture,' Julien said.

'I'm not exactly a *bergère* Louis XV, even if I am slightly tubby,' Austin joked, his voice suddenly turning hoarse. He knew if he was back in America his friends would croak, 'Drop him. Married men are poison. You'll see. He'll go running back to her after he's finished playing with you.' But over here, in France, in these posthumous, post-diagnosis, foreign days, Austin no longer expected anything to work, certainly not to be ideal; he would share a man with a woman and even meet her if need be, though he was afraid of her anger. 'What went wrong, then?' Austin asked.

'She's a bitch. In Ethiopia she was fine. But the moment we came back—starting with the wedding!' His eyes shifted from side to side, as though looking for the best escape route; then he sighted it and ran. 'My grandmother was revolted. She didn't want me to do something so bourgeois as get married.' Inspired, he laughed his laugh, a hollow tocsin of mirthless pleasure. 'They wanted me to be gay—anything rather than marry that *petit-bourgeois* bitch and her stuffy, petty family. They were so disappointed I was marrying that they wept. My grandmother pulled up her skirts at the reception and danced like Marilyn over the subway grill and my grandmother's lover clapped and shouted, "Go, Granny, show them your pussy!" (*Allez, Mémé, montre ta moule!*)'

Austin smiled painfully. He didn't see anything funny in the scene and wondered if it had ever happened. If it did, he thoroughly sympathized with Christine and her parents. 'But how old is your grandmother?'

'Oh, not that old,' Julien said with his usual vagueness. 'Her legs were still good then and she cut a fine figure, although now she's gone to fat. It's all the fault of that lover of hers, a real vulgarian called Modeste.'

'It's nice, I think, that your grandmother has a lover. In America people stop having sex at a surprisingly young age. Few of us can say the words, "my grandmother's lover".'

But Julien wasn't paying attention. He'd turned on to his stomach and was laughing, repeating to himself, '*Allez, Mémé, montre ta moule!'* The ugly words and the self-amused booming laugh didn't really go with his body, with the fine swirls of hair on his boyishly full buttocks, nor did the laugh fit the small ears pinned back to his head as though he were standing still in a ferocious wind nor with the delicate architecture of his shoulder blades, lightly dusted with black hair.

If Austin was always alert to Julien's mood, feared boring him and followed his conversational lead, Julien wallowed, oblivious, in his own worries and obsessions. He seemed to be sick with worry. He had two red welts on his forehead and small pimples clustering around the follicles where his beard was growing in. His nose was always oily. Gregg, who had all sorts of fetishes, had said to Austin, 'That Big Julien is so randy and young he even has acne, slurp, slurp.' Gregg always pronounced the words for his sound effects, and said such things as 'Sob' or 'Drool'.

'My mother committed suicide ten years ago,' Julien was saying. 'She and I loved each other—she was the great love of my life. That's why I don't speak to my father. I hate him. It was his fault. He'd married her young. He didn't like it that she was—' He hesitated, then revised his thoughts. 'That she was a concert pianist. He made her give it up. She sacrificed everything for him. Her family gave him money to start his pharmaceutical company. They gave them their house. She killed herself in Belle-Ile at the summer house her mother had bought her.' He pounded the mattress and said into the pillow, 'The thought—'

'What?'

Julien looked up, astonished, as if awakened. 'The thought that he is living there now with that slut, his mistress—'

'His wife?'

'Yes, I suppose he married her. The thought...'

Austin felt it would turn out to be a very long story and he wasn't sure Julien would be a reliable narrator. This Latin man with his black hair, with his lean neck shaggy because he'd long been overdue at the barber, with his low unstoppable voice that sometimes seemed the inefficient, power-guzzling motor draining his body of all its fuel—oh, he wasn't an impartial, objective American, respectful of the truth and impressed by any fair challenge to his version of things, ready to chuckle at his own absurdities. Julien was never the butt of his own jokes. No, he was a passionate Latin male whose body seeped anguish and oil and whose voice hypnotized his mind into believing whatever it had proposed and was elaborating.

'My mother's death was such a powerful thing for me,' he was saying; now he was sitting up and hugging a surprisingly shiny knee above leggings of hair—there was even hair on the knuckle of each of his toes. It occurred to Austin that Julien had rubbed his knee bare with worry, but he knew that couldn't have been the case. 'I was the one who found her dead. It was during my final exams for my architecture diploma, so I guess I hadn't been paying much attention to her. I knew she was unhappy. She'd asked my father if it was all over between them. She'd said, "Tell me. I'm still young, I can find someone else." In fact she was just forty-three, and she looked so young that when I'd take her out dancing everyone would ask if she was my sister.'

Austin thought he'd heard the same story all his life, a story that always seemed so odd to him. His own mother had died of ovarian cancer when he was still a teenager, but he'd never wanted to pass for her brother, nor did she dance. Of course she'd been nearly forty when he'd been born, a plump greying woman locked into another epoch by her elegant Tidewater accent and soft, unambitious ways, whereas Julien's parents had been in their twenties and his father even now was just five years older than Austin.

The story had reached a head and Austin hadn't been listening. He figured out that Julien's father had lied and pledged his renewed love to his wife, but in truth all he'd wanted was continued access to her money. 'When she realized he'd left her for that other bitch, not moved out but was spending all his time with her—that's when and why she attempted suicide. She survived and I just dismissed her when she asked me if I thought she should see a psychiatrist. I laughed at her and told her to pull herself together.'

'You were at an entirely different juncture in your life,' Austin said. 'You had to marshal all your forces to pass your exams, you couldn't afford to be swamped by feelings, hers or yours.' He'd learned in other, earlier affairs with confused younger men that a few words, wise to the point of banality, uttered at the strategic moment, could become talismanic for years to come.

Later that night, after they'd showered and dressed and dined, all alone now that the wedding party had left, Julien said, 'You know, when I was a kid I always had a best friend, one friend; you have so many friends but I'm not like that. You're always saying, "So-and-so is one of my best friends." I don't have a series of best friends. Of course I know a lot of people, but I always wanted just one friend, who'd be loyal to me, and I'd tell him everything.'

Austin must have waited for the obvious conclusion with such wide, yearning eyes that Julien finally laughed and said, 'But, *Petit*, you look like a puppy.'

'I'm sorry,' Austin said, offended.

Julien just ran over his prickliness and squeezed Austin's right leg between both of his and said, 'You're really such a *bout de chou*.'

'A *bout*?'

Julien explained that 'the end of the cabbage' was an affectionate nickname for a little kid.

'I'm hardly *little*,' Austin objected sweetly, thrilled with the new name.

They left the hotel for Paris on Monday morning.

As they saw each other with greater and greater frequency, until they were getting together nearly every night, Austin realized that he had indeed become Julien's little sidekick, his one best friend, his confidant, not his father. Julien had no idea of deference—nor of reciprocity. He never cooked Austin dinner or even offered him a coffee, and he certainly never asked Austin a question about his family or past lovers. Was his discretion evidence of his incuriosity and egotism or did he hope to win with it an immunity from Austin's prying? Austin never saw his apartment, the one where he lived alone. He covered Austin with kisses and smiled with a solar warmth, just as though the sun were setting closer and closer and peering directly into his eyes. He'd whisper, *'Petit'*, and *'Mon bout de chou'*, or say, *'Comme tu es mignon!'* (How cute you are!), but Austin knew it wasn't his face or body that was being praised, just his presence, his docility. Austin understood that straight men, married men, were used to partners who listened or half-listened to their monologues. Anyway, Austin liked listening, which he could always pass off as a language lesson since the words were in French.

Because Gregg had been the one to suggest the trip to the abbey-hotel, Austin called him when they got back to Paris.

'Well, Mother, you went and got yourself a nice Mother's Day present, I see.'

'What? Oh, Gregg...*Daughter*. I honestly forgot the day. It's only Mother's Day back in the States, isn't it? Gregg, it was a great suggestion. I never pick out guys who might actually like me.'

'I hear you. Your daughter's no better when it comes to doing for herself. So how's the meat?'

'We had lots of sex, but of course it was safe, safe, safe. Tons of frottage, *touche-pipi*, soul-kissing. No fucky-fucky—actually it was terribly romantic.'

'Do you think he's hooked enough to tell him you're positive?' Gregg asked.

This entirely cynical question opened a door inside Austin's mind. He laughed and said, 'Not yet. Maybe it's because I'm not really in love or because that beastly Little Julien dropped me so brutally, but I've never been shrewder. I'm determined to open up new sexual horizons for him—'

'Meaning?'

'His nipples are more sensitive than his wife's. He told me that. She used to play with his—'

'—perky little devils,' Gregg added.

'They *do* just perk right up,' Austin said. He knew Julien would be horrified if he could hear this tacky, heartless, camp exchange. But he, Austin, was so insecure in an affair—so eager to please, so intense in his devotion, so quick to accept the first sign of boredom as an irrevocable rejection—that in sacrilegious chatter he could reassert, at least for a moment, his freedom. 'But I want to discover his bottom for him. Not to mention the beauty of bondage.'

'*Bondage!*' Gregg shouted with outraged amusement. 'You old Stonewallers are such shameless hussies.'

'Oh, like your generation is so pure. Ex*cuse* me. Hel-*lowwuh*...' Austin was merrily imitating the new Valley Girl slang or his very dim idea of it, but it was a fashionable reference designed as an implicit rebuke to Gregg's dismissal of Austin's 'generation'.

'But won't he be horrified by *bondage*?' Gregg asked. 'Not that I should question Mother's *millennium* of experience…'

Strangely, through all this talk of tits, ropes and sexual technique, Austin knew he was communicating to Gregg his timid happiness and his fear of losing Julien when he discovered Austin's HIV status. In America, of course, Austin thought bitterly, they would have met at a Positive Boutique or on an HIV cruise and that would have been that, the introduction equivalent to an admission.

Julien complained of his health at dinner the next night (a *blanquette de veau*, mushrooms, pearl onions, carrots and veal swimming in an egg-yolk-and-cream sauce that had taken Austin all afternoon to elaborate). 'I can't seem to make this acne go away— *Petit*, this fish is excellent! I've been hacking away all day with this terrible cough, that's why I can't stay over, I'd keep us both awake. I think I'm coming down with the flu.' Austin felt a cringing, a tightening around his heart, as though someone were inching him gently closer and closer to the airplane's open hatch. Mentally he ran through all their sexual positions over the weekend but could find nothing unsafe. He hadn't let Julien suck him. They'd kissed, but was that dangerous? Julien had held their erect penises close together in his hand, but surely that wasn't 'at risk' behaviour, as the pamphlets called it. Or was it? Anyway, the disease took months or at least weeks to declare itself, didn't it?

Of course the unconscionable thing was that they were both involved in a deadly game Austin had already lost and Julien didn't know he was playing.

Usually Austin could forget the virus but now it kept ringing back like a bill collector on the phone, calling at all hours, insisting upon its claim.

'Why don't you stay home tomorrow? And I'm sorry about the rich dinner.'

'But I love pike in a *beurre nantaise*.'

Austin thought he should say it was veal, but that would destroy the illusion they both fostered that Julien, as a Frenchman, knew everything about food, wine and fashion. And because Austin felt guilty about his continuing silence on the subject of his HIV status he couldn't bring himself to irk Julien in any way. He was pleading with Julien to forgive a crime he'd not yet confessed. He'd heard of men who'd gone on a killing spree when they'd found out their lovers had infected them. If Julien was just a nice married man gambling with gay sex, shouldn't he know the stakes? The stakes that he'd already accepted, all unknowingly?

Austin made an appointment with his doctor for Julien. They went to see the man together. The office was just across the street from the Buttes-Chaumont, that vast park for the working class that Napoléon III had benignly inserted into a former quarry. Now, of course, the workshops and the little villages of workers' cottages on the streets leading off the park housed up-and-coming artists and photographers—Austin knew a gay *couturier* who'd filled his cottage with medieval kitsch (shields, tapestries, suits of armour). Even so, the neighbourhood felt forgotten and Austin had no idea why Dr Aristopoulos lived and worked there. His *cabinet* was up three flights, a cheerless suite of dim rooms, unmatched chairs, a student's lamp and a coffee table covered with last year's magazines and more recent HIV brochures. Somewhere in the neighbourhood, no doubt, Dr Aristopoulos had found a comically hostessy receptionist, a woman in her fifties who wore puffy dresses and had dyed her hair an egg-yolk yellow and who walked around in very high heels, bowing and welcoming the skeletally thin AIDS patients as though to a Pensioners' Ball.

When Julien came out of his appointment he was red in the face and almost cross-eyed with anger. As they were escorted to the door by their bobbing, tripping, smiling hostess ('*A bientôt, messieurs!*' she sang out in a fruity voice), Julien said nothing, but on the dark stairs, which smelled of the *concierge's* salted cod dinner, he hissed, 'But he's an idiot!'

'But why?'

'He wanted me to have the test.'

'The test?' Austin asked stupidly.

'The AIDS test.'

'Why?'

'Because he's worried about my acne and my cough and that wart I have on my penis.'

'But that's absurd. Unless...'

'Yes, it's absurd.'

'Unless you've had a lot of sex with men these last few years.'

Julien didn't say anything but worked his jaw muscles menacingly. When they were outside he took Austin by the elbow and steered him across the street and into the park. Two Indian women in saris were pushing strollers along in which solemn, brown-faced babies were propped up like gingerbread men with big sultana eyes. The mothers were conversing so loudly that they reminded Austin how most Parisians whispered.

Had Julien not responded because he was irritated that Austin—and probably Dr Aristopoulos—had asked him direct questions about his sex life? Or did he think the test cast doubts on his honour?

'I have to tell you something,' Austin blurted out. 'I'm HIV positive. Don't worry that you might have—from me...'

'No, no, of course not,' Julien said as a polite reflex. 'How long have you known?'

'Two years already. My counts are very good, surprisingly good.' His voice wobbled and he was short of breath. 'They don't seem to be going down. I hope you're not angry that I didn't tell you right away, but I could never seem to find the right moment.' Hey, how about the moment just before we had sex? Julien might be thinking, or so Austin imagined. 'I'm sure Dr Aristopoulos wasn't asking you to have the test because of me.'

'No, no, of course not,' Julien said, his politeness now striking Austin as ominous. Would Austin ever see him again? All he had was his work number and Julien could instruct the receptionist to say he'd call him right back or that he was out of the office for a few days—no, for an 'indefinite leave'. That's what she would say.

Julien sprawled on the grass just beside a sign that forbade doing so. An old Vietnamese man walking past shook his finger at him, laughing. Austin stood just on the other side of the foot-high fence of metal hoops, then felt foolish and joined him and felt foolish.

'Please don't worry about Dr Aristopoulos. He's positive himself; some people say he's ill, though he looks fine to me. He probably is overly cautious.'

'I don't think he's competent. Why aren't you seeing a famous specialist?'

'Several of my friends with HIV see him—'

'You have *several* friends with AIDS?'

'They're all in good health for the moment,' Austin said primly.

'I've never met—or even heard of someone infected until now, until you. It just seemed to me a media circus, just some new puritanical horror invented by the Americans.' He thought about it for a while.

'Are you worried about Christine? Have you gone on having sex with her?'

'Christine?' He smiled a mild, studied, imperturbable smile that Austin read as a signal that he had gone too far with his grubby, indiscreet American questions.

Austin changed tactics: 'You know, don't worry about…if you want to drop me…I should have been honest from the beginning.' He propped himself up on his elbows and wondered if the grass was staining his seersucker jacket and the seat of his trousers. Julien was wearing his liverish green linen sports coat. 'Do you like linen?' Austin asked wildly, then hastened to add, lying, 'I do.' He was chattering out of fear and embarrassment.

'Yes, it's a noble material.'

By now Austin had learned that Julien liked cotton, linen and silk, that he revered natural wood and stone, especially marble but even the ubiquitous Parisian sandstone extracted from this very quarry in the last century, that he despised brick and concrete—oh, Austin thought, I'll miss him.

Maybe because Austin was a foreigner and what he did and said were thrown into relief, if only through contrast, or maybe because Austin would soon turn fifty and was seropositive, he now had a heightened sense of the swath his life was cutting. In the past he'd been casual about himself. He'd never wanted to shine. He'd never been known for anything—neither his books, which were ordinary, nor his accomplishments, which amounted to nothing more than a nearly photographic memory of particular pieces of furniture and ceramics and a low-energy charm that allowed him to pass hours with the rich idlers who usually owned those things. Although he'd done well in everything related to the history of furniture itself, he couldn't talk a good line about Louis XVI as a great patron, about Mme de

Pompadour's 'rapacious curiosity' or her 'exigent tastes', which constituted an 'enlightened tyranny'—no, he wasn't a phrasemaker, nor was he ambitious like those chaps at Sotheby's in London. And he preferred spending an evening with his overgrown adolescent friends than with the countesses who owned the last great bits of eighteenth-century furniture in private hands—*finding* the furniture was always the problem. It sold itself. Over the years he'd acted as a middleman between countesses and museums in a few transactions, but he wasn't interested enough in money to persist—or rather he was too quickly bored by grown-ups, officials, heterosexuals (or rather by all these people, straight or gay, who kept their sexuality hidden).

No, he'd always seen himself as an amateur and his life as formless, but now, today, here in this suddenly hot sunlight and grass laid like velvet over the raw, gouged surfaces of the old stone quarry, Austin was alive for the first time since his high-school days to the question of his 'destiny'. Yes, he probably would die soon, probably in France in a charity ward since he didn't have French insurance nor the official residency that would entitle him to national health coverage. He had a panicky fear that he'd forget French, that his brain would start bubbling like an alphabet soup, scrambling all the words he knew in the reverse order he'd learned them, so that French would be the first to go, then the language of furniture, next all adult conversation until he ended up with just a few nursery rhymes, the song his mother had sung him to make him sleep, 'When Johnny comes marching home'.

Julien was chewing a blade of grass and squinting up at the bright hazy sky. With his right hand he alternately tugged at Austin's seersucker lapel and smoothed it, but he wasn't looking at Austin. The gesture appeared isolated from his thoughts and the immobility of the rest of his body. Julien even stopped chewing. The rancid, cooking smell of grass reminded Austin of bitter Japanese green tea, the tang so inherently rank that sugar seems laughably inadequate to it.

For the next few days Julien was sick with a bad case of the flu. He called Austin every day to tell him he was getting better, but each time he stayed on the line only a moment. The one time he did linger was to tell him the plot of a *Fluide Glacial* he was reading. Like so many adult Frenchmen he read comic books filled with grotesque sex scenes and anarchistic violence, an art form that had largely replaced fiction for many Latin men in their teens and twenties. At the giant music and literature emporium, the FNAC, enraptured solitary men, unemployed no doubt, stood or sat cross legged on the floor for hours in the aisles of the section for comics, reading and chuckling or sucking in their breath with amazement.

A t last Julien was better. Once again he started coming by several evenings a week for dinner. One night Austin took him along for a formal dinner at the house of Marie-France, a woman he'd known for five or six years. They'd met when Austin had written an article about her vast apartment along the Quai d'Anjou on the Ile Saint-Louis, twelve rooms with lamps, tables and even bronze bookcases that had been designed by Diego Giacometti, the sculptor's brother. The apartment was on the second floor and the drawing-room windows looked out through trees on to the Seine—the movement of the wind-stirred leaves and the racing, faceted water created a pointillism of living light.

It was a formal dinner for twenty served on two separate tables by two Filipino servants but Marie-France made it all seem comical, even improvised. Julien and Austin were seated apart, each beside glamorous divorcees 'of a certain age'. Austin's dinner partner kept raving about everything—her key words were *'sublissime'*, which he gathered meant 'very sublime', and *'la fin du monde'* ('the end of the world'), which also seemed to be a sign of enthusiasm. Philippe Starck's new toothbrush was *sublissime* and Claude Picasso's carpets were *la fin du monde*.

Marie-France and all her friends were so civilized that they smiled discreetly and benignly when Julien and Austin stood by the piano after dinner drinking a brandy together. On the phone the next day Marie-France said her old uncle Henri had been delighted to meet them and thought he'd bring his own boyfriend to the next gathering, which had never occurred to him previously in half a century. 'Of course *his* friend is a gardener whereas yours is an architect and *so* amusing.'

Sometimes Julien and Austin would wander through the narrow streets of the Marais during the endlessly prolonged June twilight. They'd go through the Jewish Quarter and often they'd eat at Jo

Goldenberg's, a deli up front and a restaurant behind, full of cosy booths and paintings of rabbis and of old women in babushkas. Violinists serenaded each table in turn and a gypsy told fortunes. For Austin it was like a distorted dream version of a New York deli—it took him a second to realize that *cascher* was the French word for 'kosher'.

As they ate their *kasha* and *derma*, Julien said, 'I thought it over. You must understand, I'd never met someone before who was seropositive. For me it wasn't part of real life.'

'Not even in Ethiopia?'

'Well, I suppose there are lots of cases there, but I think it's other parts of Africa, black Africa—'

'The Ethiopians aren't black?'

Julien smiled with a smile so superior it was almost sad, certainly pitying. 'Don't let *them* ever hear you say that. No, they think they're an ancient tribe, close to the Pharaohs, the Pharaonic Egyptians, and they look down on their black neighbours. It's true the Ethiopian elite is rather light-skinned, the men plump and often balding, their features quite small and regular, the women truly beautiful. Of course the Ethiopians *pretend* they're black when they think they can get some political mileage out of it. It's a clever, sophisticated nation.'

He talked on and on about Ethiopia, while Austin waited for him to come back to their love and its future. Austin was soothed by this absurd reprieve and Julien, essentially a kind-hearted man, seemed happy, too, to avoid what he must have prepared to say.

But finally a densely packed poppy-seed cake, heavy as an ingot, was served as though it was a black curse in a fairy tale, and they both fell silent after the pell-mell interrogation and speech on the subject of Ethiopian pride.

'You said you'd thought it all over?' Austin prompted, determined to make it easy for this tactful young man.

'You must understand that I was thunderstruck (*foudroyé*) when you told me about yourself. I'd never thought about it, I'd never met anyone...' Perhaps he saw from Austin's look of vulnerability that to insist on the singularity of Austin's condition only made it sound more monstrous. He ran out of energy and once again was caught in a brief moment of stasis, like a gymnast who has twisted and turned in every direction on a sawhorse and then balances upside down on his hands for a second, before choreographing a military-sharp descent to the floor.

But now Austin couldn't help him out any more. He couldn't be expected to fabricate his own marching papers.

'In any event, I realized you could—you *will*—become ill and it's a long illness...'

Austin felt he was being lectured at by an aunt or the Episcopalian minister back home about the ghastly consequences of his excesses and his thoughts emigrated inward. He was caught out not paying attention when he heard Julien saying, 'Anyway, I've decided I'm going to stay with you. I'll take care of you.' 'You shouldn't be too hasty—' Austin protested. But Julien interrupted and said, 'No, that's what I've decided. I can't imagine leaving you. I'm already too hooked on you.' Austin felt a warmth spreading through his whole body, as though he'd rushed naked through snow into a sauna. □

THE
PROBLEM OUTSIDE
Linda Polman

TRANSLATION BY
SAM GARRETT

Survivors of the Kibeho massacre in Rwanda lie among the dead, 22 April 1995.

The Problem Outside

About 150,000 refugees, standing shoulder to shoulder on a mountain plateau the size of three football fields. When I first see them, they've been standing there for almost three days. Somewhere in this sea of humanity there are supposed to be two small camps of the United Nations 'ZamBat' unit, peacekeepers from Zambia, but I don't see them anywhere.

There's no room to sit down on the plateau. The refugees are squeezed together above their belongings, their legs spread across the bodies of old people and children too tired to stand. Rwandan troops in long raincoats, guns slung over their shoulders, some wearing black berets, are posted every ten metres around the throng they've driven together. Kibeho refugee camp, the largest on Rwandan territory, was closed two days ago when the Rwandan government lost patience with the UN's mission, Opération Retour, to return these refugees to their homes. It was taking too long; the government feared the social and political consequences of 150,000 alienated Hutu citizens packed together on its territory. The soldiers of the Rwandan government have chased the inhabitants from their huts in the surrounding valleys and herded them on to the plateau. Now they're keeping them covered.

With the evacuation of the camp completed, the Rwandan soldiers, all Tutsis, have apparently run out of orders. Just like the Hutu refugees, they've been waiting for days for someone to tell them what to do. They're drawing patterns in the dust with their truncheons, taking drags off each other's cigarettes and wantonly kicking misplaced Hutu possessions into the deep valley. Down in the depths, it looks like a hurricane's been raging. Tens of thousands of huts have been knocked down, trampled, some of them torched. Cooking pots, rice baskets and muddy blankets are lying among the nondescript heaps. Here and there a soldier skims the remains to see if there's anything he can use.

Somewhere in the crowd people start pushing. An old woman is knocked off the crammed plateau and rolls on to the road that runs below, towards me. Swinging their truncheons, the soldiers drive her back into the crowd.

A few blue helmets loom up from the outer reaches of the crowd; my escort to one of the ZamBat camps. The UN is still here.

Linda Polman

'We'll have to plough right through the middle. So take a deep breath,' one of the peacekeepers warns me. I worm into the crowd after them. The refugees are paralysed with misery. They don't seem to hear the blue helmets' 'Out of the way!' or feel it when they're roughly shoved aside. Step by step, we make our way through the masses. I see only faces, dull eyes and lips chapped with thirst. The ground beneath my feet is covered with anonymous personal effects and the occasional human. I can't see the soil itself. At first I put my feet down carefully, until I become afraid of being left behind by the blue helmets. I have to be less careful, not care too much who or what I step on. 'Excuse me! Excuse me!' I hear myself mumble a thousand times over. Every time I feel my feet sink into something soft, I only hope I'm not treading on a human being. Or stepping in excrement. For the last sixty hours, the refugees have been forced to relieve themselves where they stand, or where they've fallen. The stench takes my breath away.

I trip over someone's legs, lose my balance, and fall against people. By the time I've scrambled to my feet the trail the blue helmets blazed for me has disappeared. I'm stuck, with no idea which way to go. Just when I'm about to panic, a hand clamps hold of my wrist. One of the blue helmets drags me towards him, through the human mass. Hyperventilating, I hold on to his belt with both hands for the rest of the journey.

We reach a pole, painted red and white, serving as a traffic barrier. Behind it lies the former primary school of Kibeho, where the UN commander, Francis Sikaonga, and his eighty soldiers have set up camp.

Just as the Rwandan government soldiers surround their Hutu prisoners to keep them from escaping, so the Zambian blue helmets surround their school to keep the Hutus from trampling it. The Zambians are posted at intervals behind the wire around the former playground, which is barely large enough for the three white jeeps parked there now. The badly bent iron gates are locked, and guarded by Zambians as well.

The refugees try to stay as close to the UN soldiers as they can. They crowd on to the parking lot; some have managed to find a place to sit, their legs stretched out as far as possible into the safe territory beyond the barbed wire. The refugees do nothing, say nothing, just stare at the Zambians.

I walk up to a blue-helmeted soldier in shirtsleeves who's fiddling with a broken pump. 'Smashed to bits when the people made a run on our camp two days ago.' He sounds angry, but his gaze is full of sorrow as he looks at the children with eyes and mouths open wide, gaping vainly at the drainpipe in hope of a few drops.

Two nights ago they heard gunshots, the UN soldier tells me. 'We got down behind the sandbags right away, we had no idea who was shooting whom. Maybe they were even shooting at us. The ground was shaking, but we thought it was tanks, we couldn't believe it was tens of thousands of people running. Not until we saw them climbing out of the valley towards us. They came running in from all sides, screaming, straight at us, with about a thousand government soldiers firing at them. Our commander stayed calm. It was because of him that we didn't start shooting too, purely out of fear, not even when the refugees stormed our camp. I thought we were all in for it.'

His voice has grown hoarse: 'We climbed up on to the sandbags and the roof as fast as we could. All around us people were stumbling, falling on top of each other and being trampled to death. There's the proof...' He nods at some bulky shapes beneath a neat row of blue tarpaulins next to the gate, towards which a Zambian soldier is walking at that very moment. He has a woman with him, and he lifts the canvasses one by one so she can see what's underneath: eleven children, trampled to death during the nocturnal stampede. The woman shakes her head. She's lost her child, but he's not here. The Zambian leads her back past the barbed wire. She pushes her way through, falls backwards into the wall of people and stands perfectly still, fixing the Zambians with her gaze.

The human avalanche finally came to a halt against the walls of the school. After the Zambians had ventured down from their perches, it took them hours to direct the refugees back to the other side of the trampled barbed wire. ZamBat was just dragging the last bodies away from the school gates when the government soldiers came up to Captain Francis.

'We're taking over here. The refugees are going home,' they announced. They didn't say how the refugees would get home, and it still isn't clear. The Hutus aren't allowed to walk home: the Rwandan government is afraid they'll settle down again after a few kilometres and erect a new camp. Loading the refugees into trucks and driving them to their villages isn't feasible either: the Rwandans have no trucks. The UN has a few, but United Nations troops aren't allowed to take part in the deportation of prisoners. Voluntary status is a criterion for UN passengers, and the inhabitants of Kibeho haven't volunteered for this.

The two roads winding through the mountains to Kibeho have been closed. Food and water convoys from aid organizations are being stopped and sent back. As of the day before yesterday, the Rwandans have forbidden all refugee aid.

'We've been here for sixty-two hours now,' the blue helmet says, 'waiting for somebody to do something.' He nods towards the people behind the barbed wire. 'They're hoping we'll do something. We're hoping God will. But it's the Rwandan government that will have to solve things. It's their country; what we're seeing here is their refugee policy. We're not allowed to interfere.'

Suddenly angry, he throws down his pipe wrench and gropes wildly in a crate for another tool. 'These people haven't had anything to eat or drink since the day before yesterday. They're going out of their minds with thirst. They think I'll give them water as soon as I've repaired this pump, but there's barely enough water for us.' Provisions for the eighty Zambians are also being held up at the barricades on the mountain road, along with the food and water for the refugees. In the parking lot, an American UNICEF employee— who got past the roadblocks because he wasn't carrying any relief goods—is talking to Captain Francis. The American says that he thinks he has convinced the Rwandan commander to allow a water tanker through by pointing out to him that water will help move the refugees. The Hutus can go without food for a while, but—as he's pointed out to the commander—people who are half dead with thirst can't go anywhere.

'There's a tanker with 18,000 litres of drinking water stuck at a roadblock ten kilometres from here. If the Rwandan soldiers let it through, that water could be here within half an hour.'

'That's fine,' Captain Francis says, 'except you won't be able to distribute it. All the pumps in Kibeho have been smashed. We'll repair some of them for you. But there's not much more we can do.' Francis pulls five soldiers away from the cordon behind the barbed wire and sends them into the crowd with the UNICEF man and some tools. Then he disappears as well. I hear his voice trailing off: 'I must try to negotiate. There must be an authority somewhere around here who can be reasoned with.'

Why distribute water at all, when there are only 18,000 litres for 150,000 dehydrated refugees? One decilitre, half a teacup for every parched throat. To keep the refugees on their feet, to say nothing of keeping them alive, we'd need at least 450,000 litres, three litres per refugee. And we'd need it again tomorrow, of course.

And then how do you go about distributing 18,000 litres of water among 150,000 people?

By hand. One cup at a time. There's no other way, because the blue helmets haven't been able to repair a single tap in Kibeho. All smashed to bits, they'd need more than the pipe wrench they got from the UN.

And what about the speed you'd have to work at to pour half a cup of water for 150,000 people? And where would you find that many cups in a blue-helmet camp? Francis sighs very deeply.

'OK, send that tanker of yours,' he tells the American from UNICEF. 'We'll see what we can do.'

The lorry pulls into the Zambian parking lot with stowaways on the bumper, licking drops off the welding-seams. A little copper tap is sticking out of the middle of the giant reservoir. The blue helmets open it and start filling the cups, tins and pans that are being thrown to them from the crowd behind the wire. Full cups and tins and pans are carried back to their owners, who sob in anticipation. One of the blue helmets slips and falls in the mud under the tap. The containers he's just filled spill all over him. He scrambles to his feet and goes to the end of the line of blue helmets waiting their turn at the tap.

I don't see how this rescue operation can succeed, but what these blue helmets are clumsily trying to do, I can do too. This isn't skilled work. Even a journalist can do it. I pick up the first empty can from the ground and hold it under the thin stream, then I carry it to the barbed wire and hold it up until its owner comes forward and claims it with a loud 'Merci'.

The illusion that we're rescuing refugees makes us euphoric. After discussing how we can speed up the operation, we find an empty oil drum in the kitchen. The cook asks us to bring it back before six: he needs it to fix ZamBat's dinner.

We attach a hose to the tanker and use it to fill the drum. Some of us dunk the drinking vessels the refugees are throwing at us into the water, others trot back and forth between the truck and the barbed wire. Meanwhile, the rest of ZamBat is keeping the crowd covered. The sight of water, having to wait their turn before they can take a sip, is too much for most of the refugees. They push towards us, panting. The barbed wire bulges dangerously and the people who get caught in it scream and cry. The Zambians, who are becoming increasingly panicky themselves, admonish the people to remain calm. 'Everyone will get a turn,' they lie desperately. At the back of the crowd we see government soldiers using their truncheons to chase away those who've already had water.

When the tank is empty, a few hundred of the 150,000 people on the plateau have had a couple of sips of water. Those who haven't are pleading and crying behind the barbed wire. Everyone is exhausted.

I'm drenched and shivering.

The first time I witness the logical consequences of the UN's non-intervention policy, I fly into a rage. At the blue helmets. We watch as a group of refugees, about six of them, break away from the crowd and start running into the valley. They're trying to break the siege! Rwandan troops start firing immediately. We see the refugees fall. Dead. Their bodies roll down the rocks to the bottom of the valley, and come to a halt at the trampled huts.

'They're being slaughtered!' I scream madly at Captain Francis. 'Stop them! Do something!'

Francis turns to me. 'Such as?' he says. 'Shoot the government troops?'

'Yeah, good idea,' I bite back at him.

Francis regains his composure. 'We've been wanting to do that from the start, of course. But we can't. They're better armed...'

'Then do something else, but do something...'

'There are a thousand of them and only eighty of us.'

'Then call for reinforcements.'

'We've done that, but even if all six thousand blue helmets in Rwanda came to Kibeho today, carrying the kinds of weapons we can only dream of, we still couldn't fight. There are a hundred and fifty thousand civilians between us and the government troops. We'd have to shoot right across those people in order to hit one Rwandan soldier.'

I look around: from the Zambian parking lot I can see only three of the thousand Rwandan soldiers supposedly roaming around on the plateau. The trio in the distance is peering over the edge to see whether the bodies are still moving. Apart from them, I can see only a solid wall of Hutus. Some of them are doing their utmost to catch my eye, so they can direct their pleading looks at someone.

'Besides, imagine the panic if we started shooting,' Francis continues. 'There would be another stampede. Even more casualties. Of course the government troops would return fire. More casualties.'

'OK, OK, OK, I understand. Sorry.'

'Furthermore,' he continues imperturbably, 'I've conveniently failed to mention that the mandate of the peacekeeping force in Rwanda doesn't allow force. We've been ordered to cooperate with the Rwandan authorities, not shoot at them.'

For a moment I think I can trick Captain Francis: 'But that wouldn't apply if those authorities were killing innocent people before your eyes, would it?'

'Yes it would. It does.'

I pass up what later turns out to be the last chance for a lift out of Kibeho. A few UN observers are trying to get to UN headquarters in the Rwandan capital, Kigali, to alert it to the situation in Kibeho. I'm transfixed. I watch the blue helmets watching the killing around them, eyes and mouths wide open in disbelief, as if they're screaming without making a sound. I keep watching until the sun's gone down and it's pitch-black on the plateau. Captain Francis looms up behind me.

'We're eating in half an hour. Go and have a wash first.' He leads me through the iron gates into the little school. Wash myself while people are dying of thirst all around me? And then have dinner while the Hutus outside haven't had a bite for three days? I feel the moral outrage welling up again. Francis does, too. He comes up with counter-arguments before I can start hassling him again.

'This,' he says, waving his arm to indicate the little playground, 'is normal.' I look at a soldier who is sweeping a dormitory, at another soldier lathering the chin of a colleague. In the kitchen I see the cook chopping onions. He's whistling.

'Outside,' Francis says, jerking his thumb over his shoulder, 'madness reigns. And probably cholera, too. I have to make sure the madness and disease stay outside the gates. Whether people are being killed or not, we have to try and keep fit. There's no point in dying with them. So we have to keep going, eating, drinking and sleeping.'

ZamBat's accommodation consists of three brick buildings roofed with corrugated iron. The UN soldiers sleep in bunks, in what used to be the classrooms. At the back of one of those makeshift barracks, in a former broom cupboard, a bucket of hot water is ready for me, and a bar of green soap. Francis shoves his own yellow bathing slippers under the wooden swinging doors. He calls through the doors:

'Give your hands a particularly good scrubbing. We don't have rubber gloves, and everyone and everything out there could be infected.'

On the table there is a plastic cloth with flowers and steaming dishes. 'Ah, here she is,' Francis says delightedly when I enter the staffroom with 'Officers' Mess' on the door. I'm wearing a clean T-shirt I borrowed from Captain Francis, who's seated at the head of the table in a neatly pressed uniform. His second-in-command is sitting next to him. His name is Innocent. There are also two UN Human Rights observers at the table, a Greek man and a Dutch woman. Like me, they've asked Francis to put them up for the night. They're working overtime.

As the good host, the captain piles our plates high with rice and chicken, and fills our tumblers from a gallon-pack of South African red wine. During dinner we euphemistically refer to what's happening

beyond the wire as 'the problem outside'. We call the masses of
people 'IDPs', Internally Displaced Persons: UN jargon for refugees
in their own country. Through the brick walls of the mess we can
hear IDPs being executed. Each gunshot is followed by the screams
of onlookers, fearing for their own lives. Before we've drained the
gallon-pack, at least three people have been killed.

Midnight. Francis and Innocent are on the floor under the table
with radio equipment, hands clasped behind their heads.
They're staring at the loudspeakers; the speakers are switched on, but
emit only static. Our contact with the outside world has been broken
for the last few hours. Captain Francis has given me his camp bed,
but I can't sleep. No one in Kibeho can, judging by the sounds
coming from the other side of the wall: a continuous moaning,
coughing and weeping, which is sometimes punctuated by shooting
as Hutus who have tried to escape under the cover of darkness are
captured and executed.

At three o'clock it starts raining. Until it becomes light, the only
sound I hear is the deafening pelting on the corrugated iron roof.

When I walk outside through the school gates at sunrise, the
refugees are standing there just as they were yesterday, shoulder to
shoulder, but now drenched as well. The siege of Kibeho has been
going on for seventy-six hours.

'Do you know if any reinforcements are coming today?' a
Zambian soldier asks me.

'You'd think so. It's about time they intervened.'

'Who?' the Zambian asks. A good question: who?

A little boy has wriggled his way towards us through the crowd
and stands at the wire, crying to break your heart. He must be
about five.

'What's wrong, child?' asks the Zambian on guard across from
him.

Papa et maman tombés, the child says. He raises his arm and
lets it drop again: dead. Then he rolls up a torn trouser leg and looks
at us expectantly. His leg is pink and flayed to the bone. It looks like
a peeled banana, with the peel dangling down around his ankle.

'If no one does anything about that, he'll die,' another Zambian says. He reaches resolutely across the wire and lifts the little guy into the parking lot.

'What now?' I ask.

'I don't know. Put a bandage on it and hope it'll heal?'

Other children have seen the Zambian's act of rescue and stretch out their arms imploringly, waiting to be lifted up too. Most of them have wounds they're trying to show us. Some of them are worse than the banana leg. One child points to a large hole in its skull, another one has a bone sticking out of its shin. There are about ten of them. We lift them all over the wire. More children push their way to the front. The ten in the parking lot become twenty, pressing themselves against the blue helmets. We look at their lips, cracked and white with dehydration, but smiling happily: now that they're with us, they think they've escaped death.

'What are we going to do with them?' I ask a Zambian.

'Put them on top of the sandbags? Maybe their parents will recognize them and come to pick them up.'

I don't think so: right now parents are pushing their children towards us, under the wire. Forty children become a hundred. They're squatting on top of and around the bags of sand, dehydrated infants sitting on the laps of wounded toddlers, all of them too filthy to touch. For days their excrement has been running down their legs; judging from the dried remains, they all have diarrhoea. There's hardly a drop of water left in Kibeho, and certainly not enough for bathing sick children.

'There'll be a thousand of them before long,' one Zambian says. 'They need food.'

'Water's more important.'

We can't offer them either.

'We should only allow badly wounded or seriously ill children to enter,' I suggest. A bad idea that's adopted immediately by the Zambians, to my own dismay. Responsibility for new policy is in the hands of the one who thought it up, I find out: every time a child asks to be taken in, the Zambians turn to me hopefully and enquire whether this one is in bad enough shape. Not only do they ask my opinion, the Zambians act on it as well: I get to decide who stays and who's set back across the wire with no chance of appeal. The parents pushing their children towards us disappear into the crowd before we can hand them back.

All in shock, some bleeding, others trembling with fever, the children are sitting in rows along the wall of the school building. Captain Francis frowns.

'There are so many of them,' he says. One hundred and twenty is my guess.

'I don't know how it happened. I sent back a lot, too,' I tell him guiltily.

'I ran into government soldiers over there,' Francis says. 'They stopped me and accused me of setting up a refugee camp for children. I told them not to exaggerate, that we were only babysitting for a few of them until we'd found their parents. Now I see what they mean. I'll have to explain it to the Tutsis before they come and clean up here, too.'

But the problem solves itself before Francis gets back. When gunfire breaks out nearby, the children are gone in a flash, experienced veterans of war even at their age. Later they try to get back in again, one by one, but by then I've come up with new, stricter rules for admission.

This chubby little boy, for example, can't stay: he's managed to crawl under the wire and is tugging at my trouser leg, pleading: 'I'm all alone! No papa, no mama, nobody.'

His fat little legs are sticking out of muddy Bermuda shorts. With his Nikes and the baseball cap turned around on his healthy round head, he could almost be a tourist. He must be at least ten; by my new rules, that's old enough to survive on your own.

'I don't see any blood, and you're well-fed,' I tell him, pinching a roll of fat under his T-shirt. I pry his hands off my leg and tell him to get out.

The latrines in the valley have been trampled. People have been defecating on top of each other and each other's possessions for days. When a fight breaks out, machetes are drawn excitedly from among the piles on the ground. And used: the first children with cuts are reporting to ZamBat. A few refugees attack the enemy with sticks and rocks. The government soldiers retaliate by emptying their gun-clips into one of them. Francis is out pleading for lives, at least when the executions take place within walking distance.

According to him, the Rwandan troops are nearly as desperate as the refugees. They come to him begging for food and water. He's given orders to send them away empty-handed; he can't bring himself to help them, though like the refugees they have been standing in the burning sun for days, and at night they get soaked with rain.

Francis says: 'Every shower washes the shit from the plateau over their boots. They're scared of getting cholera, and starting to realize that they may not get out of it alive either, not if this goes on much longer. There's only a thousand of them against a hundred and fifty thousand of their enemies, desperate with hunger and thirst. Refugees who have nothing to lose will attack their rivals whether they're armed or not.'

At dinner, rice without chicken, Captain Francis squeezes the last drops from the pack of South African red wine. Near us, on the other side of the wall, a shot rings out. Innocent jumps and knocks over his glass.

'So sorry,' Francis says commiseratingly. Innocent stares at the red stain spreading across the tablecloth.

'To the problem outside. May God save them,' he says.

At midnight I tiptoe over to the Zambian guards standing under the soft yellow spotlights along the wire. The Zambians ask me to roll cigarettes for them. Their smoking rations have been delayed at the roadblock as well. We whisper to keep from waking anyone. The refugees have made a little more room for themselves. Some are actually lying down, sleeping.

'It's great they can lie down, isn't it?' I say in an emotional whisper as I light the Zambians' cigarettes. The soldiers nod and look around, pleased.

'They were so tired...' one of them says.

'Exhausted,' his friend says.

'At least they can get a bit of rest before it starts again,' I say.

'It won't start again. I feel it in my bones. Tomorrow we'll see a convoy of trucks coming over the hill to pick them up and take them home.'

We're silent, smoking and thinking about trucks. We watch as someone turns over under his tarpaulin and falls back asleep. Someone else is snoring, and further along we hear humming: a Rwandan lullaby, one of the Zambians thinks. Tarpaulins rustle. Someone clears his throat and goes into a coughing fit. A baby wakes up crying.

At two o'clock the nightly downpour begins, and the crowd rises. The shooting starts again too. But by then I'm lying on my cot, eyes shut tight.

At six in the morning, I hear Francis calling for the children to be rounded up. He's heard that the Rwandan troops intend to drive the refugees off the plateau today. The children in our camp will have to go with them.

About fifty foundlings were allowed to take shelter in one of the dormitories last night. When they realize that we're planning to send them out again, they start fighting like wild cats. A few try to hide under the bunks, others clutch the bedposts so tightly that we have difficulty prying their little hands loose. But we're unrelenting. If they refuse to walk, we carry them out of the gates.

The siege of Kibeho has been going on for one hundred hours. We're heading into the fifth day. You can barely tell the people from the household goods they're dragging. Unrecognizable heaps, uniformly muddy. The crowd passes the Zambian post, shuffling elbow-to-elbow, all heading for the 'exit', a narrow mountain trail leading past the parking lot to another plateau. There's room there for trucks to park and take on refugees. A couple of UN trucks are on their way, enough to transport maybe 200 or 300 people, but it isn't clear whether they'll make it to Kibeho. The nightly rains have made the roads almost impassable, so progress is slow. But the Tutsi soldiers are obviously counting on a miracle; they're driving prisoners to the next plateau as if a thousand trucks were on their way. The refugees take each step reluctantly: death could be waiting for them at the end of this slow journey.

Climbing up on to the sandbags, we see that the whole plateau has started to move. The exodus will file past our school, where things are already backing up along the barbed wire as people stop to plead one last time. The ones at the back are pushing, causing huge pile-ups of falling people at the front. Some of them have thrown down their pots and mattresses and are struggling against the flow to rescue trampled friends and relatives.

'Move along!' the blue helmets shout to them from atop the sandbags. 'Stay calm! Don't panic! Everything will be all right if you just keep moving!'

'The Tutsis are going to kill us,' a woman cries, drawing one hand across her throat like a knife.

At the other side of the plateau I can see government soldiers trying to get people to move in our direction by beating them and firing shots in the air. A wave of people starts to roll towards us. The people at our feet can't see what's happening. They're still lying on the ground in a tangle, screaming. The wave is coming in. Then the barrier collapses with a bang and the human wave comes tumbling into the parking lot. The barbed wire disappears under the people, people disappear under people. People are pulling on me, almost pulling me down. Zambian soldiers pull me loose and drag me along. Before we can throw our weight against the gates to close them, about forty Hutus have wormed their way inside. People are screaming and banging on the gates to be let in. The tide of human beings is breaking against the school. The ones in front are squashed against the walls by the tens of thousands behind them. People are jumping up against the gates, fighting their way over the top and letting themselves fall on top of us. Blue helmets are trying to push back as many as they can.

'Here, take this,' a Zambian calls out as he balances one foot on the gate and the other on the roof. He's holding a baby by one arm. Its eyes have rolled up in its head.

'Come on, take it!' Above me, another baby is dangling from a soldier's hand. The people outside are trying to rescue their children by throwing them over the gates to us. 'Take it, take it,' the blue helmet shouts in desperation.

I grab one baby after another, some screaming, some

unconscious, others already dead. The Zambian soldiers, holding on to the top of the gate with one hand so they won't fall, catch the children and swing them over to us in one easy movement. When there are too many children to walk without stepping on them, we start carrying them off to one of the dormitories, running back and forth with our arms full. The children are shrieking, vomiting and writhing. One of them seems to have been crushed to death, another one has had the wind knocked out of him. Still another is banging her head hysterically against the stone wall. Meanwhile, the sheet iron roof is about to collapse under the weight of the people who've climbed up on it.

When I come back outside I suddenly see the chubby face of the little fellow in the Bermuda shorts, coming over the top of the gates.

'*Madame!*' he yells to me, but the ZamBat soldiers rap him on the knuckles with a stick and he falls into the screaming crowd below.

Six hours later, all is quiet outside the gates. The government troops panicked in the chaos and bombarded the crowd with mortar shells and grenades for hours. All we can do is drag away the corpses.

The parking lot has disappeared beneath a layer of bodies, some still crying or moaning. Among the motionless piles of people near the wall I recognize the faces of a few of the children I dragged out of the dormitory into the parking lot.

A few of our former boarders are still alive. One of them is lying among the busted sandbags, strangely twisted. I recognize the worn black jacket, much too large for his thin little body. His eyes are turned up in his head, but I can hear him moaning through cracked lips.

'It's not very comfortable like that, is it?' A Zambian soldier kneels down beside the child. He straightens the small body gently; first the head, then the upper body. It looks like the boy's legs are broken. The Zambian lays them across the body of another child: the only thing he can do with the space available.

'There, that's better, isn't it?' the blue helmet says optimistically, using his sleeve to wipe the mud off the boy's forehead. A rivulet of blood is flowing from the corner of the child's mouth to his ear. 'You take it easy for a while, child. A doctor is bound to be coming soon.'

The Zambian gets up. 'I know this one. He's been hanging

around at the barrier for days, trying to learn a little English from us. A good kid. I've got two myself, the same age.' Tears are running down his cheeks.

When they were standing there, dying of thirst, we couldn't help them. Now that they're lying here, mortally injured, we can't help them either. The blue helmets are lifting dead bodies from among the wounded and laying them along the wall of the officers' mess. They line them up neatly; that's all they can do. Other blue helmets are kneeling beside the wounded, holding their hands, patting them consolingly. Where am I going to start? And with what?

Clumsily, I pat the cheek of someone half buried beneath a soaked, filthy mattress. 'Hello?' I call out. And again.

She's dead, I think. What now?

The little body next to her looks dead as well. I can't even tell whether it's a boy or a girl, that's how deeply it's been trampled into the mud. Its mouth is open. I see the lips move slightly. It's alive.

What now?

The next one is alive too. So are the next three. Then two dead. Then a twisted mass; I can't make out where one set of limbs stops and the other begins. I don't even try. Dead or alive, piled up or not, I can't do anything for them. I'm only making things worse by pulling on broken arms or lifting people with collapsed lungs.

Here's another one who's still alive, but I pretend not to see him: I don't want to go over to him, even if it's only to say that a doctor's bound to be coming soon. His lower jaw has been hacked off, and I don't want to see the remaining pulp up close.

For some reason, the scalped head of the man next to the cut-off jaw doesn't bother me as much.

'What are you supposed to do in a case like this?' asks a blue helmet, studying the open skull at close range.

'I don't know. Make sure he stays upright so his brains don't fall out, I guess.' That sounds like a good idea to both of us, so we prop the wounded man upright. He falls over whenever we let go of him, until we get him balanced against the corpse behind him. He's listing a little, but he's sitting, dazed but upright. The blue helmet and I look on in satisfaction.

'We should really cover it with a bandage, otherwise it'll get dirty,' the blue helmet says.

'Isn't there a first-aid kit somewhere?'

'I've already looked in it. There's nothing but a strip of aspirin left.'

There are so many of them already, and the Zambians keep bringing in more of the seriously wounded. They drag them hurriedly into the parking lot by their wrists, lay them across the bodies that are already there. The peacekeepers arrange them in neat rows, just like the corpses, then go back to pick up more. It looks like they've discovered another slaughterhouse somewhere in the crowd.

A few Rwandan troops are standing on a garbage heap near the officers' mess, surveying the corpses. One points at the neat rows and chuckles. Another noses interestedly in a basket he's found among the corpses. Some have their guns slung around their necks, resting their wrists casually on the stocks. I'm witnessing the ultimate abuse of the UN's non-intervention policy: they're the boss around here.

The metal gates fly open with a bang. Bent over, shoulders hunched up around their ears, seven white men in flapping white coats come running in. They're carrying big cardboard boxes. For a split second there, I thought they were angels. Until I noticed the Doctors Without Borders logos on their jackets.

'Bring in the wounded,' one of them calls out. The first boxes are torn open. Rolls of gauze are taken out.

'Help has arrived,' I hear myself shouting. 'Welcome!' A blue helmet and I shake hands on the arrival of the outside world, the sane world.

'We can only stay till four,' one of the doctors says to temper our enthusiasm. He's cutting strips of adhesive bandage with a little pair of scissors from one of the boxes.

I was on my way out to pull more wounded from among the dead, but now I freeze. 'What do you mean, four o'clock?' I ask.

'Orders from HQ,' the doctor replies. 'We have to be home before dark. It's too dangerous here.'

It's a quarter past three.

There's no time to argue. The Zambians are already dragging victims over from the parking lot. They lay the man without a jaw at the doctors' feet as well. A woman lies panting on the ground, and an infant with a machete wound across its cheek is waiting for treatment too. I can see its milk teeth sticking through the flesh.

I walk outside to the first blood-soaked bundle of rags I see and pull it to its feet. Time is running out. 'Come on, get up, the doctor's here,' I growl at him impatiently. He moans and cries out when I pull at him, but finally succeeds in getting up and together we stumble through the gates. Trying to catch a lift, another wounded man has grabbed my leg. I shake him off. He's too heavy.

The Zambian soldiers are dragging more and more victims inside. I run out and grab another one, too, but have to give it up: he's no longer able to stand, and I'm no longer able to lift. I go back to help the doctors in the yard.

The first patients are already sitting against the wall of the officers' mess, stitched and bandaged, neatly in a row. They eye their bandages gratefully, and I feel happy. Around me the doctors are kneeling beside their patients, working quickly. I hold up adhesive bandages, cut sutures and prop up arms and legs for bandaging.

'Four o'clock. We're out of here,' someone shouts, and the work is literally dropped: rolls and rolls of bandages are falling all over the courtyard, trampled on by the Zambians coming in with more wounded in their arms. The jawless man, sitting upright, is leaning forward a little. Someone has placed an orange bucket in front of him, into which he's throwing up blood and little pieces of flesh. No bandage to be seen: the doctors haven't got to him yet. Nor to all the other wounded people still on the ground. I'm holding someone's leg in my hands, stunned.

'But what about all these other people? You told us yourself to drag them in here. There are still stacks of them outside,' a blue helmet says in astonishment.

'We have to go. Sorry.'

'And we have a few hundred sick children in that dormitory over there.'

'We saw them. We can't help them.'

'Hurry up,' someone says.

'Sorry. But we'll leave these boxes for you. Good luck.'

The doctors disappear through the gates. From outside comes the sound of rifle fire. The doctors come rushing in again, all hunched up.

'Welcome back,' I say.

'I heard that sarcasm,' one doctor says. 'But a dead medic's no good to you either.'

Several of the doctors take advantage of the delay to treat a few more wounded people. One of them, a man who reminds me of the young Alain Delon, is squatting against the wall, chewing ferociously on a wad of gum and staring into space. I'm bent over an unconscious woman. For some reason I seem to think it's a good idea to pour water between her slack lips. Alain Delon looks up.

'Lay her on her side. She'll choke like that,' he advises me, then goes on chewing.

The shooting outside stops. 'OK, let's go!' I hear, and the doctors run out again.

A mortar-shell explodes. The doctors come running back.

'We can go now!' someone else shouts almost right away.

'Where do they think they're going?' Captain Francis has just arrived.

'Home. They have to be home before dark,' I tell him.

We watch as the doctors run around the bodies, dashing for their Land-Rover. Then we see them stop, bend down and straighten up again with something they've found among the bodies: live babies! The deeper they dig, the more they find; they walk towards us with their arms full.

'Here. Babies. We found them,' a doctor says.

'Are you prepared to do anything for these babies?' Francis asks.

'We have to go, we're late already,' the doctor replies.

'In that case, put them back where you found them. We already have four hundred children we can't help.'

The doctor nods, dumbfounded. Then he and his colleagues lay the babies gently at our feet.

After the Land-Rover has disappeared into the human chaos, Francis bends down to pick up the dumped infants. He gestures to me to do the same. We carry them into the stifling heat of the dormitory.

Linda Polman

Hundreds of children. Motionless or vomiting. A few are trying to crawl, their little legs stained with blood and diarrhoea. Francis puts the babies among all the others, in a little open space. He comes out again with two dead children.

The doctors have left a mess of blood-soaked bandages, torn sterile wrappers and untreated patients behind in the courtyard. The patients have been defecating, vomiting and bleeding. The ones against the wall, who've already been treated, refuse to go outside again. We don't have the heart to throw the others out. The boxes the doctors left behind come in handy. The Zambian soldiers pass out the surgical gloves they found in one of them, and the Zambian medic, visibly pleased, discovers some bags of intravenous fluid. He hangs them on the window sills right away and puts a few unconscious people on the drip.

I start rushing around with half-litre bottles of iodine and big rolls of gauze: that way, the wounded will at least have the illusion of the medical treatment we promised. At the first gaping wound I see, I become hysterical. Sobbing with laughter, I bend over heads shot to pieces and half-torn limbs. I can think of only one way to treat them: dousing wounds with iodine, even the scalped heads, then covering them with bandages. I've never taken a first-aid course. To my amazement, the patients seem grateful, and the Zambians ask hopefully if maybe I could help some of the wounded outside too. Giggling foolishly, I go outside and do it, until—finally—all the iodine and bandages are finished.

The killing goes on through the night. The rain does too. When I get up, I don't really know whether I've slept or not.

The glowing sun comes up over the mountains. Outside, nothing's moving. In the silence I can hear a bird singing on the roof of the school. I settle down on a sandbag, and by the time I notice it's soaked with rain I don't care any more. I take my time rolling my first cigarette of the day, inhale deeply and enjoy the warbling. A Zambian walks by, raking the ground. He wishes me a good morning.

'And a very good morning to you,' I say. 'Get any sleep?' Only when I look where he's been raking do I realize that the Zambians must have worked all night long. The dead and wounded who were lying here yesterday, all those pots, pans, mattresses and God-knows-what that were scattered in the mud, are gone now. Amazing. Maybe it was all a dream.

For the first time since my arrival in Kibeho, I can see the other Zambian camp, on the far side of the plateau. Then I realize that the refugees are still there, it's just that none of them are standing up. The Hutus and their possessions have merged into one hideous, soaked rubbish dump, reaching to the end of the world.

We peer down the road littered with dead bodies, looking for reinforcements on the horizon. There are none. The road to Kibeho is kept closed until well into the afternoon. The reason is obvious: Rwandan troops are busy dragging away all bodies that can be seen from the road. It's hard to say how many corpses are thrown into cesspits in the valleys, or how many have disappeared in mass graves hurriedly dug by hand. However many there are, by the time the Red Cross, the UN supreme command and the president of Rwanda arrive at Kibeho by car, only the trampled possessions of the victims are left.

In the parking lot, the Rwandan president, Pasteur Bizimungu, asks Captain Francis for his estimate of the casualties. Francis cautiously puts it at 4,000. The president is not pleased.

'I think you're exaggerating,' he says coolly. He'd rather stick to the 300 his soldiers reported to him.

I discover I'm out of tobacco. I go to the washroom, collect my toothbrush and climb into a UN vehicle bound for Kigali.

The next day, after a flight from Kigali to Brussels, I'm home again in Amsterdam. I buy a paper, *De Volkskrant*, and read about the place I've just left.

REFUGEES LEFT TO ROT

Butare, April 26, 1995—The international organization Doctors Without Borders, along with the British Oxfam, has filed a complaint about the United Nations' performance in Kibeho. Although the tragedy had been in the making for days, there were only 250 UN soldiers present at Kibeho during last weekend's events. There are a total of 6,000 UN peacekeepers in Rwanda.

'They could have brought in reinforcements,' said chairman Jacques de Milliano. 'They failed to protect the refugees, and did nothing to facilitate relief operations. [...] Like last year, the UN has once again bent to the will of local authorities, and failed the population they were supposed to protect,' De Milliano said.

Later I hear that the UN succeeded in smuggling Captain Francis out of Rwanda alive. People said he was trying to give the country a bad name with his estimate of 4,000 casualties: there had been threats to his life. □

ON OBSERVATION HILL

Francis Spufford

Here I stand on Observation Hill. If the Devil made me an offer at this moment, I feel sure I would accept. The kingdom of ice and snow is spread at my feet. From Observation Hill, on 25 February 1998, I look down on McMurdo Sound, a wide fjord plated over with white; and on the shore, McMurdo Base, the largest scientific station in the Antarctic. Its labs, its dorms, its industrial landscape of gasoline storage tanks and warehousing, all fill a hollow in the tip of Hut Point Peninsular on Ross Island. When we landed this morning, the three-dimensional glory of this scene was folded neatly flat, a lateral panorama. Sunrise behind Ross Island had lit the horizon to the west in pinks and golds but the near slopes of the land were still in deep blue shadow, chill as a wine cellar where the sun has never reached. Our Russian tour ship was moored off McMurdo's ice pier, in a black lane of open water trembling between liquid and solid. The rubber boats ferrying us to shore picked up a glassy crust at the waterline, and left a slow, oily rocking where they passed. American guides met us, and led us up through McMurdo to the road that goes to the airstrip: the only road in Antarctica, and therefore inevitably known as Antarctic One. When Antarctic One crossed the saddle in the ring of hills around McMurdo, we struck off to the side, up the volcanic cone of Ob Hill. The last 300–400 feet were a hard-breathing scramble up a seam of dark clinker that forms a ridge in the snow. Then suddenly we were in sunlight. But not sunlight in the usual sense, seen from within the swathing greens and living haze of the biosphere it fuels so generously. The sun rising here has a hard white glitter, like a welding torch. Clearly, it was a bright star, close by. Here, I thought, you don't need to read about the ozone hole overhead, or to see satellite photographs of the solar wind bombarding the poles, to know that some of the filters in the sky have been withdrawn. Your body feels it, distinctly. There are fewer veils between you and what lies beyond. You get a glimpse into the furnace.

And now McMurdo is a strew of coloured cubes and cuboids down below, linked by dirt roads along which toy pick-ups crawl, scattered with radar that register at first glance as Orthodox onion domes. Officially, McMurdo exists for research and logistics. The United States' National Science Foundation runs it, and hires the skills of the drivers and cargo handlers who keep it running from Antarctic Support Associates, a contracting company. Hercules supply aircraft thunder down from New Zealand, bringing ice and ozone specialists and fuel and stores for distribution to fifty field camps. All very utilitarian: yet somewhere along the line McMurdo reached critical mass with all that activity, and gained the kind of identity that sustains itself. The inhabitants call it Mac Town, and even in the last week of February, with the summer contingent of more than a thousand people flown away, and a skeleton crew of 160 battening down for the coming winter—muffling empty buildings, draining fluids from the overhead supply lines—the streets still have a little urban bustle.

History has a place down there too. I can pick out the hut that gave the area its name. The low brown building on the far side of the harbour, ringed with veranda like an outback farm, was the only architecture on this part of the continent when Captain Scott's first expedition put it up in 1901. That was the beginning of the 'heroic age' in Antarctica, when expeditions from Britain and Australia and Norway began to strike inward from the coasts. Now the hut is bevelled into this strangely urban landscape, and lumps of concrete block the access road to its door in case a forgetful driver should run tyres over the historic site. Present and past, the things humans do are assertive here.

The further out I gaze, the more my body feels purely given over to seeing. From Ob Hill—a mere 700 feet tall—I see clear to Erebus, the great live volcano presiding over the southern closure of the Ross Sea, trailing its permanent banner of steam. I see the jagged peaks of the Trans-Antarctic Mountains, continuous as the teeth of a comb, marching away south towards the polar plateau on the far side of sixty-odd miles of frozen sea. I see the beginning of the Ross Ice Shelf, blindingly blank, and the shadowed areas around the shores of the island where the ice has buckled and split under pressure. What the land begins, the sky completes. It feels as though the pinnacle of the hill has lifted me to the centre of a globe, white in its lower hemisphere, blue above. There are places—all north of here—that happiness or trouble have filled with more significance than an Antarctic hilltop could ever have for me. These are the substantial scenes of my life, and they are not spectacular; but I never wanted to be anywhere, in any place, so much as I have wanted to be here, standing beside the jarrah wood cross to the memory of Captain Scott and the other British explorers who died on his second expedition in the heroic era's defining catastrophe; the cross erected by the survivors in this flood-tide of light and air, where it testifies to the promise and the penalties of desiring the spaces it overlooks. I spent six years in well-heated libraries studying the tradition of British fascination with the poles through the words it generated. Now here I am in the place itself. The wind bites, reducing the temperature to an effective minus fourteen centigrade. My nose runs helplessly. I'm flicking crumbs of frozen snot from my moustache.

The hilltop is narrow. We cluster around the cross, careful of the precipices to the side. IN MEMORIAM, says the nine-foot upright, in leaded letters like the rough work of a country undertaker. They've lasted through nine decades, and storms that have toppled the cross itself twice. CAPT R F SCOTT R.N. DR E A WILSON. CAPT L E G OATES INS.DRGS. LT H R BOWERS R.I.M. PETTY OFFICER E EVANS R.N. WHO DIED ON THE RETURN FROM THE POLE MARCH 1912. TO STRIVE, TO SEEK, TO FIND AND NOT TO YIELD.

When Robert Scott sailed here in early 1911, leaving behind a baby son named after Peter Pan, he fully expected to leave the first human footprints at the South Pole—to return in triumph, the Neil Armstrong of Edwardian Britain. He had reconnoitred the ground on his earlier expedition; he was the expert. He had the moral right to the pole, at least in his own mind, and also a kind of national right based on the idea that exploration was part of the British genius. Culturally, practically, geographically, in January 1911 he thought he saw his way clear before him. Roald Amundsen arrived suddenly in the Ross Sea in February. The genuine expertise of the small Norwegian team cruelly exposed the shortcomings of Scott's mixed bag of scientists, sailors and gentleman volunteers. Amundsen drove stripped-down Inuit dog sledges. Scott had never mastered that art, with its delicate combination of dependence and ruthlessness. He'd brought along a bit of this and a bit of that by way of transport, but where it really mattered he preferred the headbanging certainty of pulling the sledge himself, which was the way the Royal Navy had always travelled in the Arctic. It was a lethal preference, this time. Of the five Englishmen who eventually stood at the pole, looking at the month old Norwegian flag planted there, none survived. Edgar Evans died first, probably of a brain haemorrhage. Oates tottered suicidally away into a blizzard, so that his gangrenous leg should not hold up his desperate companions. The others died in their tent eleven miles from a supply depot, of some combination of hunger, cold, exhaustion and scurvy. Unable to survive himself, Scott instead used pencil on paper to create an image of the expedition that could. He gave the deaths a majestic cadence. He wrote funeral music in words for the five of them, as if a vast sombre orchestra were playing them off the stage.

No one is buried on Ob Hill. Evans and Oates were never found. The search party who discovered the bodies of Scott, Wilson and Bowers built a snow cairn over them where they lay, and they sank down into the slowly flowing ice of the Ross Ice Shelf, every year a little thicker with accumulated snow. If their pocket of canvas stayed intact in the moving ice, their bodies may have travelled whole and deep-frozen all the way to the sea. By one calculation, they would have floated free in about 1980: around the time of Ronald Reagan's first inauguration, three black bundles bobbing for a moment in a slush of ice fragments. Or, they may have been crushed to what Thomas Hardy called 'human jam'.

I have a strong mental image of each of these dead men. I can picture them; I know things about them that they didn't know about each other. I have the one-sided intimacy with them gained by reading their story and, because I read and studied that story alone, I'm touched by the illusion common to every individual in the crowd of witnesses surrounding public heroism, that a connection exists between them and me singly. I've also gone a step further and recreated them in a story I told, so that I put my living hand inside the glove of facts known about them and made it move. Seeing their memorial now, I'm filled with a confused intention towards them. I'm elated, pitying, exasperated, moved, humbled. I wish something to them, to these five literal long-dead men rather than to the mobile, tenacious images that have endured in British culture, leading the purely metaphoric existence of myth. But, as a theologian of Edwardian England asked, what do we pray for when we pray for the dead? That they may have peace: there's nothing else to ask. 'May light perpetual shine upon them,' says the Anglican burial service. Well, *lux perpetua* does shine on their monument, at least in Antarctic summer—this world's light in the form that dazzles most and holds least heat, the light we might imagine belonging to an immaterial world. In the nineteenth century commentators constantly linked polar whiteness with celestial whiteness, connected the frozen sea with the glassy sea where the saints lay down their crowns. For the first time, I really see why. For the first time I begin to have some understanding of the explorers' own sense that heaven was close; that, ringed by this horizon, you stand near heaven's door.

British cross, American town. I have a Cuban celebration planned for this moment. Sheltering a match in the lee of someone else's parka, I take unpractised puffs on a Montecristo, and as I add my small curls of blue smoke to the amazing blue above, I begin to think about this aerial perspective on the Antarctic. Sight and stories coincide. So many things began here. The first leg of Scott's journey to the pole ran southward from Hut Point across the dazzling ice to the hidden gap between White Island and Minna Bluff. His unwieldy caravan of motor sledges, ponies, dogs and foot sloggers dwindled into the distance, just down there. Over to the east I see Windless Bight, the ice-filled, crevasse-cracked bay of Ross Island where in the winter dark of June 1911 three travellers crossed, using the enforced pause before the polar attempt to fit in a side journey in search of emperor penguin eggs: Edward Wilson and Henry Bowers, remembered on the cross for their deaths the next year, and a young man named Apsley Cherry-Garrard, who as well as choosing the inscription on the wood memorialized his friends in *The Worst Journey in the World*, the greatest book of Antarctic travel ever written. Right there's the ground they covered, dragging several times their weight in supplies, sometimes lighting their way in the crystalline stillness, when the moon was down, by holding up a candle.

But the cross stands upon a brink of time as well. We visit it as the century closes. Half the affiliations on the cross refer to dead things: Bowers's Royal Indian Marine has gone the way of the Raj whose navy it was, Oates's Inniskilling Dragoons vanished with British Ireland. The landscape of power has been creased, folded and shaken. The great powers have changed and changed again. Perhaps Scott's expedition is not so far away if we count years by the human body's clock. It is not yet out of reach of the human lifespan—my living grandmother was born before this monument was built—nor quite out of reach of the linkages of personal knowledge. At this moment I am sharing the hilltop with a retired professor who in the 1940s used to stand watch against incendiary bombs on Cambridge University's rooftops with one of the Scott expedition's scientific veterans. But the cross surveys the twentieth century from the far side of a gulf. It represents a moment, virtually the last possible moment, before the process began that dragged the century we recognize into being: our twentieth century, which was not the one Scott's men expected, with its horrors and its liberations that were both in their way unpinnings of the rules the Edwardians worked by. The explorers' time was no more innocent than any other. It had events that covered the whole moral spectrum. The Inniskilling Dragoon and the marine lieutenant were part of the enforcement apparatus of a white-supremacist empire. Oates's regiment, stationed near Alexandria a few years before, had hanged an Egyptian villager for killing a British soldier, and issued picture postcards of the execution. Yet the Shoah and the Gulag were still unimagined. If history were visible, you would be able to see them from Observation Hill as livid presences on the horizon; and much closer, the precipice at the cross's foot, there'd be the war that loosed fascism and Bolshevism on the world, and set up a turbulence that didn't die down till 1989, as well as winning votes for women in Britain and freeing millions from deference; that took the rigidity of the Edwardian order of things off to the breaker's yard, and began to pound on it. A year after the survivors returned to England, most of them were in uniform. For Cherry-Garrard the First World War was one trauma on top of another. It bled back into his memoir of the expedition, becoming an inescapable point of reference and a yardstick of suffering. When he wanted to convey how bad the winter journey had been, he told a story from the botched landing at the Dardanelles. A British officer was blinded in no man's land and crawled back and forth between the Allied and the Turkish trenches, shot at by both sides, all sense of direction gone, until after two days he cried out, 'Oh God, will nobody help me?' and was finally rescued. It was as if Cherry-Garrard could scarcely remember the expedition without the war coming in, whether as a parallel or as a terminus or as the greatest of all possible contrasts.

Scott's leadership in the Antarctic followed a pattern more than a century old. So, I wrote in my Antarctic history about the particular rigidity that afflicted the British in the polar regions (with a few honourable exceptions) as the result of a long tradition that privileged moral force over practical competence. Better to break than bend, might have been the tradition's motto. It celebrated a brittle kind of integrity. And of course I wasn't immune. It still tugged at me while I analysed it, still had the power to move me. Now suddenly, cigar in mouth, I'm struck by the resemblance between the cross on Ob Hill and the thousands of crosses, statues and obelisks that were built in every British village and city soon after, also inscribed with dead men's names. And I wonder if the stubbornly unadaptable behaviour in the Antarctic, about which I am emotionally ambivalent, is anything more than a miniature rehearsal of the tactics of the trenches, about which I'm not. Defiance of the environment is something they could be said to have in common. Scott sent his expedition walking straight into the ice, underequipped, underprepared, and underfed. Field Marshall Haig sent hundreds of thousands of soldiers walking straight towards machine-guns. Better to break than bend. The difference is that Scott's strategy killed Scott. He was not a staff officer tucked away in a chateau behind the lines. But is that enough of a difference? If the two things really were the same phenomenon at different scales, the expedition just a foretaste of the Somme, I should ignore the landscape. I shouldn't let the sublime immensity I'm seeing now influence my reading of the explorers' behaviour in it. The military caste of Edwardian Britain, which three out of five of the dead men belonged to, cultivated mildness as a style: self-effacement, understatement, the unraised voice. It was a remarkable manner for an officer class to choose, and in the snow, facing environmental adversity, it looked very like gentleness. But perhaps I should be seeing it as a fatalism so profound it became a kind of violence, a spiteful refusal to look out for themselves. Many of the disastrous decisions of Scott's last expedition achieved their full destructive effect because of a kind of complicity among the participants—almost an agreement to make the worst of things. Scott should never have decided at the last moment to take five men along on the final stretch to the pole, when he had supplies for four and a four-man tent. The person he should have sent back was Oates, who didn't want to go on to the pole anyway. But, since Scott wanted him there as a representative of the army, Oates didn't feel able to volunteer the information that the scar tissue in his old Boer War wound was already dissolving, thanks to the vitamin-free diet. Therefore Scott set out to do one of the most punishing foot journeys on the planet with a team member who was concealing an open hip wound. Absurd. I began my work on the Scott expedition with a pleasure in gestures of defiance that has eroded over time, as I grew older and more acquainted with their miserable consequences; this new thought I am having now crumbles another section of my original romance with the explorers.

And yet as I gaze from Observation Hill I find myself admiring them more, not less. It is impossible to ignore the landscape. This is not the Western Front. What happened here was particular, an encounter with a particular environment that brought particular qualities in the hybrid knot called 'Englishness' to the fore, and often did so, I realize now with force, in silence. Neither Englishness nor the spirit of a place are things that are easy to define. The traditional strategy is to coax a sense of them into existence obliquely. That's what I did writing about the British at the poles: built a cage of words and hoped that the living bird would appear inside it. Guile, indirectness, but always within the medium of language. An account led by words is appropriate in a way to British exploration, because one of the weaknesses of the tradition was that it was very literary exploration, almost willing to give higher priority to eloquent descriptions of journeys than to the journeys themselves. And by being more enthusiastic about the human spirit and what it could do than about human hands and what they could contrive, it slanted naturally towards language, which is the spirit's tool kit. But I now see I was missing a good half of the encounter. I missed all this silent space around me; I missed the bodily reality of all the actions done in it. My respect grows for the rhetorically minded crew who nevertheless existed moment by moment in Antarctica, leading the life of the body, out there below me. That part of the experience is irrecoverable—as is almost the whole achievement of their unrhetorical rival Roald Amundsen, because like the grace of a great athlete it is better seen than described; it is living in the world done superlatively well.

What I see from Ob Hill is literally indescribable. The forms of the mountains, the forms of the ice defy translation into the linear forms of grammar. A mountain is not a sentence any more than it is a triangle. The modern ecological movement has built an explicit philosophy on respect for the world as it is in itself, apart from our understandings of it, and an aesthetic too; but reverence for place is a much older urge, the integrity of rock and water have been felt for much longer. I was struck, reading James Gleick's *Chaos* on the ship coming here, by the frequency with which the Romantic poets came up as forerunners of his new mathematics of natural forms, their painstaking observations of the world's foliate richness, and endlessly varied flow, anticipating in inevitably failing words the new science's determination to trace the actual shapes in which nature is organized. Captain Scott was an heir of the Romantic project (and General Haig was not). The colours and textures of Antarctica touched him like a message whose meaning is never quite clear. I remember—perched at a height that smooths out the surface down below, and makes day-long traverses across the ice into vistas to be grasped in one greedy glance—that the stupid practice of Scott's men hauling their sledges had a consequence other than exhaustion and snail-speed progress. It imposed attention to each square foot of snow. In a mode of frustration and constant physical effort, it forced them to be aware of the exact properties of the crystals underfoot, powdery or crusted, sandy or sticky. On the Ice Shelf—the 'Great Ice Barrier' to them— a footfall would sometimes force open an air pocket under the surface, and the snow would give a faint sound like an animal's cry. It was a discipline. They learned the land minutely.

They grew more intensely present in it. Dr Edward Wilson, the expedition's surgeon and chief biologist, wrote a poem of rapture:

Francis Spufford

'We might be the men who were meant to know/The secrets of the barrier snow...' That knowledge—in the skin and in the bone—was their return on the seemingly losing proposition of dragging dead weight across Antarctica. It was the secret recompense for being British in the snow. It's not enough to die for, in my opinion, but it is enough to keep my view of the dead complicated.

There is another poem which I cannot leave this hilltop without reading. The cross quotes Tennyson's 'Ulysses', an inspired choice by Cherry-Garrard. It is the fullest Romantic statement there is of the lure of departure, the urge to be always moving, always seeing vistas like this one; yet it is a poem without ease, a driven poem that leaves room for doubt about its own heroic voice. It makes the perfect memorial here, where so many ironies have to be acknowledged. Tennyson took the story of Ulysses refusing his happy ending on Ithaca in favour of one last voyage, not from *The Odyssey*, where the old hero is quite happy to hang up his sea boots, but from Dante, where Ulysses is explaining how he came to be damned. Is it a sin to refuse peace? To prefer over any real life the possible life that dances ahead of you just as long as you never stop travelling? I pull out the book from the pocket of my scarlet, polar-weight parka, the fat skiing gloves on my hands making me clumsy at working the Velcro fastener. All of us standing on Ob Hill's tip, around a monument to men who died in threadbare canvas suits, are bulked out, and rounded, by our technological insulation until we're slightly bear-shaped. I make the noises which indicate that poetry is about to be committed in public. I'm embarrassed, in an English way, but I'm also vainly pleased that as I begin to read, people gradually fall silent, and the space for the poem expands. 'I am a part of all that I have met;' says Ulysses, 'Yet all experience is an arch wherethrough/Gleams that untravelled world, whose margin fades/For ever and for ever when I move.' On Observation Hill the corollaries for Tennyson's images are all around. The ice shines out under the blue-black sky's arch, and the margins are cast so wide they defeat the eye. The lapse of time between the cross and us seems immense too, and yet, as Tennyson intended, a part of what the poem defies. 'Come my friends,/'Tis not too late to seek a newer world.'

Perhaps, Ulysses says, they will all drown, or perhaps (it does not seem likely) reach the destination that can finally satisfy the need for destinations. 'It may be we shall touch the Happy Isles,/And see the great Achilles whom we knew.'

I think of Henry Bowers, the youngest of the five named on the cross, and an easy victim for later times' condescension, because he was kind and muscular and unsubtle. If the expedition had not killed him, he would have been a patriotic sitting duck for the war that followed. 'Though much is taken, much abides; and though/We are not now that strength which in old days/Moved earth and heaven; that which we are, we are...'

It turns out that I cannot quite get out the affirmation of the last line. I don't have the gall to leave a silence. I say: 'To strive, to seek, to find, and not to yield... yeah.'

I stay a while longer on Observation Hill. This is not a sight I shall see many more times in my life. Then something happens inside me, and I start down towards the town in long sliding plunges. I'm glad that the only person near is the most oblivious member of the party, whoopee-ing downslope on his backside, because I find that the compound emotion I felt beside the cross has lurched, and resolved into a plainer sorrow over lost things, no matter how stupid or flawed; into unambiguous grief. □

THE BLACK BOOK OF COMMUNISM

CRIMES, TERROR, REPRESSION

STÉPHANE COURTOIS, NICOLAS WERTH,
JEAN-LOUIS PANNÉ, ANDRZEJ PACZKOWSKI,
KAREL BARTOSEK, AND JEAN-LOUIS MARGOLIN

Already famous throughout Europe, this international bestseller plumbs recently opened archives in the former Soviet bloc to reveal the actual, practical accomplishments of Communism around the world: terror, torture, famine, mass deportations, and massacres. Astonishing in the sheer detail it amasses, the book is the first comprehensive attempt to catalogue and analyze the crimes of Communism over seventy years.

"Revolutions, like trees, must be judged by their fruit," Ignazio Silone wrote, and this is the standard the authors apply to the Communist experience—in the China of "the Great Helmsman," Kim Il Sung's Korea, Vietnam under "Uncle Ho" and Cuba under Castro, Ethiopia under Mengistu, Angola under Neto, and Afghanistan under Najibullah. The authors, all distinguished scholars based in Europe, document Communist crimes against humanity, but also crimes against national and universal culture, from Stalin's destruction of hundreds of churches in Moscow to Ceausescu's leveling of the historic heart of Bucharest to the widescale devastation visited on Chinese culture by Mao's Red Guards.

As the death toll mounts—as many as 25 million in the former Soviet Union, 65 million in China, 1.7 million in Cambodia, and on and on—the authors systematically show how and why, wherever the millenarian ideology of Communism was established, it quickly led to crime, terror, and repression. An extraordinary accounting, this book amply documents the unparalleled position and significance of Communism in the hierarchy of violence that is the history of the twentieth century.

78 halftones, 6 maps 1120 pages • $37.50 • £23.50 cloth

HARVARD UNIVERSITY PRESS

US: 800 448 2242 • UK: 0171 306 0603 • www.hup.harvard.edu

James Buchan was the *Financial Times* Middle East correspondent in the 1970s and 1980s. His new novel, *A Good Place to Die*, will be published by Harvill later this year.

Linda Polman is a freelance journalist based in Amsterdam. She has written books on East Africa and the Haitian boat people. 'The Problem Outside' is a translation from her most recent book, '*K Zag Twee Beren*' ('We Did Nothing'), an account of UN peacekeeping operations throughout the world.

Edward Said is the author of seventeen books, including *Culture and Imperialism* and *Beginnings*. He is Professor of English and Comparative Literature at Columbia University. 'Self-Consciousness' is taken from his autobiography, *Out of Place*, published later this year by Granta Books in Britain and Pantheon in the United States.

Zadie Smith was born in north-west London in 1975 and continues to live there. 'The Waiter's Wife' is taken from her first novel, *White Teeth*, to be published by Hamish Hamilton next year.

Francis Spufford is the author of *I May Be Some Time*, a cultural history of polar exploration, published by Faber in Britain and St Martin's Press in the United States. He is writing a book about compulsive reading, *Reading Silence*, to be published by Faber next year.

Jasmina Tesanovic is a writer, film-maker and co-founder of the first women's publishing house in Serbia, '94'. Her stories have been translated into Italian, Hungarian, Austrian and English. 'The Diary of a Political Idiot' is an edited extract from her forthcoming book *Normality: A Moral Opera by a Political Idiot*, which will be published in Spain by Plaza y Janés and Portugal by Temas/Debates.

Larry Towell has been a Magnum photographer since 1989. *The Mennonites* will be published by Phaidon Press in autumn next year. Another collection of his photographs, *The World from My Front Porch*, will be published next year by Aperture.

Edmund White has published six novels, most recently *The Farewell Symphony*, as well as books about Proust and Paris. He is an officer of the Ordre des Arts et des Lettres. 'Telling Him' is taken from his seventh novel, *The Married Man*, to be published next year by Chatto and Windus in Britain and Knopf in the United States. He lives in New York.

Joy Williams has published three novels and two short story collections. In 1993 she received the Strauss Living Award from the American Academy of Arts and Letters. She lives in Florida with her husband and daughter.